GRAVITY SHIFT

How Asia's New Economic Powerhouses
Will Shape the Twenty-First Century

The rapid growth, diversity, and strategic importance of the emerging Chinese and Indian economies have fired the world's imagination with both hopes and fears for the future. In this perceptive analysis of changing institutions, demographics, and politics, Wendy Dobson paints a thoughtful and surprising picture of India and China as economic powerhouses in the year 2030. Examining past events and current trends, *Gravity Shift* offers bold predictions of the changes we can expect in key economic and political institutions in China and India, changes that will inform and shape tomorrow's business decisions.

Dobson's work anticipates that by 2030, China's economy will be larger than those of the United States, India, and Japan, though China's population will be aging and its growth slowing. India will also come into its own, making major strides in modernizing its vast rural population, vanquishing illiteracy, and emerging as an innovative manufacturing powerhouse. A China–India free-trade agreement could well become the foundation of a cooperative Asian economic community. As the world re-evaluates business practices in the wake of the global economic crisis, *Gravity Shift* provides a clear vision of how India and China will reshape the Asian region and inform and transform global economic institutions.

WENDY DOBSON is Co-director of the Institute for International Business at the University of Toronto's Rotman School of Management. She is the author of numerous books and articles on Asia and the international economy, including *Multinationals and East Asian Integration*, which won the Ohira Prize for the best English-language book on Asia.

GRAVITY SHIFT

How Asia's New Economic Powerhouses
Will Shape the Twenty-First Century

Wendy Dobson

UNIVERSITY OF TORONTO PRESS
Toronto Buffalo London

Rotman/UTP Publishing
University of Toronto Press Incorporated
Toronto Buffalo London
www.utppublishing.com
Printed in Canada
Reprinted in paperback 2010

ISBN 978-1-4426-4052-8 (cloth)
ISBN 978-1-4426-1165-8 (paper)

Printed on acid-free paper.

Library and Archives Canada Cataloguing in Publication

Dobson, Wendy
Gravity shift : how Asia's new economic powerhouses will reshape
the twenty-first century / Wendy Dobson.

Includes bibliographical references and index.
ISBN 978-1-4426-4052-8 (bound) — ISBN 978-1-4426-1165-8 (pbk.)

1. China – Economic conditions – 21st century. 2. India – Economic
conditions – 21st century. 3. Institutional economics. 4. International
economic relations. 5. Economic forecasting – China. 6. Economic
forecasting – India. I. Title.

HC427.95.D62 2009   330.951'06   C2009-904008-5

University of Toronto Press acknowledges the financial assistance to its
publishing program of the Canada Council for the Arts and the Ontario
Arts Council.

University of Toronto Press acknowledges the financial support for its publishing
activities of the Government of Canada through the Canada Book Fund.

To my parents, Kenneth and Una Dobson,
two adventurers, married in Hong Kong in 1935

Contents

Preface

No events better capture the shift of the world economy's center of gravity that began three decades ago than the summit meetings of the Group of 20 major economies. For the first time, the leaders of China and India spoke with voices equal to those of the advanced countries at the international gatherings held in Washington, DC, and London in 2008 and 2009.

Thirty years ago, the world's seven largest economies were still forming what would become the G7, and 'globalization' was not even part of the lexicon. The intact Berlin Wall still symbolized the Cold War division of Europe, China was just beginning to open its economy to the outside world after the chaos of the Cultural Revolution, and India, despite the promise of its Green Revolution, seemed mired in endless poverty. Few people – even someone like me, who had worked in India in the 1960s and had visited China in 1978 at the start of the Four Modernizations – could have imagined the economic transformation of these two huge countries that would lead the world to beat a path to their doors.

Predictions, then, are perilous, but in this book I look ahead twenty years to the world of 2030, when next-door neighbors China and India, already the two most populous nations on earth, will, if present trends continue, also have the world's two most dynamic economies. Indeed, the size and dynamism of the Chinese and Indian economies are already reshaping Asia. Can they sustain their current high growth rates? What impact will their rapid growth have on the world economy? Will these two economies produce everything? Will the effects of their industrialization on pollution and greenhouse gas emissions overwhelm the global commons? Will the economic dynamism of China and India shift the patterns of power and bring in a new world economic order, as is often popularly assumed?

In shaping answers to these questions, I begin by explaining what drives the economic growth of these two giants. I do so not by a simple recitation of estimates of population and production; these are, after all, just numbers – large and important numbers, to be sure, but they tell us little about how the Chinese and Indian economies work. Rather, I view each country through the prism of its institutions.

Institutions matter because growth is not just a function of an increasing labor force, or rising savings, or new sources of natural resources or innovation. Nobel laureate Douglass North and R.P. Thomas argue in their pathbreaking book, *The Rise of the Western World*, that these factors *are* growth, not its causes. An economy's incentive structures influence whether it grows, stagnates, or declines over time. An expanding labor force is an asset if workers have incentives to be productive, but it is a burden if they do not. Economic growth is sustained by labor market institutions that reward education, skills training, and productive employment; by financial institutions that allocate capital efficiently and reward savers; by legal institutions that record and protect property rights; and by economic institutions that encourage a nation's openness to trade and finance. With a better understanding of a country's institutions, especially those that differ from the familiar Western ones, one can discern a much more nuanced picture of the potential growth – and the inherent weaknesses – of the Chinese and Indian economies than is possible with mere numbers.

Changes in key institutions kick-started the rapid growth of China and India, as we will see in the first chapter. Sixty years ago, China adopted the central planning model; today, China's approach is better described as 'bureaucratic capitalism.' No longer is China highly centralized. In place of monolithic direction from Beijing and the Chinese Communist Party, far-flung ad hoc experiments – ranging from new ways to reward farmers for their work to new ways to transfer nonagricultural land to industrial use – are closely observed, copied, and rolled out across the country if they work. Yet how can one square such decentralized efforts with the popular perception of a top-down autocracy? For its part, India is sweeping away the vestiges of the socialist ideology that informed economic policymaking after independence, yet its democracy frequently is gridlocked by competing interest groups. Can its democratically elected leaders and an activist judiciary cut through this political paralysis?

Still, growth and development are not ends in themselves but the means to improve people's living standards. By 2030, both China and India will have populations of one-and-a-half billion, but in size their labor forces will be moving in opposite directions, with China's shrinking and India's continuing to grow. In the second chapter, we will see why, and what it means for the future. In China, hundreds of millions have been pulled out of absolute poverty and into jobs in the modern economy, but how can China's strategy for future growth compensate for a shrinking labor force? In India, too, absolute poverty has declined, and the country is becoming renowned for its highly skilled professionals in the information technology (IT) industries. But 90 percent of India's growing labor force is still casually employed; what is it about that society's educational and labor market institutions that they seem unable to realize the full potential of its population?

Mobilizing and channeling savings into more productive sectors that create good jobs can help offset these demographic challenges. As we will see in the third chapter, both countries could provide tomorrow's jobs and new products by financing small and medium-sized private enterprises, yet they do not – in neither country do such firms obtain adequate funding from formal financial institutions. China, with the world's highest savings rate, is brimming with financial capital, but these savings are being used, not to fund small entrepreneurs, but to deliver rapid industrial growth. The government stabilizes the exchange rate, administers interest rates, and owns the banks, and capital is priced cheaply and directed largely to the state sector. Although this strategy served its growth objectives, it built up large stocks of foreign-exchange reserves, nearly half of which are now invested in U.S. government bonds. Indeed, China's unique monetary and financial framework means that the interdependence of the Chinese and U.S. economies has become a central feature of the gravity shift. India's financial system is more developed and market driven – its stock markets are models for emerging markets. But the Indian government has also co-opted the country's financial system by requiring financial institutions to hold the bonds it issues to finance its deficit spending.

In the fourth chapter, I turn to science, technology, and innovation, which could help offset the two countries' demographic challenges and financial weaknesses. Both countries still depend on the technologies of others, despite their recent exploits in space. The process innovations of India's experienced IT services entrepreneurs have created world-famous companies and brands, and its auto parts and pharmaceuticals sectors are not far behind. Yet this well-earned innovatory fame merely dramatizes the yawning gap between India's export successes and a domestic economy in which even existing knowledge has not diffused to the myriad tiny enterprises that create most of its jobs. In China, research and development (R&D) is more state driven, meant to achieve ambitious nationalistic goals to reduce dependence on foreigners. But such targets ignore the realities of China's dynamic nonstate enterprises, which, in the face of intense market competition, drive innovation in labor-intensive activities that are more in line with the country's comparative advantage.

Thus, the impressive strengths of China and India, which are shifting the world economy's center of gravity, are offset by persistent weaknesses. China's pragmatic combination of cheap capital and labor, economic openness, and unique mix of state and market institutions has delivered rapid growth, but also a lopsided, investment-driven economy featuring rising income inequality and environmental degradation. India has chosen equity over growth but has achieved neither very successfully, and large swathes of its population are still excluded from the modern sector. Accordingly, in the fifth chapter, I look at the chances that the governments of these two emerging giants will do what is necessary to remove these impediments to sustainable, long-term growth.

And what are the implications of that growth for the rest of us? China's and India's strengths and weaknesses, in fact, present both opportunities and risks, which we will explore in the sixth chapter. Their rapid growth promises to expand the size of global markets and raise global productivity, from which everyone can benefit. They also provide new opportunities in areas where neither country has a comparative advantage. In such areas, global multinationals with an edge over domestically focused Chinese and Indian rivals can target the two countries' vast local markets, while leveraging each country's comparative advantages – particularly in the form of low-cost labor – to serve their global customers.

At the same time, the advanced industrial countries face the challenge of adjusting to the gravity shift in order to stay ahead. Their imperative will be to exploit their technological advantages in the knowledge-based manufacturing and services industries. Their ability to meet this challenge, however, will depend on the success of their educational institutions and social safety nets to help workers make the transition to new skills and occupations. Attempting to obstruct the gravity shift by resorting to protectionism will not work, since they would simply fall behind if they closed themselves off from the competition. The United States faces a particularly daunting challenge: an expanding world economy has made it convenient for the United States, which spends more than it saves, to borrow from China, which saves more than it spends. Indeed, China is now the world's largest creditor and the United States its largest debtor. In recessionary times, however, China worries about the long-term costs of finding itself in the same boat as the United States. The way in which the two countries manage their relationship will be key for their future economic growth.

In the final chapter, we will look at the global implications of the gravity shift, which, by 2030, will be well advanced. By then, even under conservative assumptions about growth, the Chinese and Indian economies combined could be nearly twice the size of the slower-growing U.S. economy. Many observers look at these numbers and predict that the rising economic prominence of the two Asian giants will reshape the world's political order. Such predictions eventually may prove correct, but they are unlikely to be borne out in the next decade, or even two. Both China and India will have to address their domestic stumbling blocks if they are to maintain their rapid growth trajectories; both countries realize they cannot continue with business as usual. The Chinese must keep their economy from moving to a markedly slower growth path, while Indian voters will push their government to adopt policies that will sustain a high growth rate.

Moreover, translating economic clout into political power will depend on a number of factors, including the ability of China and India to weather the current global recession, their willingness to cooperate, rather than compete, with each other and with their Asian neighbors and to take on a more active role in global governance institutions. What seems clear, however, is that the world order of 2030 will be multi-polar, unlike the period after the collapse of communism in Europe, when the United States was dominant. While the United States is likely to continue to lead, global economic progress will depend on the willingness and ability of the major countries to forge a common vision and to work together. The G20 leaders' summits are a first move in this direction by recognizing the gravity shift caused by the emergence of Asia's new economic powerhouses.

GRAVITY SHIFT

How Asia's New Economic Powerhouses
Will Shape the Twenty-First Century

chapter one

Why Are They Growing So Fast?

> The man who removes a mountain begins by carrying
> away small stones.
> – Chinese proverb

By 2030 China and India together could account for as much as a third of the world's economy, according to prominent economic historian Angus Maddison.[1] How will this happen? Even though the two giants have deeply different societies, they share the experience of a common economic transformation – from relatively stagnant, centrally planned, inward-looking, and self-sufficient to a market-based economy rapidly integrating with world markets. In each country, the turning point came during a crisis, when the government changed the rules of the game, kick-starting a sea change in their economic behavior.

China's turning point was especially evident to me during a 1978 visit to Lushan, a hilltop town in Jiangxi province, high above the south banks of the Yangtze River. On a sunlit side street, a small group of peasants dressed in heavily patched blue shirts and trousers were engaged in intense discussion. At their feet was an assortment of produce and carrying baskets, and in their hands they held simple scales with which to weigh the produce they had brought to trade. This was a market – hitherto banned since the founding of the People's Republic in 1949 – and part of an experiment in which agricultural collectives were giving land to individual farmers to manage and allowing them to pocket the proceeds from selling whatever they could produce over and above government quotas and taxes. With the introduction of such incentives, farmers increased production dramatically.

India's turning point came later. In 2006, an executive in Noida, a high-tech enclave near New Delhi, described to me how it had affected his life. In the early 1980s, after completing his engineering studies, he had asked his father to provide financial backing for his first business venture in the chemicals industry. For more than a decade, he produced and distributed chemical products to his Indian customers. Then, in 1991, India experienced a major financial crisis and found that it could not pay for its imports. The crisis triggered a radical change in government economic policy. Doors to trade and foreign investors that had been closed in the 1970s were reopened, forcing Indian executives to face the bracing winds of foreign competition. Initially, the chemicals executive's response was 'How will I cope with the loss of government protection and the aggressive foreigners?' Soon, however, he reasoned, 'If foreigners can come here, why can't I go there?' By 2006, his small business venture had grown into a science-based pharmaceutical company with assets of more than half a billion US dollars and sales of a third of a billion dollars.

These two accounts illustrate how changes in institutions and incentives free people, finance, and technological innovation to become drivers of economic growth. For much of the twentieth century, outsiders perceived both China and India as overpopulated basket cases whose governments had turned their backs on the world. Ejecting foreign imperialists and capitalists in the late 1940s, they were determined to mould their own destinies. In China, the founding of the People's Republic in 1949 was followed by the upheavals of the Great Leap Forward from 1958 to 1960 and the Great Proletarian Cultural Revolution of 1966 to 1976. India, upon independence from Britain in 1947, had been partitioned to create the Muslim state of Pakistan amid wrenching communal violence. Hundreds of millions of people continued to depend on subsistence agriculture, and though their lives were ameliorated somewhat by the Green Revolution of the 1960s, India's economic progress did not spread far in the face of Prime Minister Indira Gandhi's socialist policies, the imposition of emergency rule in 1975, half-hearted economic liberalization in 1980, and her assassination in 1984.

None of these crises affected the rest of the world much. But languishing economic growth mattered to the governments of China and India, and economic crises opened windows of opportunity for reform of both economic policy and institutions. In the 1970s, Deng Xiaoping compared the performance of his country, 80 percent of whose population was still rural, with that of its rapidly growing neighbors, dubbed the 'Asian Tigers.' Agriculture dominated the economy and productivity was low; every available space not used for brick kilns, railroad tracks, or roads was cultivated and fertilized by hand. Outside the major cities, the air was crystal clear. The only vehicles on the roads were large Red Flag limousines for officials, and buses and bicycles for everyone else. Foreigners visiting Shanghai and Beijing stayed in government guest houses or in the handful of hotels permitted to house them.

As part of the economic reforms that began in 1978, China's leaders allowed peasants to sell their surplus production and encouraged the opening of markets like the one I saw in Lushan. In response, production and incomes in the Chinese countryside increased dramatically. Building on this success, the state began slowly to withdraw from the economy and to encourage foreign investment in special economic zones, where doors were opened cautiously to international trade. Deng Xiaoping spoke of the ladder-step doctrine whereby 'some [that is, those in the urban coastal areas] will get rich first.' The doctrine was underpinned by the one-child birth control program, which slowed population growth, and *hukou,* the household registration system dating back to the early days of the People's Republic, which restricted the movement of rural peasants into the large coastal cities.

India's window of opportunity opened in 1991, when the price of imported oil rose and its export markets disappeared with the collapse of the Soviet Union, its main trading partner. These two crises caused India to run out of foreign exchange. Seizing the opportunity, then-finance minister (and later prime minister)

Manmohan Singh freed up the exchange rate and abolished protectionist institutions such as the 'license raj,' a costly and time-
consuming system of official permits that businesses had to obtain
in order to import and export and that fostered official corruption. As India's markets re-opened to foreign competition, Indian
businesses like the one at Noida were free to compete with the rest
of the world.

These economic transformations remain incomplete. Indeed,
popular accounts portray China as the world's manufacturing
workshop and India as its back office, descriptions that accurately
reflect their interactions with the rest of the world. But these ste-
reotypes gloss over the inequalities and contradictions that still
exist in the two countries – between dazzling riches and grinding
poverty, sometimes on the same city block; between modern cities
and feudal rural areas; and, in China's case, between economic
openness and an autocratic political regime. There are, in fact,
many Chinas, but what stands out for the outsider are the differences between the coastal region, which is modern, industrialized, and outward looking, and the inland and western regions,
which remain largely agrarian, relatively untouched by economic
reforms, and more ideological and conservative in their attitudes.

There are also many Indias. Despite its back-office, high-tech
successes, much of the country is still not industrialized. Former
finance minister P. Chidambaram has spoken of two Indias: First
India, an educated, sophisticated, urban elite eager to compete
globally, and Second India, the deprived rural and urban poor,
struggling to survive. Among India's states, too, there are the urban, modernized ones with modern infrastructure, a favorable
investment climate, and populations that are three-fourths literate, and the poor, agrarian, 'lagging' states with little investment,
abysmal infrastructure and public services, and where six in ten
adults cannot read.[2]

China has gone farther than India in diffusing economic opportunity into the hinterland, but it still has more to do. China has
followed its east Asian neighbors in opening up to the world, its
people and enterprises are high savers and its government plays
a strong guiding role in investing those savings in infrastructure

and industries that export to world markets. Low-cost skilled labor and considerable foreign investment drive growth, facilitated by a stable and favorable exchange rate. Jobs in modern industries attract tens of millions of people out of the rural economy. Growing at an average annual rate of 9 percent for the past thirty years, China's economy has doubled in size nearly four times in that period. Yet, incomes of those still in the countryside are only a third of those in urban areas, and China's rural poor are increasing the pressure for a better deal.

India has been more ambivalent about opening up its economy. Until the 1990s, Indian industry was inward looking, protected from international competition, and heavily regulated to prevent 'capitalist excesses.' Since the heady days of the Green Revolution, growth in the agricultural sector has declined, and productivity and incomes remain low – indeed, in 2006, India's Planning Commission described a 'crisis of the agricultural sector.'[3] Government subsidies remain an entrenched feature of economic life and are proving difficult to reduce. Persistent deficits and the requirements of servicing the large public debt crowd out the public funding needed to modernize India's inadequate physical infrastructure. India's growth surge, which reached an 8 percent trajectory only in 2003, is one sided, driven by entrepreneurs in IT services and sophisticated, capital-intensive 'techno-manufacturing,' rather than by the labor-intensive manufacturing found in China and every other successful developing country. Moreover, these successes have had little effect on the lives of those in Second India, including the 60 percent of the total population that still depends on agriculture. Unless more productive higher-paying jobs can be created in the services sector, they will have to be found in labor-intensive manufacturing.

Sustaining High Growth

The crucial question for both countries and for their future roles in the world is whether they can sustain their current high economic growth rates in the decades to come. One way to address this question is to use a simple economic framework known as 'growth accounting.' An economy grows when the population grows and becomes more productive, when savings are mobilized and channeled into productive investments, and when labor and capital are used more efficiently through the application of new techniques and innovations. In its early stages of development, the economy grows by bringing people into the labor force, real-locating population from rural agriculture to urban industry, and saving more. Eventually, however, just adding another unit of capital to a fixed amount of labor produces ever-smaller increments of output or gross domestic product (GDP), and growth slows down. The trick is to invest in the technologies and innovations that make it possible to get more output from existing inputs – that is, to increase productivity through innovation.

Japan, South Korea, and Taiwan, whose economies were once similar to China's, illustrate what is possible. At their most rapid rates of industrialization, the Japanese economy averaged 10.5 percent growth a year (from 1960 to 1970), the South Korean economy 9 percent a year (from 1982 to 1991), and Taiwan's at 8 percent a year (from 1980 to 1989). At these rates, their economies doubled in size in a mere seven to nine years.[4]

Although most studies of the Chinese and Indian economies look at just one or the other, a few compare the two using the growth accounting framework. One of the first such studies, published by Goldman Sachs in 2003, attracted international attention with its projected growth of the group of countries dubbed the BRICs (Brazil, Russia, India, and China) out to 2050.[5] Using assumptions about growth in employment, investment, productivity, and appreciating real exchange rates, the study concludes that, measured in US dollars corrected for inflation, the BRICs economies would be half the combined size of the G6 economies (France, Germany, Italy, Japan, the United Kingdom, and the United States) by 2025 and exceed them within forty years. The Goldman Sachs study predicts that, by 2042, China would catch up with the United States, while, by 2050, India would still be closing the gap (see Figure 1). More recent comparisons highlight how China's high rates of investment are driving its strong growth, but conclude that it cannot sustain this performance over time, while

Figure 1: China and India Gaining on the United States

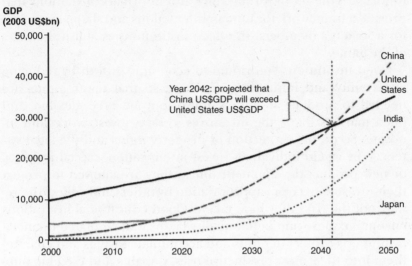

Source: Dominic Wilson and Roopa Purushothaman, 'Dreaming with BRICs:
The Path to 2050,' Global Economics Paper 99 (New York: Goldman Sachs,
2003), p. 19.

India's growth, though slower, has been more balanced, relying on
increases in both labor and capital, and hence more sustainable.[6]

Institutions: The Software of Growth

The two countries' differing rates of labor force and investment
growth can be explained, in large measure, by differences in their
institutions. For the tools with which to understand how to think
about and measure institutions and the roles they play in the
process of economic growth, we are indebted to Nobel laureate
Douglass North and R.P. Thomas.

Economic growth depends on human and physical capital and
technology, but, as North and Thomas famously questioned in
1973, 'if all that is required for economic growth is investment
and innovation, why have some societies missed this desirable outcome?'[7] Their answer is that a country's institutions, the 'software'

of development are what actually drive – or inhibit – growth: institutions are the set of formal rules and informal conventions that
provide a framework for human interactions and shape incentives
for a society's members. In effect, institutions establish the rules
of the game.

Good institutions contribute to economic growth by reducing
uncertainty and improving efficiency, so that fewer inputs are
needed to produce an added unit of output. Free, flexible, and
open markets shape the incentives to save, invest, work, and innovate. So do the protection of property rights and the legal system. Why would individuals invest in education, capital projects,
or new product development unless they are allowed to protect
their investments from appropriation by others and collect the rewards of the risks they have taken? Good educational institutions
encourage more and better-quality labor; well-regulated financial
institutions protect deposits and accumulate savings and channel
them into their most productive uses. Capable and credible public institutions and bureaucracies carry out functions that substi-
tute for the market when the market fails; they also stabilize and
regulate markets and make it possible to achieve social objectives.

A country's economic institutions are determined collectively,
in large part because of their roles in enlarging and distributing
the economic pie. In turn, economic institutions are determined
by a country's political institutions and how political power is distributed among various interest groups. Of course, the converse
is also true: economic institutions can influence the relative af-
fluence of various groups, which gives those with more economic
resources a greater say over political institutions. At the extreme,
some groups may develop monopoly positions in, say, an industry or a natural resources sector, which could lead to 'poor' institutions, slow economic growth, and persistent poverty.[8] Good
economic institutions, ones that successfully promote growth and
long-term prosperity, are usually associated with political institutions that ensure power is shared and is subject to checks and
balances to prevent one group from extracting economic gain at
the expense of other groups. In short, good institutions are more
likely to be found in countries with a combination of political sta-

bility, governance by the rule of law, the absence of corruption, and effective government that provides credible policies, a professional public service, regulatory oversight that promotes competition, and transparency and open markets.[9]

Of particular relevance to our focus on China and India is how outdated or obsolete economic institutions can be improved. Institutional change can be a slow process because of the close connections to political institutions and political power. The process of wresting opportunities and incentives from powerful groups requires considerable political will and clear objectives that promise to make everyone better off. Studies of the transition from central planning to market economies in China and Eastern Europe, for example, find some significant common features. The first important factor is initial conditions: change is unlikely to be successful if there is little supply of or demand for better institutions. Further, the changes must be structured so that they have wide popular support and also benefit those in charge; many institutional innovations fail because they lack incentives for entrenched interests and those with political power. Another common feature of successful transitions to good institutions is the presence of catalysts such as those that flow from increased competition when economies are opened to world trade, from increased education, and from increased political accountability. Events in neighboring countries can also be a powerful catalyst for change, especially when evidently successful outcomes in the neighbors help to build support for similar changes at home.

The World Bank carries out regular surveys of countries' governance institutions and publishes rankings of what it finds. In 2007, India ranked far above China (and many other countries) on a 'voice and accountability' measure of the process by which governments are selected, monitored, and replaced, and also above China on the factors of the rule of law and control of corruption. China, on the other hand, scored far above India on political stability, government effectiveness, and regulatory quality.[10] In the following discussion of the two countries' institutions, I qualitatively assess variables such as these to help explain both the promotion and obstruction of long-term growth in China and India.

Economic Institutions and Reemergence

Changes in China's and India's economic institutions are important in explaining their future prospects and growing prominence
in the world economy. In fact, these changes signify the *reemer-
gence* of the economic importance of these two countries following nearly two hundred years of foreign domination and internal
strife.

This perspective draws on the remarkable work of Angus Maddison, a British economic historian who has assembled available
statistics reaching back to the beginning of the Common Era to
develop population and economic data that can be compared
through time and across countries.[11] His statistics show that, between 1300 and 1820, China and India together accounted for
more than half of the world's total economic output. Their shares
then shrank to less than 20 percent around the beginning of the
twentieth century and to a low of 10 percent in the early 1970s,
when they began to expand again. The shrinkage was not just because their growth slowed but also because of faster growth in the
rest of the world, particularly with the launch of the United States
on its long growth trajectory and the take-off of the Japanese
economy after World War II. Using quite conservative assumptions about future growth rates, Maddison estimates that, by 2030,
the combined shares of China and India will again be 30 percent
of the total (see Figure 2). In achieving this remarkable outcome,
the two countries' institutions will play a significant role.

China's Institutions

Historically, China's distinctive political institutions were much influenced by the size of its population. Maddison estimates that,
in 1300, China had as many as 100 million people – a third of
the world's population at that time. Then, China was the world's
leading economy and largest market, slightly ahead of India and
more advanced than western Europe in technology and administrative capabilities. China's huge population was unified, and order maintained, by the emperor, who ruled as the son of heaven,

Figure 2: Share of World Economic Output, Selected Economies, 1300–2030

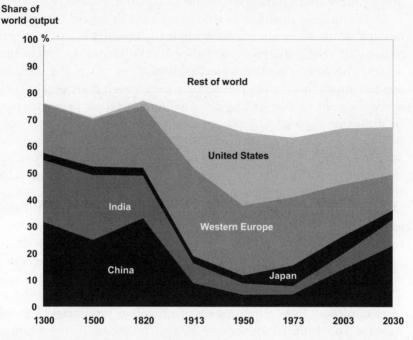

Source: Angus Maddison, 'Asia in the World Economy 1500–2030 AD,' *Asian-Pacific Economic Literature* 20 (2, 2006): 33.

holding power through virtue and piety. He also ruled according to custom, and if his rule was unjust or ineffective, his mandate could be revoked by custom, or he could be deposed by violence if necessary. Beginning in the seventh century, the system was administered by an elite bureaucracy, strong relative to commerce, whose mandarins had higher status than merchants. Selection for the bureaucracy was by a rigorous system of examinations that provided a channel for the best and brightest, regardless of background, to enter state service. The country was well administered, and it carried on state-to-state commerce both overland on the Silk Road and along maritime trade routes traveled by China's well-developed navy. Trading partners paid tribute in acknowledgement of Imperial China's superiority, in exchange for its trade and protection; indeed, tribute was regarded as an act of political submission, and Chinese immigration to tribute states often followed.

The economic institutions that supported this growth began to decline in the fifteenth century, when the country turned inward to focus on its agrarian base and close itself off from the rest of the world. The navy was abandoned and the fleet destroyed. Maddison attributes this shift to the bureaucracy, which consisted of rent seekers intent on preventing any challenge to their preeminence by entrepreneurs and merchants. Potentially lucrative economic activity was subject to bureaucratic 'squeeze,' while licensed or state monopolies were the only entities permitted to engage in larger projects. Bureaucrats were also the ones who decided to turn inward and close down the ship-building industry.[12] Eventually the bureaucracy deteriorated as it became corrupt and the vaunted examinations increasingly archaic and irrelevant. The examination system was abolished in 1905, but the Communists revived the bureaucracy itself to govern the far-flung countryside.

In the nineteenth and early twentieth centuries, China was wracked by chaos caused by internal strife and weaknesses that were exploited by foreign powers. To this day, memories of helplessness and humiliation before British gunboats in the Opium Wars of the mid-nineteenth century contribute to China's strong sense of nationalism and sensitivity to foreign interference. The Communist Party's rejection of the western world in 1949 did little to restore China's economic prominence, and by the 1970s population was growing faster than production and living standards were declining. Indeed, it took the leadership transition following Mao Zedong's death to reject the institutions of the closed and planned economy. Initial conditions, however, were favorable for change. Seeing what their East Asian neighbors had accomplished through their export-led industrialization strategies, Mao's successors sought to learn and apply their lessons to Chinese development. Deng Xiaoping is also reported to have sought the help of the World Bank, telling its then-president, Robert McNamara, at a meeting in 1980, 'We are very poor. We have lost touch with the world. We need the World Bank to catch up. We can do it without you, but with you we can do it better and quicker.'[13]

Reforms began in the rural areas. The government raised agricultural procurement prices in 1978 at a time when farmers in the agricultural collectives in some of the poorer provinces were already experimenting with better ways to reward members – for what they produced rather than how long or hard they worked. These ad hoc experiments had a positive impact on production, and when one of the provincial leaders was promoted to premier, the new approach formed the basis of the national Household Responsibility System, introduced in the early 1980s. Households were permitted to farm land leased from the state and keep some of the proceeds. This change in incentives caused a surge in agricultural production. By 1984, grain output had increased by a third and China became a net grain exporter.[14] As agricultural productivity rose, labor was freed up to move into other sectors, particularly industry.

Reform of China's state-owned enterprises began in 1980 in a similarly experimental manner. Initially, they were allowed to retain some of their profits and to buy and sell to some extent outside the plan. These partial changes introduced market signals, increased competitive pressures, and created some of the financial incentives of a bottom line. In the vigorous competition that ensued, some enterprises in southern China encouraged the Chinese diaspora to invest and trade.[15] When these competitive pressures squeezed enterprise margins and government revenues, the government reduced its financial support and pushed enterprises to fund more of their own activities, creating a virtuous circle of competition that rewarded successful enterprises, which then pushed for more deregulation. In the mid-1990s, enterprise reform moved into high gear with wholesale restructuring of state-owned enterprises that forced them to become profitable, merge, or close. By the end of that decade, the state-owned commercial banks were also restructured to turn them into competitive stand-alone institutions.

Political scientist Susan Shirk, in describing the reforms of this period, emphasizes the careful calculus of China's political leaders. Although they aimed to retain political power and speed up economic growth, they had no clear initial strategy. Rather,

changes were improvised and incremental, as later summed up by
Deng Xiaoping's famous dictum, *mozhe shitou guo he*, or 'crossing
the river by feeling for stones.'[16] Great care was taken to create
win-win outcomes. This was accomplished in industry by gradually expanding the market sector without jettisoning the planned
sector. In economic terms, this two-track approach looked messy,
but it was a great political success in that it protected incumbent
managers in the old system while profitable opportunities in the
market sector proliferated – indeed, were encouraged by changes
in taxation and profit sharing. The growing success of the market system eventually attracted managers in the planned sector to
change over.[17]

In short, China has grown so fast *because* institutional reforms
were ad hoc and seemingly incomplete. Deng Xiaoping's leadership was pragmatic rather than ideological. Reforms were from
the bottom up and experimental, beginning in the rural areas
where most people lived; as living standards improved, support
for reforms widened, and those that were successful were rolled
out across the country. Significantly as well, the institutional reforms were win-win: the potential losers, incumbent managers
and village officials, who might have undermined the changes by
dragging their feet, instead were presented with opportunities to
benefit.

The reforms were also widely regarded as necessary to restore
China's rightful place in the world. Party members studied the rise
and fall of great powers in the past half-millennium, and in 2005
state television aired 'The Rise of the Great Powers,' a series of
programs portraying the histories of the European countries and
the United States. The lesson – that political and economic stability are essential to sustain growth – reinforced that drawn from
periods of turbulence in China's own history, such as the Warring
States period (around 200 BCE) and the more recent chaos of the
Great Leap Forward and the Cultural Revolution. In this context,
China's fifteen-year-long negotiations to join the World Trade Organization, finally achieved in 2001, were used as further impetus
to open the economy and bring the country's nonmarket institutions in line with international standards.

In presenting this thumbnail sketch, one is reminded that outsiders are like blind people touching various parts of the proverbial elephant – or dragon – and attempting to interpret what they experience as the whole. They may see China's economic system as a partly reformed, centrally planned economy with an autocratic government opposed to democracy and determined to hold onto political power at any cost. China's leaders, however, might have a different view: that growth at any cost is necessary to preserve social harmony – that it is imperative to create sufficient jobs to replace those lost in the ongoing restructuring. The freeing of market forces – and political stability – helps to deliver those jobs, which also provide the legitimacy for the Party's continued grip on power. The ultimate objective is transformation and balance, but along a path of correct, small, nonlinear changes that rectify the gross imbalances and hardships of the past. Sinologist John Fairbanks captures the magnitude of these challenges using U.S. metaphors:

> To modernize ... China has had farther to go and more changes to make than most countries, simply because it has been itself for so long. The result has been a tremendous hold of inertia which has made China's revolutionary changes spasmodic, sometimes inhibited, and sometimes destructive. If modernization can grow out of one's recent experience as it has in the United States, people are under much less strain than if modernization requires a rejection of the Virgin Mary and the Founding Fathers, a denial of the values of one's grandfathers, and an acceptance of foreign models.[18]

This pragmatic, step-by-step approach has delivered economic openness, fast growth, urbanization, and more productive jobs, pulling hundreds of millions of people out of absolute poverty. But it leaves substantial unfinished business for the future. China's economy contains a unique mixture of central planning and market institutions that drive rapid growth but have unintended consequences and complexities, which I explore in later chapters. The casual observer might expect that, with nearly two-thirds of industrial production now originating from nonstate enterprises,

the roles of the government as owner, producer, regulator, and
political gatekeeper would have been replaced by the market. Yet
this is not the case. The central government, through the State
Assets Supervision and Administration Commission, still owns the
largest enterprises at the economy's commanding heights in the
energy, utilities, heavy machinery, transportation, communications, and defense industries. The five largest banks, accounting
for more than half of all banking assets, are owned by the Ministry
of Finance, the investment arm of the State Administration for
Foreign Exchange, and some other domestic entities such as the
National Council for the Social Security Fund.[19]

Ownership is separated from regulation, with other ministries
such as Energy, Environmental Protection, and Railways responsible for regulating the industrial state-owned enterprises. The
China Bank Regulatory Commission is responsible for prudential
oversight of the banks but their deposits and lending rates are
administered by the central bank. Ownership is also increasingly
mixed since most of the largest banks and state-owned enterprises
are listed on public stock exchanges. Yet bureaucrats, not public shareholders, decide the fates of these institutions. The ongoing restructuring of China's telecommunications sector (which
serves 550 million mobile subscribers) provides an example of
the dilemma. Several years ago, the central government decided
to break the huge state telecommunications monopoly into four
competitors, two in fixed lines (China Telecom and China Net-
com) and two in mobiles (China Mobile and China Unicom).
By 2008 China Mobile dominated the market. To promote more
competition, bureaucrats further restructured the companies to
create three full-service operators (China Telecom, China Mobile,
and China Unicom), each offering a complete range of mobile
and fixed-line services. Their boards of directors, now including
independent directors, oversee independent valuations of company transactions, ostensibly to safeguard the interests of minority
shareholders. Banks also have minority shareholders, but government appointees dominate their boards, just as Party committees
exist in each institution.

These dilemmas of mixed ownership are not unique to China.
What distinguishes the State Assets Supervision and Administra-

tion Commission and the Ministry of Finance as owners is that they have clear marching orders: to encourage economic growth, increase the efficiency of their charges, and promote them as future national champions. There are few signs that majority government ownership is transitional. As one China scholar quipped, the Chinese Communist Party should be renamed the 'Chinese Bureaucratic Capitalist Party.'

A second complexity is that the role of government varies at different levels. China is not a monolith run from Beijing. Its administration is highly decentralized, with provincial and local governments setting their own priorities and strategies and exercising different types of intervention. Governments in the southeastern provinces of Guangdong and Zhejiang are particularly market and capitalist friendly, open to and supportive of experimentation and enterprise innovation. Even so, enterprises exist in silos in which bureaucratic and political support is still necessary for significant business and social initiatives or innovations to proceed. These vertical relationships between productive enterprises and officials take time and resources to create and maintain – time that could otherwise be spent on horizontal relationships with other enterprises, leading to new ideas, products, or financing. Success or failure depends not only on market competitiveness but also on these complex vertical relationships.

Similarly, the Party is not a monolith. It has seventy-four million members and a political apparatus that reaches from Beijing, through China's thirty-one provinces, to thousands of municipalities, counties, townships, and villages. Governance is decentralized, so the Party leadership must rely on the loyalty of local officials in order to govern. Its influence over them is exercised through education campaigns and a system of regular evaluations of cadres, who are assessed for promotion by their contribution to growth and stability and, more recently, to clean and environmentally 'green' GDP.

The Party leaders' dilemma, however, is that, without an independent judiciary or press freedom to provide checks and balances and accountability, local corruption and abuse of political power are widespread, so much so that they undermine the Party's legitimacy. Striking accounts, such as Ian Johnson's in *Wild Grass* and Chen and Wu's *Will the Boat Sink the Water?*, detail repressive violence, brutality and even death to villagers and educated peasants who assert their rights or expose corrupt local officials.[20] Flagrant abuse of the environment and lack of transparency in land leases and transactions around urban areas lead to thousands of demonstrations annually and occasional violence by farmers and householders over perceived injustices and murky land deals between local officials and developers. An independent investigation by *Caijing* magazine of schools that collapsed in the 2008 Sichuan earthquake concluded that lack of funding was not to blame; rather, the problem was misuse of funds by local authorities. One study found that money earmarked by higher levels of government for structural improvements had been used by local authorities for cosmetic purposes.[21]

China has a long history of money and power. At its most serious, as one private sector participant observed, 'those with money are willing to exchange it for power and those with power are willing to sell it for money.' Officials are careful about actually selling their influence, usually to someone they trust and usually only once – for resources of a magnitude sufficient to secure their family's economic future. Other reports reflect the attraction of the rents to be captured relative to the risks of exposure; for example, individuals in a northeastern province apparently paid to obtain official positions, with higher levels of government commanding larger payments.

It should be noted, however, that the widespread and informal *guanxi* relationships within networks of families, businesses, and officials, differ from the forms of corruption I have just described in that they do not necessarily involve money and bribery so much as provide information channels and the basis of long-term financial and other business relationships. These are significant relationships because they emphasize mutual trust to complete and enforce transactions in the absence of formal contracts and legal enforcement that are familiar in the West.

Practices are also changing as new laws are introduced and as alternative transactions channels open up. Hong Kong is a significant external channel for enterprises large enough to list on its stock exchange. The international exposure to foreign investors, shareholders, and analysts requires a shift of focus and mindset from the bureaucratic and political power games of traditional China toward efficiency and international competitiveness. Companies that have taken this route, such as personal computer giant Lenovo, not only list in Hong Kong but also recruit foreign managers in order to subject themselves to international incentive structures and market scrutiny of their strategies and operations. As we will see, since 2005 China's state-owned banks have also been exposed to this kind of scrutiny as they modernize and restructure their business practices.

A significant unintended consequence of the Party's emphasis on investment-driven growth is rising income inequality, although this problem is not unusual in developing countries, since rapid growth is often unbalanced, with some regions, sectors, and individuals gaining more initially from the new opportunities than others do. To create jobs and sustain growth, the central government has encouraged foreign investment in export-oriented manufacturing and all levels of government have made huge infrastructure and real estate investments. After thirty years of rapid growth, China's income inequality is not so much rural versus urban as inland versus coastal, with the inland provinces still dependent on state-owned enterprises while in the coastal provinces both rural and urban incomes have risen with the dynamic growth of nonstate enterprises.

Eventually, income inequality will have to be addressed by equalizing opportunity, so that growth diffuses to areas and groups left behind and public services help people adjust to economic change by increasing their skill levels. Outcomes can also be modified by redistributing income. Since the mid-1990s, as employees of state-owned enterprises have lost their 'iron rice bowl,' job-based entitlements to free housing, pensions, education, and health care services, social organizations have helped to fill the gaping hole in the social safety net. Harvard University China scholar Tony Saich shows how such citizens' organizations have been integrated into vertical structures where elites represent their perceived interests, rather than organizing into a more diffuse civil society.[22] In the countryside, institutions such as the *chijiao yisheng*, or 'barefoot doctors' – rural workers who received paramedical training to provide basic health care in rural areas – were not replaced when the communes were dismantled. Instead, people have had to rely on their own resources and those of their extended families to pay for medical care. In the Eleventh Plan (2006–10), reducing inequality was made a priority, with increased public spending on education, medical insurance, health, and social services, particularly in rural areas. The structure of a US$586 billion fiscal stimulus package introduced in November 2008 also reflected these shifting priorities toward rural development.[23]

In summary, China's ad hoc and incomplete institutional reforms to replace the plan with the market have created win-win outcomes that have attracted widespread support. Going forward, however, further institutional reforms will be needed to support the market and correct its failures. Transparency, accountability, property rights, and legal recourse are essential to the efficient operation of markets but are inconsistent with the traditional bureaucratic mindset. This basic ambiguity in China's institutions raises questions about the country's prospects for sustained long-term growth, a theme that runs through the rest of this book.

India's Institutions

Modern India is easier for westerners to understand because it uses the English language and has familiar British institutions, including a parliamentary democracy, an independent judiciary, a free press, and the rule of law. Yet, for much of its history, India lacked a unified political community or the drive, so evident in Chinese history, to protect its territory or its borders. Repeated invasions brought diverse populations to the country. As Sunil Khilnani articulates in a 1997 work,[24] modern-day India is an 'idea' that is distinctive in its democratic ways and willingness to accommodate diversity. Yet, although this idea has prevailed so far, a competing vision that emphasizes 'Hindu-ness' and a mistrust of diversity is a cause for concern.

India scholar Francine Frankel notes how the popular view in

India that the country is destined to be a great power rests on beliefs that can be traced back to its ancient culture in the era between 1500 and 500 BCE. Powerful Vedic beliefs about the origins of the universe, the ritual power of Brahmins in maintaining that order, and the hierarchical relations flowing from such ordering created patterns of stratification that made it possible to preserve social order without a state.[25] Those patterns form the caste system, one of India's most pervasive institutions. Economist Deepak Lal argues that caste began as a response to the challenges of political instability and the traditional agrarian society's requirement for a steady labor supply despite the uncertain annual monsoon rains.[26] Caste provides stability and certainty by defining both social roles and economic tasks. It is a hierarchy of groups rather than of individuals, and is maintained by the threat of ejection of offenders from the group. While most Indians argue that caste has declining relevance in urban areas, it is still a reality in the village, where the stability it offers is offset by the difficulties of changing one's caste and aspiring to a different, better future.

Indian elites pride themselves on India's moral contributions to the world from the great religions that arose there. India had a major cultural influence on China during the first millennium, as travelers moved back and forth overland along the Silk Road and through Tibet. Chinese monks studied Buddhism at Nalanda University in Bihar, and Buddhism was adopted for a time in the Chinese court. These links were subsequently severed as nomadic tribes from central Asia invaded border areas in both countries, looted urban centers, and destroyed the Buddhist monasteries. Trade routes were closed, and Confucian traditions were restored in China.

Between 1300 and 1700, much of northern India was part of a Moghul (Muslim) empire that reached its height during the fifty-year rule of Akbar (1556–1605) and his immediate successors, Jehangir and Shah Jehan, who were famous for their curiosity and religious tolerance.[27] Aurangzeb, the ruler who followed them between 1658 and 1707 reversed these policies and, in the political and religious conflicts that followed, the empire went into decline. The British – beginning with the British East India Company, which arrived in 1600 – exploited the political weakness and uncertainty that ensued, playing off India's diverse groups against one another, first for commercial interests but later for political gain. The British government took over the administration of India from the British East India Company following the 1858 Sepoy Mutiny, or what many Indians call the First War of Independence, but India remained a collection of kingdoms, princely states, and tribal areas until its unification at the time of independence in 1947. In the lead-up to independence, the British faced increasing pressures for self-rule from Indian nationalists (*hind swaraj*) led by Mohandas (Mahatma) Gandhi, an Indian-born, British-educated lawyer.

Consistent with the 'idea' of India, ethnic, religious, and regional diversity is not just tolerated but celebrated. India is home to four of the world's major religions. Hindi is the national language, but there are twenty-two recognized languages, including English, the language of commerce – indeed, India is the world's largest English-speaking country. At independence, India became a federation with powers divided between the central government, twenty-eight state governments, and seven union territories. To the surprise of many, the strong political and legal institutions introduced by the British were retained. As in China, however, ethnic minorities and their issues challenge national unity and create insecurity. India faces insurgencies in the northeast and persistent tensions over Kashmir, while China's insecurities are heightened by the Uighur and Tibetan minorities occupying the vast western regions. Neither country shrinks from the use of force, but India has diffused tensions better by co-opting minority groups and, since 2000, has created three new states to accommodate them.[28]

Unlike China, India did not have a revolution. Rather, Gandhi and his followers relied on nonviolent protest to press for independence from British rule. He had a vision of India as a republic of villages: decentralized, self-sufficient, and agrarian. The nonviolent protests he led were steeped in an ascetic philosophy that emphasized nonmaterialism and rural poverty, values that widened the base of support for the resistance movement beyond the elites.

Independence, however, was a deeply traumatic event. In August 1947, just three months after the British announced their intention to leave, India was partitioned to create the Muslim state of East and West Pakistan.[29] Historian Ramachandra Guha asserts there were three reasons for partition: the strength of the Muslim leadership's demand for a separate state regardless of the human consequences, the fact that the leaders of the independence movement underestimated Muslim resolve, and the divide-and-rule approach of the British, which exploited these divisions for their own purposes.[30] Millions of people were uprooted, and as many as a million lost their lives in the violent migration that followed. Tensions with Pakistan have persisted and are a source of such insecurity in both countries that each has taken the extreme step of acquiring nuclear weapon capabilities.

Independent India's first rulers enjoyed widespread popular support. Jawaharlal Nehru, India's first prime minister, was, like Gandhi, a British-educated lawyer, and the two worked closely together to achieve self-rule. Both held political philosophies that left an indelible impact on the country's economic institutions. Nehru's antipathy to western colonialism led him to turn the country inward and to build a heavy industrial base that he thought would promote self-sufficiency. His political popularity was such that Parliament and the people rarely denied him the road he chose to take. With a few interruptions, much of his power passed to his daughter, Indira Gandhi, and subsequently to her son, Rajiv. Mrs. Gandhi shared her father's antipathy to foreigners and acquired a strong taste for government intervention to address the country's poverty-related problems. Her policies had long-lasting effects on the country's institutions. She introduced a number of pro-labor laws, nationalized industries and the banks, and imposed restrictions on international trade and finance. During the period of Emergency Rule between 1975 and 1977, she shut down the independent media, imprisoned opponents, and suspended democracy. She pressed the civil service, one of India's legendary 'good' institutions, into her own service. In this autocratic environment, corruption flourished and spread to all levels of bureaucratic and political relationships. In the 1980s, Rajiv

Gandhi reversed some of these restrictive policies, but India has not yet fully jettisoned the ideas and institutions adopted during those years.

India's antipathy toward western powers helps to explain why there has been less of the overt curiosity about the sources of western growth that is so evident in China. In the early years of independence, Indian politicians looked to the Soviet Union, but more recently to their East Asian neighbors. Mahatma Gandhi's ascetic values provided the basis for protectionist, labor-intensive policies to promote small craft industries, particularly in textiles, which have tended to discourage large-scale manufacturing operations and employment to the present day. Nehru believed India should have its own heavy industry run by Indian technicians. He channeled public funding into technical education, laying the basis for India's fabled Indian Institutes of Technology, but in doing so he diverted funds from primary education and basic literacy. Having its own heavy industry might have strengthened India's economic independence from foreign industrialists, but it did little to create jobs for the huge surplus of labor or to educate the millions of rural illiterates.

For all its economic weaknesses, however, India's political and cultural institutions are both unique and resilient, as Ramachandra Guha eloquently argues:

> As a modern nation, India is simply *sui generis*. It stands on its own, different and distinct from the alternative political models on offer – be these Anglo-Saxon liberalism, French republicanism, atheistic communism, or Islamic theocracy ... So long as the constitution is not amended beyond recognition, so long as elections are held regularly and fairly and the ethos of secularism broadly prevails, so long as citizens can speak and write in the language of their choosing, so long as there is an integrated market and moderately efficient civil service and army, and – lest I forget – so long as Hindi films are watched and their songs sung, India will survive.[31]

As this sketch implies, the economic circumstances of Indians have improved, but only in fits and starts up to 2003, when growth reached rates of 8 to 9 percent that continued until the global financial crisis in 2008, during which the rate has declined to below 6 percent. Many Indians argue that economic change is difficult to implement because India's political structure as both a democracy and a federation produces chaotic and messy decision-making. Disparate and competing goals and interest groups mean that change is achieved only in the most laborious fashion. Yet, for the first forty years after independence, India was a one-party state. Its leaders had the authority and the public support to undertake modernizing change but did not do so; instead, the economic legacies of Gandhi and the Nehrus led to inward-looking protectionism, which inadvertently allowed powerful interests to vest that now obstruct change.

Since 1985, when India's states began to acquire more autonomy, this top-down approach gradually has shifted to bottom-up politics. The formation of regional and caste-based parties led to coalition governments that have ended the Congress Party's grip on power. India was ruled by the National Democratic Alliance (NDA) between 1999 and 2004, after which the United Progressive Alliance (UPA) took power. Nandan Nilekani, a chief executive of IT giant Infosys, notes wryly, however, that terms like 'alliance' and 'united' fail to capture the reality of Indian coalition politics, which are fractured by religion, caste, class, and region. In this chaotic democracy, leaders have trouble exerting authority to achieve economic transformation. Outcomes may be unexpected ones or achieved only through laborious compromises among competing groups – or not at all.

An example of an unexpected outcome can be found in efforts to eliminate the discriminatory effects of the caste system. After independence, India's first justice minister, Bhimrao Ambedkar, was a *dalit,* a member of one of the lowest castes. He introduced an affirmative action program, intended to be temporary, which established 'reservations' or quotas for *dalits* and scheduled tribes and castes that entitled them to specified numbers of government jobs and university and college admissions. Access to modern education and jobs as channels for economic advancement, it was thought, would allow them to leave caste behind. The scheme,

however, had at least two unintended consequences. One was
that it helped to create so-called vote banks – organized by politicians around narrow interests that they then use to attract voters
by promising favors in return – which have since spread to other
political causes. Reservations attracted politicians who promised
the extension of entitlements to members of low castes in return
for their support. As the program was expanded to include more
and more subgroups, ethnic identity replaced competence and
qualifications in the minds of many voters when choosing their
political candidates.

The second consequence was that, rather than withering away,
the caste system has become more deeply entrenched. The original reservations have expanded under political pressures from
representatives of subgroups attracted to the entitlements. In early 2008, for example, traffic was brought to a standstill in Delhi for
forty days as the *gujjars*, a caste of animal herders from the north-
western state of Rajasthan, took to the city streets. Their goal was
to draw attention to their request to be downgraded to a designated caste, which would make them eligible for a quota category in
which they would be more competitive. Such actions highlight the
persistence in rural India of caste-based social and labor divisions.

India's federal structure diffuses authority among different levels of government, requiring compromise to get things done and
changes to be incremental. Under the constitution, the states have
authority over areas key to India's economic future, including education, agriculture, agrarian reform, and land revenues. Some
of these powers overlap with those of the central government. In
recent years, opposition parties have won control in a number of
states and, as competition with the central government for national resources has increased, state budget deficits have contributed
significantly to the total public sector deficit. The central government is not blame free either, since coalitions have found it politically expedient to spend rather than to argue over whose priorities
to support (a tactic common to most democratic coalitions). Partial economic reforms introduced during the 1991 financial crisis opened the economy and freed up the exchange rate but left
much undone, including removing regulatory restrictions on la-

bor and capital. Nearly twenty years later, socialist and communist political parties and special interest groups aligned with politicians make further changes slow and difficult to implement.

Ironically, it was Rajiv Gandhi who moved India forward when he became prime minister following his mother's assassination in 1984. He did not share her fondness for government intervention or her antipathy for foreigners and began to deregulate industry and remove some of the restrictions on trade, the exchange rate, and foreign investment. He also eased price controls and began to deregulate the telecommunications sector and education. In the 1988–91 period, growth jumped to an annual average of 7.6 percent from 4.8 percent during the 1981–88 period, creating popular support for more reform.[32]

Reform has continued, sometimes in dramatic fashion when democratic institutions have asserted their authority. India's increasingly activist judiciary, for example, has cut through political gridlocks by recognizing citizens' constitutional rights. In other cases, the prime minister has pursued laborious efforts to align narrow interests with those of the country as a whole. In the 1990s, the World Health Organization designated India's capital, New Delhi, as one of the world's most polluted cities. In response, a nongovernmental organization (NGO) initiated a public interest litigation before the Indian Supreme Court arguing that the Delhi Municipal Administration, by failing to protect the environment, was violating residents' constitutional rights. The Supreme Court agreed to hear the case, and subsequently ruled that the municipal government had to reduce air pollution by, for example, moving polluting industry away from urban areas and requiring cleaner forms of public transportation. To that end, the municipal government converted its entire public transit system, including taxis and rickshaws, to compressed natural gas. The quality of Delhi's air is still questionable, but the unconventional means by which political gridlock was circumvented suggests that reforms are possible.

One investment the capital's municipal government made to help clean the air was the construction of a rapid transit system, Delhi Metro, which demonstrates what incorruptible managers working in a nonpoliticized framework can achieve. This infra-structure project was badly needed when it was opened in 2002 as a sparkling paragon of mass transit efficiency. Financed by Japanese development aid, it was built on time and on budget, led by an experienced official who ran the construction project on condition that there be no bureaucratic or political interference. There was not.

Can the lessons of Delhi Metro's success be applied to the plethora of essential transportation and power infrastructure projects required throughout the nation? Subsequent infrastructure projects suggest the answer might be yes. During the 1999–2004 period, the NDA ruling coalition pushed forward a series of transportation infrastructure projects – the Golden Quadrilateral highway project that circumnavigates the peninsula was NDA prime minister A.B. Vajpayee's major legacy to the country. Momentum slowed, however, after the UPA government was elected in 2004 and has only recently been restored. Since 2006, there has been a surge in infrastructure spending, with US$500 billion allocated to the modernization of transportation, ports, and power infrastructure. These large investments are the result of years of central government efforts to build a multi-party consensus in support of both the public spending and the involvement of private investors in public-private partnerships.

Telecommunications reform is an outstanding example of how a new door of opportunity was opened for Second India when top political leaders aligned diverse interests around a national goal. Traditionally, telecommunications was the exclusive domain of the Department of Telecommunications with its staff of half a million. After years of effort by weak coalition governments in the 1990s, a strong coalition with a clear mandate from the 1999 elections (and the help of direct intervention by the prime minister's office) restructured the sector. The government's role was pruned back to policymaking, regulation, and dispute settlement. Service provision was thrown open to the private sector (along with a single, restructured public sector service provider).[33] The reforms paid off handsomely, unleashing lively competition in the mobile phone market and crash connection programs that reach deep into rural India.

The civilian nuclear cooperation agreement with the United States is another example of government's using its authority to achieve change. This pact was held up throughout much of 2008 by opposing political interests, which argued it gave the United States too much potential influence over India's foreign policy. Realizing that the window was closing for the final step of U.S. congressional approval as the George W. Bush administration entered its final months, Prime Minister Manmohan Singh called the opposition's bluff by risking a no-confidence vote in Parliament. The agreement was ratified but left an atmosphere of mistrust over the tactics used.

These cases illustrate that reform is possible when leaders assert their authority, but they are entangled in a seemingly impenetrable thicket of competing interests. Nandan Nilekani asserts that 'governments are forced to frame agendas that will keep them popular with voters who have made growth and rising incomes a condition for granting political power.'[34] In the May 2009 general election, voters rewarded the UPA coalition with a strengthened mandate. Expectations are high. Leaders possess the authority and public support for economic change that could set the stage for more successes on the order of the telecommunications reforms. But will they take the tough decisions that could unleash India's full economic potential?

Realizing Their Full Potential

Despite the significant changes taking place in the institutions and policies of China and India, the transformations are incomplete and disconnects remain. In China, tight political control increasingly is disconnected from a free-wheeling market economy. The Chinese Communist Party's pragmatism and focus have delivered economic growth, but its determination to retain its grip on power could yet make it a victim of its own success. Nowhere does this matter more than in finance and technology, on which China increasingly must rely as its population ages and its labor force shrinks. Corruption, lack of property rights, and growing income inequality are creating inexorable pressures for further change.

India's disconnect is between the wealth of political freedom and the poverty of economic opportunity for Second India. In India's bottom-up democracy, with its plethora of special interest groups that are making themselves heard, change of any kind is laborious and uncertain. What is it about India's institutions and politics that doors open to new technologies and physical infrastructure surges ahead, yet good jobs remain out of reach for millions of people? Why are so many Indians still dependent on agriculture? Can India create higher-paying jobs in modern sectors, the way China has? In the next chapter, we seek answers to these questions.

chapter two

Developing Human Capital

Education is light, lack of it is darkness.
– Russian proverb

One factor that will differentiate China's economic future from that of India is the characteristics of their human assets. By 2030, each country will have a billion and a half people, but China's population will be shrinking while India's continues to grow. More than that, however, the relative quality of their respective labor forces will be key to their ability to sustain economic growth.

Changes to China's institutions have freed up productive jobs and raised incomes, first in agriculture and then in manufacturing. These institutions are unabashedly capitalistic, so much so that they are being adjusted to give labor more say. India's institutions, in contrast, while allowing the college educated to thrive in First India's modern sector beyond the bureaucrats' reach, have restricted the growth of good jobs in impoverished, rural Second India, many of whose people still depend on agriculture. Education, of course, is the primary building block for developing human assets. Yet, until recently, education per se as the route to personal economic success could not be taken for granted, as the stories of a Chinese professor and an Indian farmer illustrate.

Michael He[1] is a professor at a Beijing university. His life, like that of many middle-aged Chinese, has taken a circuitous route as China's political and economic institutions have changed. He is a

member of the 'class of 1978,' all of whom, after the decade of disruption caused by the Cultural Revolution, were permitted to take
college entrance examinations. His father was a journalist who, in
the 1960s, criticized China's foreign policy and was punished by
banishment to the countryside, along with his family. No formal
schooling was available to Michael, who taught himself by reading
the writings of Chairman Mao Zedong. He nonetheless passed the
college entrance examinations and chose to study navigation in
order to see the world. Later, he obtained advanced degrees from
the Chinese Academy of Social Sciences and became an academic
and entrepreneur.

Kumar's story[2] provides insights into both the importance of
education as a channel for mobility in India and India's penchant
for direct intervention to create such channels. He is one of the
better-off rural millions, living in Uttar Pradesh, the largest of India's lagging states, but restricted by his caste to farming. Yields on
his farm are falling, but he is more fortunate than his neighbors in
that he has some options. Because of his caste entitlement to education, he has completed a bachelor's degree and is determined
to use the same means to enter medical school. He hopes to leave
subsistence agriculture behind using an institution designed to
promote such mobility.

China's Labor Market Institutions

Both China and India face the huge challenge of creating employment opportunities for the two hundred million or so 15-to-24-
year-olds in each country who will enter the labor force by 2030
(see Table 1, panel C). China has made more progress than India,
however, in channeling its population into productive, higher-in-
come jobs in modern sectors, for several reasons. First, universal
primary education is a legacy of the central planning era: 91 percent of Chinese are literate.[3] Second, China's population is aging: between 2010 and 2020, the number of 15-to-24-year-olds will
shrink by an average of nearly four million a year (Table 1, panel
C). Indeed, China's total population is expected to peak at 1.46
billion around 2030 and then begin to shrink (panel A). Third,

Table 1: Population and Labor Force, China and India, 1990–2050

	1990	2000	2010	2020	2030	2050
A. Population (*millions*)						
China	1,142	1,267	1,354	1,431	1,462	1,417
India	862	1,042	1,214	1,367	1,485	1,614
World	5,290	6,115	6,909	7,674	8,308	9,150
B. Labor Force (*population ages 15–64, millions*)*						
China	755	855	973	996	983	870
India	503	633	780	916	1,021	1,098
Labor Force (*population ages 15–59, millions*)*						
China	721	815	918	923	874	760
India	483	607	749	868	962	1,004
C. Size of Group of New Labor Force Entrants (*population ages 15–24, millions*)						
China	247	197	229	180	178	148
India	165	202	234	245	242	206
D. Urban Population (*millions and % of total population*)						
China	375 (27)	455 (36)	607 (45)	756 (53)	879 (60)	n.a.
India	219 (26)	290 (28)	367 (30)	479 (34)	613 (41)	n.a.
E. Rural Population (*millions and percent of total population*)						
China	834 (73)	815 (64)	744 (55)	665 (47)	579 (40)	n.a.
India	641 (75)	756 (72)	853 (70)	905 (66)	893 (59)	n.a.

n.a. = not available.
*Panel B contains two estimates of labor force size: the first is 15-to-64-year-olds, which is the common measure in international use; the second is 15-to-59-year-olds, which is most commonly used in China and India.
Sources: Data for panels A, B, and C are from United Nations, *World Population Prospects: The 2008 Revision Population Database*; data in panels D and E are from idem, *2006 Revision Population Database*.

China is urbanizing: in the Eleventh Plan (2006–10), the government has committed to move forty-five million people from rural to urban areas and to create jobs for all of them.[4] By 2030, two-thirds of China's population will be urban, up from less than a third in 1990 (panel D).

In the mid-1990s, China made nine years of education compulsory, but saddled local governments with the bills. In response, many resorted to school fees or failed to compensate teachers, as a result of which many students were either denied education or received inadequate schooling. The Eleventh Plan, which extols an educated population as a source of China's future comparative advantage, proposes to change all this. The state intends to supply free primary school education in rural areas by 2010 and nationwide by 2015. So far, it is ahead of target. In 2000, 20 percent of the working-age population had high school education, with nearly 40 percent achieving grade 9. Less than 1 percent had a college education in 2000, but between 2001 and 2008 the number of college graduates increased dramatically from one million to six million a year. Educational attainment in rural areas is still a problem, however: as many as 19 percent of rural females and 8 percent of males are thought to be illiterate. Twice as many girls as boys still do not go to school, and educational access for the children of migrant laborers in urban areas is still subject to discrimination.[5]

Since 1978, employment in China has undergone two transformations: labor has moved out of agriculture, and it has moved out of state enterprises into the evolving nonstate sector – which includes a variety of ownership forms such as urban collectives and township and village enterprises, as well as private ownership by both domestic and foreign entities. Agricultural employment is estimated to have fallen from 70 percent in 1978 to as low as 32 percent in 2004, much below official estimates.[6] After 1978 labor moved off the farms and, agricultural productivity increased. It also rose as restrictions were relaxed on where people can work: under the household responsibility system, families were permitted to start businesses in nearby villages and towns, producing goods and services that others wanted to buy.

Beginning in the mid-1990s, the state sector was radically restructured, which further enhanced productivity. In 1995, state-owned enterprises were estimated to have employed 113 million people; by 2004, this number had dropped to 67 million as nearly two-thirds of such enterprises were closed, merged, or sold.[7] At the same time, labor market institutions were changed radically to give employers freedom to hire and fire. This restructuring caused considerable hardship, but the strong growth of private and foreign-invested enterprises in manufacturing and services created sufficient jobs to offset the unemployment effects. By the end of 2002, as many as 108 million people were employed in manufacturing.[8]

As this restructuring proceeded, migration from rural to urban areas surged. When most of the small, unprofitable, rural state-owned enterprises were closed, many of their former employees found jobs in the industrializing urban areas. Young male employees found jobs in construction while young females entered labor-intensive manufacturing sectors such as textiles and apparel and electronics. One of the unfinished tasks in the transformation of urban labor markets is the segmentation that persists between jobs in the formal sector, which employs more than a hundred million workers, and the informal sector, which employs another one hundred and sixty million casual laborers and self-employed workers.[9] *Hukou*, the system of compulsory household registration which has been used to regulate migration, is breaking down in smaller cities and towns as it comes under criticism for denying those with rural registration access to government jobs, housing, education, and social services that are available to those with urban registration.[10]

Until recently, contract laborers had few rights, and stories of employer exploitation and unpaid wages were rife. The Labor Contract Law, implemented in January 2008, strengthens workers' rights, employment conditions, and compensation, and sets out rules – such as written contracts, rules for severance that respect seniority, and severance payments – for full-time employees. It also restricts companies' ability to hire casual workers and fire without compensation, and allows for the arbitration of disputes. Like other laws, the Labor Contract Law is being phased in gradually and is subject to the interpretation of local governments; nevertheless, it imposes universal standards previously ignored by exploitative employers seeking cost advantages over those who followed fairer practices. The law also recognizes the role of the All China Federation of Trade Unions as representing workers' welfare, although not as collective bargainer. Even so, high-profile efforts have successfully targeted large foreign employers such as Wal-Mart, which was unionized in 2008.

Rural labor markets remain active, with an estimated 76 percent of rural 16-to-20-year-olds holding down off-farm jobs.[11] China's rural-to-urban migration tends to be circular, with young male migrants moving back and forth between city and village, often returning to assist with planting and harvesting. Although land reform legislation was approved in October 2008, it has been dismissed as relatively minor in effect, since powerful interests in local governments, the real estate industry, and the ministry of construction continue to resist such reforms to keep the costs of land compensation from increasing and reducing their rents. Insofar as the legislation provides more clarity of land tenure, however, it reduces farm families' uncertainties about the security of their land allotments. It could also open the way for transfers of nonagricultural land to industrial uses and new development possibilities for villages that might attract would-be migrants to opportunities closer to home.[12]

In summary, China's labor market institutions are evolving in ways that raise the cost of labor and provide new alternatives to the labor-intensive manufacturing and services that have provided millions of jobs outside agriculture. Wages will rise as the supply of young people declines over the next two decades, productivity increases, and the Labor Contract Law is enforced.[13]

India's Labor Market Institutions

So far, movement of labor out of agriculture is proceeding in India at half the pace that it is in China, despite China's continued restrictions on labor migration.[14] Labor-intensive manufacturing has not yet taken off in India the way it has in China because India's particular institutions hinder the ability of workers to acquire skills and of employers to create large numbers of jobs in the modern sectors. Reform of these institutions or the creation of alternative ways to employ workers is needed to absorb the huge number of young Indians who will be looking for jobs in the years ahead. Former finance minister P. Chidambaram has warned: 'One thing is clear, unless the disconnect is eliminated, the Second India will limit the promise the First India sees for itself in the Asian century.'[15]

India's population is youthful and rural. By 2020, a quarter of a billion Indians will be between 15 and 24 years of age, a number that exceeds that of all but four of the world's most populous countries – even China has not had such a large population in that age group since the 1990s. By that date, two-thirds of India's population (down from three-quarters in 1990) will still be living in rural Second India, where the growth rate of the agricultural sector has been declining, reflecting poor monsoons in some years and declining public investment and services.

By 2030, India's population will still be growing, but at a slower rate. Moreover, the population of labor force age will be growing faster than the total population, prompting enthusiasm about a demographic dividend if the expanding labor force is able to support the very young and aged dependents. Such enthusiasm is misplaced, however. As long as Second India is denied education and productive employment opportunities illiterate and uneducated young people will be a liability, not an asset.

From where will the jobs come for all these millions? Surely not from the headline-generating IT services and techno-manufacturing industries; these employ only about three million people, drawn from India's supply of postsecondary graduates. India's Planning Commission expresses the hope that the country will 'create productive employment at a faster pace than before, and target robust agriculture growth at 4 percent per year.'[16] It is depending on agriculture and general employment creation to raise incomes, yet almost 60 percent of the labor force is still in agriculture, which in 2007 contributed just 18 percent of the country's output, compared with 53 percent by services and 29 percent by manufacturing.[17] Yet, productive jobs outside agriculture are critical for India's long-term economic prospects. Can India create tens of millions of higher-paying jobs, as China has done?

Comparisons of industrial employment in the two countries show startling differences (see Table 2). Although only rough comparisons are possible because of the differing ways in which these statistics are reported and defined, there seem to be twice as many employed Chinese as Indians. And twice as many Chinese are employed in manufacturing (or 'industry,') with many others in construction, trade, and services.[18]

Table 2: Patterns of Employment, China and India, 1990 and 2000

Industry	China		India[a]	
	1990	2000	1990[b]	2000[c]
	(millions and % share)			
Agriculture	342 (53.0)	334 (46.0)	242.5 (65.0)	238 (60.0)
Mining	8.8 (1.0)	7.1 (1.0)	2.7 (0.1)	2.3 (1.0)
Manufacturing	86.2 (13.0)	80.4 (11.0)	42.5 (11.5)	48 (12.0)
Utilities	1.9 (1.0)	2.8 (1.0)	1.4 (1.0)	1.3 (1.0)
Construction	24.2 (3.7)	35.5 (5.0)	11.7 (3.0)	17.6 (4.5)
Trade	28.4 (4.3)	46.9 (6.5)	28 (7.4)	37.3 (9.3)
Transport	15.7 (2.4)	20.3 (2.7)	10.3 (3.0)	14.7 (4.0)
Finance	2.2 (1.0)	3.3 (1.0)	3.5 (1.0)	5 (1.0)
Services[d]	37.1 (5.7)	41.7 (6.0)	32.1 (8.6)	33 (8.3)
Other and residual[e]	99.2 (15.3)	149.2 (21.0)	n.a.	n.a.
Total employment[f]	648 (100.0)	721 (100.0)	374.5 (100.0)	397 (100.0)

Size of potential labor force by age

	(millions)			
Ages 15–64	755	855	503	633
Ages 15–59	721	815	483	607

[a] Indian statistics are based on National Sample Surveys and include both organized and unorganized employment; the segmentation may lead to underreporting in both categories.

[b] Fiscal year 1993/94.

[c] Fiscal year 1999/2000.

[d] Services include government, commercial, and social.

[e] The large numbers in China reflect huge changes in employment during the decade as people laid off from state-owned enterprises entered private or self employment, neither of which was well covered by statistics.

[f] Percentages may not add up due to rounding.

Sources: Ray Brooks and Ran Tao, 'China's Labor Market Performance and Challenges,' IMF Working Paper WP/03/210 (Washington, DC: International Monetary Fund, 2003); India, Planning Commission, *Planning Commission Reports on Labour and Employment* (New Delhi: Economica, 2002); United Nations, *World Population Prospects: The 2008 Revision Population Database.*

Why Do So Many Indians Depend on Agriculture?

In contrast, India's dependence on agricultural employment reflects outdated labor market institutions that restrict employers' options, the lack of physical infrastructure such as reliable electricity supply, roads, bridges, and ports, and the difficulties workers face in leaving the agriculture sector.

India's labor market institutions are a legacy of socialist policies and the close connections between Mohandas Gandhi and the trade union movement, which helped him push for independence. The Congress Party sought to protect workers from capitalist exploitation by their employers by acquiescing to pressures from the unions and imposing laws and regulations on dismissals and contract hiring. If an enterprise has less than ten employees and uses electricity (or less than twenty and does not use electricity), it is classified as unorganized and is subject to minimal labor market regulation. Larger enterprises are part of the organized sector and are regulated by the Factories Act of 1948 and subject to a plethora of regulations on employment and benefits that increase with the firm's size.[19] Significantly, the 1947 Industrial Disputes Act made it virtually impossible for large firms to lay off workers or to close without government permission, and even firms with as few as a hundred employees must now obtain such permission after a tightening of requirements by Indira Gandhi, who became increasingly irritated with union militancy and strikes during her tenure.[20]

Faced with union wage demands on the one hand and the inability to adjust their work force size on the other, Indian entrepreneurs moved away from labor-intensive manufacturing into capital-intensive activities, or turned to casual labor in the informal sector. Today, the organized sector includes public and private corporations, cooperatives, and registered manufacturing units, and accounts for less than 10 percent of total employment. It is a small – and shrinking – enclave of highly paid, secure workers in large private sector corporations, state-owned enterprises, and government jobs in which rules, rather than competition, prevail. In contrast, the unorganized informal sector provides more than 90 percent of India's employment and is a vast pool of casual workers who earn low wages, receive few benefits, and are vulnerable to discrimination.

The effect of dozens of central government and hundreds of state labor laws has been slower output growth, less robust employment growth, and lower productivity. As one study concludes, 'Regulating in a pro-worker direction was associated with lower levels of investment, employment, productivity, and output in registered manufacturing. It also [increased] informal sector activity.'[21] In other words, supposedly pro-labor restrictions turned out to be anti-labor in their effect because they encouraged employers to engage in small-scale production and create fewer productive jobs. Other restrictions have magnified this outcome. For example, in the early 1970s, having already reserved craft industries for small and family enterprises, the central government restricted large business conglomerates to certain heavy industries. These interventions effectively denied small firms the opportunity to take advantage of the economies of scale they needed to be competitive and channeled large firms into capital- and skills-intensive production.[22]

Not surprisingly, such restrictions help to explain why India's organized sector is shrinking. Unions in that sector continue to resist reforms despite evidence that the laws and regulations impose high unemployment costs on the rest of the labor force. Although most small-scale reservations have now been removed, those that remain, as well as restrictions on hiring and firing, continue to limit firm size, discouraging employers from achieving efficient scale in their operations – even through the setting up of multiple small plants. A 2006 World Bank study found that plants in India's textiles and apparel industry have just 10 to 20 percent of the capacity of their Chinese counterparts.[23]

Another reason for India's continued dependence on agricultural employment is its inadequate infrastructure. Labor-intensive manufacturing – mainly textiles and apparel, furniture, sports equipment, simple electrical equipment, and certain auto parts – relies on readily available transportation and information infrastructure to link these activities to local and international supply chains.[24]

India's governments recognize the growing bottlenecks. The UPA coalition prepared a US$500 billion investment plan to upgrade and expand infrastructure, kicking off what could become a decade-long program. The program has been designed with broad political support from coalition members at the center and in the state governments. Investment by the central and state governments will account for 70 percent of the total; to reduce the impact on stretched public finances, private investors will provide the remaining 30 percent through public-private partnerships in telecommunications, seaports, and airports, and through private investment. Governments will expand power, roads, urban water supply, and sanitation, and divide their investments in telecommunications, railways, airports, gas distribution and liquid natural gas terminals, irrigation, and commodity storage facilities.[25]

While the long-term strategy must be to create employment alternatives outside agriculture, that sector also urgently needs attention. Productivity and incomes would rise if investments were made in research and training, inputs such as irrigation, and better market support services for farmers' produce. Financing is made difficult by the large fiscal burden of central government subsidies for food and fertilizer and state government subsidies for power and irrigation. These subsidies mainly benefit better-off landowners, but reforms are difficult because of vested interests and the mistrust of other rural groups, which fear losing the support they already obtain if subsidies are reallocated.[26]

Modernizing India's Labor Force

India's restrictive labor laws and lack of infrastructure seriously undermine the creation of jobs in the modern sector by restricting its scale. But even if India could overcome these problems, as China has done, its vast population would still be less productive than it could be because of India's cultural attitudes toward women and barriers to education and mobility.

ATTITUDES TOWARD WOMEN

At the turn of the twenty-first century, although India's labor force was 75 percent of the size of China's, total employment in India was only 55 percent of that in China. One explanation for the difference is the relative rates of participation by women in the labor force in the two countries.[27] In China, labor force participation by women is near-universal and stable; Mao Zedong's nostrum that 'women hold up half the sky' has shaped attitudes and practices in modern-day China, even though gender discrimination is still common. In contrast, India's national statistical surveys, which probably understate participation in the unorganized sector, show that female labor force participation is below 33 percent and declining. Economists explain this trend by the lower rate of literacy and, therefore, of employability of females, by expectations that married women, as a matter of family honor, will devote themselves to home and family (values that are not uncommon in other parts of Asia), and by the lack of labor market opportunities in the formal sector, particularly for women with some education.[28] Casual employment in the unorganized or informal sector consists of heavy or unpleasant jobs deemed unacceptable for women. Extensive discrimination with respect to hiring and wages – against not just women but also members of the scheduled castes and rural workers – are also common practices in the informal sector.

Looking to the future, as fertility rates fall and educational attainment increases for Indian women, even more of them will become available for economic activity outside the home. Fortunately, the participation of women in the labor force is slowly becoming more socially acceptable.

EDUCATIONAL ACCESS AND QUALITY

Literacy, education, and skills are important factors in finding employment in the modern sector. Here again, China and India display startling differences. For example, in the decade between 1995 and 2005, India's literacy rate averaged 61 percent, while in China the rate was 91 percent.[29] The remarkable paradox, however, is that, in a country with the largest number of illiterates on earth, India's colleges and universities produce two and a half million graduates. What accounts for this paradox?

Part of the answer resides in political choices about the allocation of education funding. Prime Minister Nehru's self-sufficiency policy emphasized heavy industry and, as a corollary, priority funding was channeled into engineering and technical education to supply the skills needed to run those industries. In 1950, India's constitution aimed that, by 1960, the state should endeavor to provide free and compulsory education to all children up to age 14. Indeed, the first Five Year Plan (1951–56) allocated more than half of the education budget to primary education. But by 1966, both technical and secondary education funding had increased at the expense of primary education.

Change is under way but progress is slow. The constitution was amended in 2002 to mandate free and compulsory schooling for all 6-to-14-year-olds, 90 percent of whom now go to school, and in 2006 employment of children in many personal services was banned. The government claims that 94 percent of the population lives within a kilometer of a primary school and 84 percent within three kilometers of an 'upper primary school.' Still, the dropout rate is high, and parental choice and social barriers inhibit educational access for many.

Take the case of Banwasi, a *dalit,* one of the lowest castes, who lives in Uttar Pradesh. Her husband is a self-employed weaver, and she works as a casual agricultural laborer. She cannot read – indeed, literacy in her caste is among the lowest in the country. Her father did not send her to school because her impoverished family needed her earnings as a casual laborer. Besides, school was an unpleasant experience for low-caste children like her, who were frequently segregated and discriminated against by higher-caste students and teachers.[30]

The central issue now is the quality of education. In government schools, teaching quality is poor. Teachers are organized sector employees with secure jobs and benefits, but little accountability for their attendance or performance. In 1998, PROBE, a government-sponsored report on basic education, found that, in the four most populous lagging states, teaching was actually taking place in only 53 percent of village schools – teachers were absent in one-third of the schools and, when present, only half actually taught. This is not necessarily the fault of teachers; other institutional factors, such as conventions governing the conduct of young women, are part of the reason, as an example illustrates. In 2006, in a small town in western Rajasthan, I witnessed students

dressed in blue uniforms converging on the school late one morning. This was when their teacher, a conservatively dressed young
woman with a somber expression on her face, arrived by bus from
Udaipur, many miles away, where her family lives. At the end of
the day, she would catch the bus back to Udaipur and return in
the late morning the next day.

NGOs are heavily engaged in raising the quality of education
in India. One of the best known is Pratham, founded in 1994 in
Mumbai by two individuals concerned about educational quality
in the slums and now the country's largest nonprofit organization.
UNICEF provided startup support, and the organization subsequently expanded its work to other states. More recently, ICICI,
India's largest private bank, whose headquarters are close to Mumbai's slums, has taken on the role of Pratham's 'parent.' Pratham
estimates that half of India's two hundred million children of primary school age cannot read or write. Eleven percent fail to enter
school and 65 percent drop out before reaching the equivalent of
grade eight. Pratham's volunteer teachers work cooperatively with
government-run institutions to supply accelerated teaching techniques that result in visible changes in learning outcomes within
three months. Indeed, outcome measurement is an important
part of its program to influence public opinion on the quality of
primary education. In Uttar Pradesh, Pratham reached 2.1 million children between November 2006 and May 2007 in twenty
districts, and its random testing demonstrated that the number of
grade one children who could not read had dropped by 59 percent as a result of its programs.[31]

Parents have also responded to the low quality of public school
education by turning to private education, where teachers are
directly accountable to their employers. Importantly, private
schools teach English. On any morning in New Delhi, children in
neatly pressed uniforms can be spotted trickling out of the urban
slums into taxis that take them to their private schools. The returns to education are so clear to their parents that they cut down
on living expenses to find the money for high-quality education
for their children. By 2006, more than half of India's secondary
schools were private and were attended by a quarter of the student population.

LABOR MOBILITY

Geographic mobility is another factor for success in finding employment. Urban jobs tend to be more productive than rural jobs, and their higher real wages attract rural migrants. In theory, if labor markets are allowed to function without interference and labor is able to move freely, rural and urban wage rates should be equalized through time, assuming workers' similar education and experience. But, as we have seen, both China and India still have barriers that segment labor markets. India's segmentation is between the organized and unorganized sectors, while China's is between the large state-owned enterprises and the smaller non-state and private enterprises.[32]

One study comparing labor mobility in the two countries suggests that China's *hukou* system creates a working class with rural origins that acts as an exclusionary mechanism not unlike India's caste system.[33] This observation might be dated in China's case, however, since the more important barrier to migrants seeking better jobs is the lack of a high school education – nine years of education is no longer sufficient for urban services and manufacturing jobs in China, as wages rise and employers put more emphasis on labor productivity. In India, though, caste is a more pervasive factor, restricting labor mobility since one's surname frequently identifies one's religion, caste, and provincial origins. Indians are free of formal restrictions on migration, but caste influences who leaves the countryside and where they move to in urban areas.

In China, wages are now largely determined by competitive forces, although higher urban wages offer incentives for rural workers to migrate.[34] In contrast, wages for casual labor in India show only small rural and urban differences, implying there are few incentives to migrate.[35] Even so, rural-to-urban migration does occur in India, particularly among 15-to-44-year-old males, who move to jobs in towns or cities, even in other states. In contrast, females who migrate tend to do so only within their rural area because of the social custom that a woman moves to her husband's village when they marry.

In summary, the suggestion that India's large population promises a 'demographic dividend' is unrealistic. Unless the popula-

Table 3: Population Projections, India's Lagging States, 2001, 2026, and 2051

State	2001	2026	2051
	(millions)		
Bihar*	109.8	166.1	194.2
Madhya Pradesh*	81.2	118	137.2
Uttar Pradesh*	174.5	271	319.3
Orissa	36.7	45.5	47.4
Subtotal	402.2	600.6	698.1
Lagging states (% of total)	39.0%	42.3%	44.0%
India total	1,027	1,419	1,579

*Projections incorporate population numbers for the newer small states that have been carved out of these three states. The 2026 and 2051 projections are standard variants; the authors also present high and low projections incorporating alternative demographic assumptions.
Source: Tim Dyson and Pravin Visaria, 'Migration and Urbanization: Retrospect and Prospects,' in *Twenty-first Century India: Population, Economy, Human Development, and the Environment*, ed. Tim Dyson, Robert Cassen, and Leela Visaria (New Delhi: Oxford India Paperbacks, 2005), table 5.11.

tion of labor force age can be drawn out of unproductive jobs in agriculture, this 'dividend' risks becoming a future source of social instability.

The Future: Where Will India's Young People Find Work?

As we have seen, between 2010 and 2020, the number of 15-to-24-year-olds in China who are looking for jobs and education each year will shrink, while the number in India will grow by some eleven million. Where will they all find work? For many, the challenge is complicated by their lack of employability: nearly 40 percent of those over age 15 are illiterate, and although literacy rates are rising, many young people in Second India will not find work outside agriculture without huge improvements in educational standards, facilities, and attainment, particularly in the lagging states, where public services are poorest. As Table 3 shows, by 2050 these states will account for 44 percent of India's population.[36]

Clearly, changes in labor laws are essential to expand labor demand. Yet the UPA coalition elected in 2004 chose to paper over the problem in two ways: with more subsidies and by appointing a commission to study the problem. The National Rural Employment Guarantee Act of 2005 guarantees a hundred days of work a year at the minimum wage to any rural household seeking employment. In a lengthy 2007 report, the National Commission for Enterprises in the Unorganised Sector, set up to analyze working conditions and recommend improvements in the supply of jobs and in working conditions, advocates protective measures for these workers, supplementary measures for small farmers, measures to encourage growth in the nonagricultural sector, and measures to expand employment in the sector. One of its many recommendations is to universalize the National Rural Employment Guarantee Act, which initially targeted only the poorest areas.[37]

Faster urbanization would also help – for example, if India were to reach China's current 45 percent ratio by 2020, an additional 140 million people would have moved into urban areas by then. As it is, India is predicted to have more than seventy cities with a population of more than one million by 2026.[38] In the populous lagging states, though, urban wages are not sufficiently high to attract migrants, and conditions in city slums are little better than those in the villages. Rural workers are also unable to compete for available urban jobs because of their poor skills. Accordingly, the eastern part of India, in particular, is likely to remain relatively rural, and rural males will continue to move in large numbers out of states such as Bihar and Uttar Pradesh.[39]

The relative dynamism of the leading states further complicates the picture for the lagging states. One study describes a situation in which the leading states take all the 'oxygen.'[40] The lagging states need people with management and leadership skills to aid their necessary large-scale increases in labor-intensive manufacturing. But these same skills are in great demand in the dynamic peninsular states, which are bidding up the prices of skilled labor. A greater supply of skilled labor would help to offset such wage pressures, but restrictions on out-of-state registration in postsecondary institutions and occupational licensing obstruct the mobility of people from the lagging states.

Why not just skip the stage of development that relies on manufacturing and create the necessary jobs in the dynamic services sector? The problem is that those jobs need people with postsecondary education, and the lack of availability of higher education in Second India means that few young people there have this option. Higher education is traditionally important in India and became a priority after independence, when it was decided that the state would finance and regulate the system under the University Grants Commission. Government would pay for education that students could ill afford, and high standards would be enforced by a standardized curriculum and teachers' qualifications.

Today, India has 335 universities and 18,000 colleges. Some university departments, the Indian Institutes of Technology, and the Indian Institutes of Management are world class, and the system has produced brilliant graduates. But, in a world in which new areas of study are emerging, India's centralized and regulated system has been static: faculty have guaranteed salaries, but creativity is neither encouraged nor rewarded. As well, many students from better-off families who might otherwise pressure for change can afford to be educated abroad. Students who remain are nevertheless motivated to perform because of the potential rewards in the knowledge economy if they do well in the centralized examinations. If they do not do well, however, they are ignored. Employers of college students, many of them in the IT services industry, complain about the unevenness of the education system: they find that only a fraction of India's university graduates are employable and so must invest their own resources in training to bring new employees up to their standards.[41]

Some change is occurring, as state governments respond to pressures for more choice and better quality by permitting private colleges and universities. The central government also recognizes that the system is underfunded and has committed to double overall public spending on education. Further restructuring is required, however, to allow even more private delivery of higher education, more autonomy to institutions, and more emphasis on the quality of educational attainment.[42]

Casual India

The gap between First and Second India persists, in large part, because of bad institutions. The nearly one billion people in rural India need higher-quality, universally available education if that gap is to be reduced. Employers need more flexibility in their employment decisions to hire in those sectors that offer good jobs. Yet, such changes are opposed by vocal groups many of whom have come to depend on secure organized sector jobs.

Instead of a frontal assault on the underperforming public education system and restrictive labor laws, Indians find ways around them. Economist Arvind Panagariya argues that the state has demonstrated its inability to deliver quality educational services,[43] so parents turn to the private sector for accountable teachers and better-quality education. Why not build on this trend? Instead of channeling public funds into the dysfunctional system, why not give them directly to parents in the form of education vouchers? This would help parents who are already taking matters into their own hands by buying private education for their children. Parents then could choose the institution that best meets their children's needs. As market accountability is introduced into the system, productive institutions would prosper and dysfunctional ones would fail.

For their part, entrepreneurs and producers have long been resigned to labor restrictions, and make their production and hiring decisions accordingly. Were they to attempt to replicate the employment-creating scale of China's labor-intensive manufacturing, India's regulations would be a major stumbling block. Large organizations with thousands of employees either live with the higher cost of doing business or are complicit with state government officials. Some states have modified the powers of inspectors, while others look the other way, which only compounds the problem of corruption.

Yet, manufacturing employment is rising anyway, although predominately in rural, small-scale enterprises that rely on casual labor: between 1998 and 2003, half the growth in employment outside agriculture was in small-scale manufacturing operations in the unorganized sector in rural areas.[44] Over roughly the same period, the textiles and apparel, nonmetallic mineral products, furniture and wood products, and beverages and tobacco industries accounted for three-quarters of all new manufacturing jobs, all of them casual jobs in small, unorganized sector enterprises outside the purview of inspectors.[45] But these employers not only provide no security; they also have to depend on workers without skills. The Asian Development Bank estimates that India has as many as eighty million young workers who are in need of up to two years of training to 'repair' their skills, since almost two-thirds of them have little or no education. The vast majority of these workers hold low-quality jobs in the unorganized sector whose employers cannot afford to provide on-the-job training. Government, the Asian Development Bank argues, should not attempt to fill the training gap, but should leverage the private sector's demonstrated capabilities. The NGO Pratham has developed a successful approach to basic literacy and numeracy in the public schools; can its methods be adapted to similar offerings in occupational training?

Second India might be described better as 'Casual India,' because no one wants to take on the archaic labor laws that keep contract laborers and the self-employed in the wings, rather than at center stage, as the curtain rises on India's future. Outsiders who see what China's labor-intensive manufacturing has achieved are left scratching their heads, wondering why India does not simply change the laws. The inertia of the curious mixture of attachment to myths about the merits of rural life, the convenience to elites of a sea of cheap labor, and militant voices in the unions and the organized sector who oppose changes to their comfortable status quo creates perverse political incentives. Those who would gain have no voice and can vote only with their feet, engaging in modest self-employment or taking up the jobs that are gradually appearing in small-scale rural enterprises, while investing in the private education they see as opening doors for their children's futures.

India's underuse of its growing labor force is the country's Achilles' heel. Some Indians point out that most people have jobs,

but this is not the issue. The source of vulnerability is the growing economic divide between the few million with good jobs and
the hundreds of millions with casual jobs.[46] China's very different
challenge is its shrinking labor force.

Can China and India compensate for these seemingly intrac-
table problems by emphasizing other drivers of growth? One
way would be to foster the entrepreneurial talents of owners of
the small and medium-sized enterprises that create most of the
new jobs as well as the products and technologies of the future.
Such enterprises need funding to grow, however, and in the next
chapter, we will look at how effectively the two countries' financial
systems channel funds for startups and expansion to these small,
risky entrepreneurial ventures. Is either country up to the task?

chapter three

Finance: Sharper Scissors Required

'Sonia Gandhi keen to capitalize on crisis.'
– *Financial Times*, 22 November 2008

'Chinese officials lecture Paulson.'
– *Financial Times*, 5 December 2008

The financial systems of China and India are no match for the depth, sophistication, and diversity of the U.S. system. They are relatively conservative, in both their structure and oversight, and the world financial crisis that began in 2008 served to strengthen the confidence of Mrs. Sonia Gandhi and Chinese financial officials of the wisdom of that conservatism. Yet their government-owned, bank-dominated systems leave much to be desired. While small savers may have been protected by the government ownership Mrs. Gandhi extolled, government intervention in both countries' financial systems diverts national savings to social and political goals. Both financial systems are works in progress; beyond the banks, equity and bond markets need to be developed, particularly in China, to meet the needs of increasingly complex economies.[1]

One simple way to think of a financial system is to imagine a pair of scissors, where one blade collects savings while the other directs those savings to productive users by screening and monitoring borrowers and investments. Unlike a pair of scissors, however, sound, liquid, and diverse financial systems do not roll off a production line but must be developed. In subsistence agricultural economies, finance is informal: money is lent primarily on the basis of whom one knows. As economies become more complex, however, borrowers and lenders no longer know each other, and an information 'asymmetry' develops where lenders know much less than borrowers about whether they will be repaid in full and on time. To solve this information problem, formal financial institutions mobilize and pool the savings of many households and enterprises, and screen borrowers and issuers of bonds and commercial paper to determine their ability to repay. A modern financial system also facilitates payments in economic exchange, and helps to sustain fast growth by attracting necessary capital, processing information about enterprises and investment projects, and helping to direct savings to productive uses such as innovative firms.

Global finance has undergone a revolution in the past thirty years as advances in telecommunications and computer technology have made it possible to move capital with a keystroke – indeed, finance is now borderless. In the largest advanced industrial economies, managers and regulators have been unable to keep pace with the proliferation and complexity of financial innovations or adequately to protect investors and consumers against the risks they face. In the 2008 financial crisis, bank rescues by the U.S. government and temporary bank nationalizations by European governments prompted Sonia Gandhi to praise her late mother-in-law Indira Gandhi's controversial bank nationalizations in the late 1960s. The complex financial instruments and flawed government policies and regulatory regimes that were among the root causes of the global crisis are not the standard to which emerging markets should aspire. Rather, their goal should be sound regulation, liquid markets, and financial institutions and instruments of sufficient diversity that households, enterprises, and governments can make long-term investments and manage the associated risks.

The financial systems in China and India have some distance to go to reach such a standard. Their financial capacity is smaller than one might expect given these countries' huge populations

and the rapid growth of their economies – in 2007, their combined financial assets (bank deposits, debt securities, and equity)
totaled an estimated US$16.6 trillion, compared with US$4.7 trillion in 2003.[2] Moreover, they lack sufficient diversity to sustain
long-term growth, and government, rather than market forces,
still plays an important role. Yet, even though China seems to be
awash in capital, with a financial stock four and a half times that
of India, equity and corporate bond markets are underdeveloped,
and banks dominate the system: more than half of Chinese savings
are held in banks, compared with a third in India and a fifth in
the United States.[3] India's system is more diversified and sophisticated, but both countries' systems are behind what is technologi-
cally possible.

One reason for their underdevelopment is historical. For decades during the last century, they cut themselves off from world
financial markets by erecting barriers to capital flows and the entry
of foreign firms and, more recently, by managing their exchange
rates. In China, the communists nationalized the financial system
on taking power, and a single government bank issued currency
and collected deposits. Even today, after many years of reform,
although enterprises may reinvest their savings in their businesses,
Chinese households have few alternatives to the banks, which pay
interest at low rates set by the central bank after political approval
by the State Council. India's savers have more options, but many
households mistrust formal finance, preferring tangible assets of
gold and land.

In both countries, governments still have strong ownership
and conservative regulatory roles. Banks are largely state owned
– as in most developing countries – despite evidence that financial and economic development is slower in countries with large
state involvement.[4] As well, the official institutions that support
and regulate financial markets are underdeveloped, and neither
central bank is fully independent. In China, the People's Bank of
China reports to the State Council; in India, the Reserve Bank of
India is legally responsible to the central government, although it
has some de facto independence because of the central government's declining political clout. In China six regulatory agencies

share sometimes-overlapping responsibilities,[5] while in India such responsibilities are distributed among a number of agencies both inside and outside the financial system.

In short, neither country's financial scissors are as sharp as they could be. Measured by the amount of capital required to produce an additional unit of output, India and China are estimated to use 40 percent more capital than Japan did at a similar stage of its development.[6] Both countries' governments remain heavily involved because they use financial institutions as instruments to achieve significant political objectives: in China, jobs and political stability, which are the central goals of the Chinese Communist Party, and in India, access to financial institutions for rural and low-income savers and borrowers. Within these broad political constraints, both governments are pursuing reform agendas – China faster than India. The evolution beyond banks to create equity and bond markets is reflected in the stories of two young employees in financial institutions.

Nomita works in India's financial services industry, in a Mumbai brokerage firm. She takes online questions from customers who use her employer's stock portfolio management website. Over the past two years, volatility in Sensex (the Bombay Stock Exchange Sensitive Index) has made investors nervous; her job is to interest them in her employer's wealth-management offerings. She grew up in Ahmedabad, Gujarat, where her father, a real estate agent, paid for her to study in the private school system. Instead of leaving the country for a job in North America or Europe, she moved to Mumbai, where she earns 225 thousand rupees (US$5,600) a year for a six-day work week. She lives with an uncle while she earns enough money to take MBA studies that eventually will enable her to start her own financial services business.[7]

Xiaodong is a graduate of Peking University, and recently landed his first job in the newly formed fixed-income department of one of China's largest commercial banks. Like Nomita, he is a migrant, having grown up in a village in an inland province where his parents still live. He managed to change his *hukou* household registration from rural to urban when he graduated from college, and joined a state-owned enterprise. From there, he headed to

Beijing where, with hard work, he was admitted to the elite Peking
University for Master's studies, which he initially financed himself.
He thought about applying for PhD studies abroad, but decided
to seek a job in China's booming financial services industry so that
he could look after his parents.[8]

China's Evolving Financial System

People like Xiaodong head for the banks to find a good job because
banks are at the heart of China's financial system, and banking
reform has been a major feature of the country's modernization
since 1998. The bank regulator, the China Banking Regulatory
Commission, was created only in 2000.[9] China's equity and bond
markets are works in progress. There are two stock exchanges, in
Shenzhen and Shanghai, both of which were established in 1990.
Most of the 1,500 companies listed on these exchanges are large
state-owned enterprises. Domestic share ownership on the Shanghai Exchange soared in 2006 and 2007 as savers diversified their
portfolios beyond bank deposits, but between October 2007 and
October 2008, the exchange lost 73 percent of its value. Foreign
participation is heavily regulated through the Qualified Foreign
Institutional Investor program to prevent the volatility that can occur when foreign investors move into and withdraw funds from
local markets.[10] China's bond market is dominated by government
and policy banks, which accounted for nearly 75 percent of outstanding issues in 2008. The number of private issuers is very small;
most corporate bonds are issued by state-owned enterprises.[11]

The banking system consists of five large state-owned commercial banks, a dozen joint stock commercial banks, more than a
hundred commercial banks owned by municipal governments,
and more than thirty thousand rural and urban cooperatives. The
state-owned commercial banks dominate the system, accounting for more than half of banking assets, and have thousands of
branches and hundreds of thousands of employees throughout
the country, but they are growing more slowly (15 percent annually) than the joint stock banks (33 percent) or city commercial
banks (29 percent).[12] Governments retain majority ownership in

all banking institutions, but private investors and foreign strategic investors have been permitted to acquire equity positions. In experimental cases in rural areas, 100 percent privately owned small banks and lending companies are now permitted.

When China joined the World Trade Organization in 2001, it committed to open the banking sector to foreigners by 2007. In preparation, the big banks began to transform themselves into competitive commercial banks. More than US$500 billion in bad loans were removed from their books.[13] The largest banks then took on strategic foreign investors, for their expertise rather than their capital – a move that attracted more than US$20 billion in investments. Finally, to force changes in their mindset and management style, some listed their shares on the stock exchanges in Hong Kong and Shanghai. The idea was to expose their directors and managers to international competition and the inevitable pressures from international investors and analysts for greater transparency and a focus on efficiency and profitability, rather than the bureaucratic and political goals of growing market share. These offerings attracted significant investor interest. In late 2006, the Industrial and Commercial Bank of China raised US$19 billion, and between 2005 and 2008 Chinese banks raised an estimated total of more than US$50 billion.[14]

By 2007, with their newly raised capital and the economy and exports booming, the big banks were flush with cash. In March 2009, the *Financial Times* ranked the Industrial and Commercial Bank of China, the China Construction Bank, and the Bank of China as the world's three largest, measured by market capitalization, with two other Chinese banks in the top fifty. (In contrast, the only Indian bank on the list was the State Bank of India, at number 50.) Chinese banks were also encouraged to 'go abroad' to develop global capabilities[15] by following their customers into southeast Asia and Africa, taking small equity stakes in U.K. and U.S. banks to learn advanced banking technologies and products, and obtaining banking licenses to enter the U.S. market.[16]

Most of these initial investments were failures, suggesting Chinese banks still have much to learn about operating abroad. For example, CITIC Securities' bid for a share of Bear Stearns, the

U.S. investment bank later acquired by JPMorganChase, was eventually cancelled. China Investment Corporation's stake in the May 2007 initial public offering of Blackstone, the U.S. private equity firm, was widely criticized when the share price dropped immediately thereafter. China Development Bank's July 2007 investment in Barclays included an agreement to invest further if Barclays' bid for Dutch bank ABN-Amro succeeded – which it did not. The value of China Minsheng Bank's 2007 stake in UCBH Holdings (San Francisco) also plummeted.

China's intensive restructuring and repositioning of its banking system is intended to create internationally competitive, efficient financial institutions, and efficiency – as measured by the share of total loans that are nonperforming – has improved. Nonperforming loans dropped from 28.6 percent for the original big four banks in 2000 to 6.7 percent for all the major commercial banks by the end of 2007.[17] The real test, however, will be the ability of these institutions to withstand significant economic adversity such as the Chinese economy began to experience in 2008. There are reasons to be skeptical that they will emerge unscathed if the downturn is prolonged. Evolving incentive frameworks explain why.

Since 2004, incentive structures for bank managers have been modernized as the oversight and prudential standards of the China Banking Regulatory Commission have been formalized. But they have not changed sufficiently to reduce the banks' traditional reliance on corporate customers, many of them large, well-known borrowers with government connections – by the large banks' own published financial statements, corporate customers still account for between 70 and 80 percent of their loans.[18] The implication is that banks are exposed to government-owned and -connected firms whose viability is protected in an economic downturn.

Banks' boards of directors include government officials and Party members, although some directors are independent. Bank heads are Party loyalists and serve as members or alternates of the Central Committee[19] – indeed, the chief executive officer is often also the institution's Party secretary, and business performance is discussed at Party meetings.[20]

China's Monetary and Financial Framework

Chinese banks also must function within the country's larger economic policy framework, which supports its investment-led growth strategy.[21] The exchange rate is heavily managed, and interest rates are administered. Since the Asian financial crisis of 1997–98, the exchange rate has fluctuated within a narrow range, appreciating 21.4 percent between 2005 and early 2009. To stabilize the exchange rate, the central bank intervenes to sell yuan[22] to counter upward pressures from China's strong export earnings and large inflows of foreign direct investment, and then withdraws the resulting liquidity by issuing bonds to the banks.

These practices reduce the independence of monetary policy, and the administered interest rates reduce commercial banks' appetite for risky credits because they can rely for a good part of their income on the spread between what they must pay savers and what they charge borrowers.[23] The central bank sets their deposit and loan interest rates, paying savers low returns and allowing the banks healthy spreads from higher lending rates. Allowing market-determined rates would be risky, as the fixed exchange rate is vulnerable to speculative capital inflows that would put upward pressure on the exchange rate and require the printing of yuan and the issuing of bonds. When administered interest rates fail to achieve desired growth results, the central bank imposes outright prohibitions on new lending.[24]

India's Evolving Financial System

India's financial system is much smaller than China's, but more diverse. There are two vibrant and well-developed stock markets, as well as venture capital and futures markets, but a smaller banking system. The Bombay Stock Exchange (BSE) was founded as long ago as 1875. In the early 1990s, the National Exchange was created to compete with the BSE, which was experiencing serious governance problems. Most of the five thousand listed companies are private, many of them small in size, and both exchanges have developed disclosure and governance practices that are widely regarded as state of the art. The Indian financial system also benefits from its well-developed legal system, a well-established system of financial regulation, and a market-based monetary framework. Market forces determine the exchange rate, although the central bank does intervene at times and interest rates are largely market determined. Yet the financial system has policy constraints similar to those in China: government ownership of banks is still at high levels and political factors influence how banks allocate their capital and what interest rates they can charge. Unlike China, which for years has had the advantage of a balanced budget, India's governments habitually run large deficits.[25] Much government spending is oriented towards consumption subsidies and public sector wages and the deficits have constrained governments' ability to undertake infrastructure investments.

As in China, government dominates the bond market but in a different way; it requires commercial banks, insurers, and provident funds to buy and hold government bonds in their capital bases.[26] India's corporate bond market is one of the world's smallest, with capitalization less than 10 percent of GDP. It is difficult and costly to use because of stringent government regulations, inadequate infrastructure, complicated procedures for legal recourse, and ineffective bankruptcy laws. Corporate funding requirements frequently are met by issuing foreign currency convertible bonds and private placements to international institutional investors, a channel that avoids the costs and obstacles facing issuers of domestic instruments but makes them vulnerable to external shocks such as the 2008–09 credit crunch.

India's banking system has 218 scheduled commercial banks, of which a hundred are owned by governments, private investors, and foreigners; most of the rest are regional rural banks, which have tens of thousands of branches throughout the country. Specialized state-owned intermediaries, such as the National Bank for Rural Development, the Small Industries Development Bank of India, and various state finance corporations promote the social objectives of finance. Most commercial banks were nationalized in 1969 to support Indira Gandhi's anti-poverty drive. As public sector banks, they were expected to try to reach small savers and borrowers in the effort to dilute the banks' traditional dependence on cozy relationships with wealthy preferred borrowers. After a balance-of-payments crisis in 1991, the government loosened its grip and allowed the public sector banks to issue up to 49 percent of their equity to the public. 'New private' banks were also formed, in which foreign investors were allowed limited stakes. One of these private banks was ICICI Bank, now the second-largest and fastest-growing bank in India.

In addition to the statutory requirements that affect their capital structures, India's banks must direct 40 percent of net bank credit to 'priority sectors' such as small-scale industry, with 18 percent of the total directed to agriculture and 10 percent to 'weaker' sectors. The effect is ambiguous, however. Although banks have created thousands of rural branches to attract rural savers, small, low-income borrowers are costly and high risk to service, and few loans are made to them. Not surprisingly, banks are not the best way to achieve social goals, and there are unintended side effects. For example, rural savings in the government-owned banks are transferred to government consumption through the required investments in low-risk public sector bonds, which crowd out higher-risk productive investments. Public sector banks also are less efficient than other banks and account for a higher share of non-performing loans. In 2007, the leader of an independent Expert Group leveled withering criticism at public sector banks, charging they were 'the least efficient, most poorly managed, most bureaucratic, most overstaffed and the least well compensated';[27] in addition, they are losing market share to private and foreign banks.

Sharpening the Scissors

In both China and India, then, much remains to be done to turn their domestic banks into efficient risk managers, able to withstand financial volatility and adversity. The authorities are moving slowly, which means that the financial systems have not damaged either country's growth prospects, but they have not enhanced them either. Instead, they finance industries of the past and deny formal finance to the entrepreneurs and industries of the future.

China is vulnerable both to a slowdown in its export markets and to declining asset values in the stock market. As investors meet margin calls by disposing of other assets, stock values will decline and banks' nonperforming loans will increase. Although China's financial resources seem sufficient to handle these problems,[28] further bailouts would continue to distort incentives and divert public funds from other, more productive priorities.

Thus, the financial system's 'scissors' do not yet 'cut' as well as they could. Savings are collected but are used in ways that waste capital – in India by diverting it to government consumption, and in China by diverting it to large, well-connected enterprises. Governments intervene in the financial systems in the belief that they know the best uses for savings. But as their economies become more complex and market oriented, can they continue to afford such inefficiencies?

Reform of China's government-dominated financial structure has been useful, but has not gone far enough to have a significant effect on the growth of the economy. It is estimated that, if further reform enabled smaller, more productive enterprises to obtain needed funding, growth could increase by as much as 13 percent a year. Similarly, if enterprises in China obtained their funding the way they do in other countries, with lower-cost bond markets supplying 60 percent (instead of 3 percent) of enterprise finance and banks supplying only 40 percent, enterprise funding costs in China might decline by US$14 billion a year.[29]

In India, a similar calculation would see enterprise borrowing costs reduced by US$2.3 billion annually if lower-cost financing were available from corporate bond markets. Additionally, it is estimated that borrowers would save nearly US$20 billion annually through more efficient banking services, which could be achieved by reducing government intervention and adopting best international practices, integrating informal finance into the formal system, and introducing an electronic payments system throughout the country.[30]

One can envisage at least four ways in which the efficiency of China's and India's financial systems could be improved: by reducing government ownership, by introducing more competition, by improving the infrastructure of financial institutions, and by upgrading the regulatory oversight needed for more complex and innovative financial systems.

Less Government Ownership

The problem with majority government ownership of financial institutions is that it creates incentives that are political, rather than commercial. China is experimenting with private ownership in a few newly created but small institutions located outside the major cities, but the government gives no indication of wanting to reduce its stake in existing state-owned banks. Still, it is likely that, once all the major banks have been restructured – one of the largest, the Agricultural Bank of China, is still a work-in-progress – the government will free up market forces by deregulating borrowing and lending rates, which, in turn, would shrink interest spreads. When deposit insurance – another reform still in the works – is finally introduced, monitoring of investors and depositors will intensify as the explicit government guarantee is modified and removed. Chinese banks already face increasing competition from the developing bond markets; as their margins shrink and balance-sheet growth declines, pressure to consolidate the banking sector is likely to grow.

In India, with the 'new private' banks turning in superior growth and financial performance, plans are under way to reduce government ownership below 51 percent of total equity. This objective, however, is politically controversial, particularly considering that, in autumn 2008, the largest U.S. and European banks effectively were nationalized by government injections of equity to keep them solvent. In the wake of these extraordinary developments, Mrs. Sonia Gandhi criticized 'greedy western finance' and praised the relative stability and soundness of Indian government banks. As 2009 dawned, the prospects for further reform seemed to diminish.[31]

More Competition

Another way to improve the two countries' financial systems is to increase competition by permitting the entry of foreign institutions and by developing corporate bond markets. China has made good use of foreign talent in its big banks and, to a lesser extent, in the stock market, where foreign institutional investors are permitted to invest in equities on a restricted basis. But the introduction of a wider range of modern financial products – the kind sold by Xiaodong, whom we met earlier – is still in its early stages.

India, in contrast, while more ambivalent about foreign ownership of banks, has permitted wide use of foreign portfolio finance and foreign stakes in brokerage firms – hence the proliferation of jobs like Nomita's in Mumbai. Foreign ownership in the insurance sector is also held to a low level. A half-hearted road map introduced in 2005 allowed foreigners to hold a stake of up to 24 percent in weaker private banks in need of restructuring. It was intended to allow such stakes to rise to 74 percent in other private banks in 2009, but that has not yet happened, and political reaction to the global financial crisis seems likely to cause further delay. Foreign stakes in the large public sector banks that dominate the sector are off the table.

Corporate bond markets increase competitive pressure on banks by providing lower-cost, longer-term finance. Politicians and regulators in both countries have been reluctant to free up private sector corporate bond issuance because of concerns about the poor quality of corporate disclosure by issuers and about poorly informed investors. Zhou Xiaochuan, China's central bank governor, outlined in 2005 a litany of institutional weaknesses: bankruptcy laws that had only recently been adopted, default procedures that were not yet based on market principles, a lack of transparency that credit rating agencies demand and an absence of modern accounting standards on the part of issuers, a lack of market discipline, and inadequate knowledge on the part of investors.[32] Nonetheless, state enterprises increasingly have turned to the bond market. In 2008, PetroChina floated a RMB 60 billion bond issue, the largest in history, when its profits were squeezed between high world oil prices and government-mandated price caps on its refined products.

Bond market reform is also under debate in India, where two successive blue ribbon panels on the financial system – the 2007

Mistry Committee and the 2008 Rajan Committee – urged reforms to increase supply and demand and improve the functioning of the marketplace.[33] Governance and technology can be addressed administratively, but legislation is required to loosen tax provisions and reduce institutional restrictions on insurance, pension funds, banks, and foreign investment. Such change seems unlikely without a crisis or other catalyst. As both reports observe, one catalyst might be the growing demand for long-term finance to break India's transportation and power infrastructure bottlenecks.

Better Infrastructure

A third source of greater efficiency and competitiveness is better financial market infrastructure to address some of the deficiencies outlined in China by Governor Zhou: electronic payments systems, credit rating agencies to provide investors with information on listed companies, and information and disclosure regulations vital for evaluating and managing risk. In India, the national stock exchanges have adopted high standards for disclosure and transparency. Further liberalization of listing and disclosure regulations to allow firms to take advantage of favorable market conditions would be beneficial to companies that seek finance from institutional investors. In China, bankruptcy laws have been passed but are not yet being enforced, while bankruptcy in India suffers from the more general problem of the overburdened legal system.

Smarter Regulation

A fourth source of improvement in the two countries' financial systems is smarter regulation, driven by the need for soundness and efficiency, rather than political objectives. In neither country are financial regulators independent from the central bank or from the political authorities. China's banking regulator must satisfy both the People's Bank of China and the State Council before it can implement regulations. India has a plethora of overlapping agencies that includes the Reserve Bank of India, the National Housing Bureau, and overseers of cooperatives, insurance companies, and securities. The central bank's multiple roles as bank regulator and owner of several large banking institutions also constitute a conflict of interest. Both countries have examined the idea of a single regulator along the lines of the United Kingdom's Financial Services Agency, but have taken no action.

Becoming More Interconnected

Even though the efficiency of the financial systems of China and India lag those of more developed countries, both are becoming prominent sources and destinations in international financial markets as their governments free up two-way flows of long-term capital. But, with the large exception of the Chinese government's international holdings of foreign-exchange reserves, their shares of world stocks and flows of foreign direct investment (FDI) and portfolio capital are still modest. In 2004, they each accounted for less than 1 percent of the world's foreign portfolio flows,[34] while, in 2007, China's share of the world's inward stock of FDI was 2 percent and India's just 0.4 percent; their shares of the outward stock of FDI were even smaller, at 0.6 percent and 0.1 percent, respectively.[35] Nevertheless, among the emerging market economies, China has been an increasingly prominent destination for FDI (US$83.5 billion in 2007) and a source of both portfolio investments and outward FDI.

Since 2006, Chinese individuals and companies have been permitted, even encouraged, to invest abroad. The Qualified Domestic Institutional Investors scheme permits portfolio outflows through authorized intermediaries. By 2006, state-owned enterprises had invested US$80 billion in FDI and US$200 billion in securities and other investments as they sought to acquire brands and secure access to energy and other natural resources. Since the China National Offshore Oil Corporation's unsuccessful 2005 attempt to acquire U.S. multinational Unocal, Chinese enterprises have sought smaller stakes, sometimes in partnership with others. In 2007, a sovereign wealth fund, the China Investment Corporation (CIC), was created to invest an initial US$200 billion of foreign-exchange reserves in nonfinancial assets. To calm fears that

CIC's investments would be motivated by political considerations, its head, Lou Jiwei, stated that its investment strategy would follow 'commercial goals.'[36] The pace of diversification has been slow, however, and CIC's initial assets were allocated to domestic, not foreign, assets. Investment decisions in foreign companies have not been particularly successful, however, and CIC has begun to commission professional fund management firms to diversify and manage its investments.

India, which attracted US$23 billion in FDI inflows in 2007, has a higher international profile as an outward investor, even though its outflows in 2007 (US$13.7 billion) were only two-thirds those of China. The reason is that Indian entrepreneurs have 'brand': their acquisitions are intended to extend their successful business models beyond India, many of them well-known names in pharmaceuticals, engineering, and IT services. Example include such high-profile transactions as Tata Steel's acquisition of Corus, the Anglo-Dutch steel firm, for US$8 billion in 2006 and Tata Motors' acquisition of the Jaguar and Rover brands from Ford Motor Company for US$2.3 billion in 2008.

China's receptiveness to FDI inflows contrasts with India's ambivalence (although that is waning). Their attitudes toward portfolio investment, however, are the reverse. India permits private equity and portfolio investment in the shares of Indian companies on the rationale that such investments reduce the cost of finance and subject Indian firms to the scrutiny of sophisticated institutional investors. China, however, restricts portfolio investment into the country through the Qualified Foreign Institutional Investor scheme that attracted foreigners into domestic stock markets. By 2007, investment under that scheme had reached 3 percent of China's tradable market cap (compared with 40 percent in South Korea and 7 percent in Taiwan).[37]

By far the largest stock of capital invested abroad is the Chinese government's holding of foreign-exchange reserves, which totaled almost US$2 trillion at the end of 2008, with some US$750 billion invested in U.S. government bonds (in contrast, India's foreign-exchange assets totaled US$278 billion in September 2008). Since the late 1990s, China's current and capital account balances have been in surplus, in part because it still restricts capital inflows and outflows, its exports exceed its imports, and it has attracted rising interest from foreign investors. Converting the large inflows of foreign exchange into yuan, however, created upward pressure on the value of the currency, which the central bank countered by printing money to keep the exchange rate stable. The bank also invested much of the foreign exchange in low-risk foreign financial assets, particularly U.S. government bonds, effectively providing a new source of liquidity and low long-term interest rates that contributed to the U.S. housing boom. Of course, U.S. financial innovations and regulatory weaknesses were also prominent factors in the subsequent housing bust.

The large and persistent surplus in China's balance of payments has attracted international pressure to allow market forces a greater role in determining the value of the yuan. For the Chinese government, however, permitting a stronger yuan presents a dilemma that a Chinese economist has described as follows:

> The authorities know the yuan should be allowed to appreciate, but they want to know how fast this will happen as restrictions are removed and what will be the relative impacts on exporters and importers. Which export sectors will be most heavily affected? What will be the impact of import competition on China's farmers? The structure of the economy is changing so fast, it is almost impossible to predict the likely impacts with any certainty.[38]

China's financial prominence has a lot to do with the government's preference for a stable currency as an adjunct to its rapid growth strategy. This goal has proved to be unsustainable, however, both at home, by helping to keep the cost of capital artificially low, and abroad, by providing an advantage to exporters that competitors see as unfair. China's cheap capital and high rates of industrial investment cannot be sustained, because they clearly are diverting resources from domestic consumption. Moreover, rising social discontent is spurring measures to rebalance public spending and incentives to encourage higher incomes and domestic consumption. One way to do this is to improve access to formal finance by small and medium-sized private enterprises.

Financing the Future: Small Private Enterprises

The most interesting dimension of the Chinese and Indian financial systems is what they do *not* do: they do not finance private small and medium-sized enterprises (SMEs), which are productive, grow quickly, and are essential to each country's economic future.

SME Finance in China

China's future growth engine is its huge and growing number of small entrepreneurial firms among the nonstate enterprises that now account for nearly two-thirds of industrial production. Yet these small companies are unable to access formal bank finance because they lack collateral in the form of real estate or capital equipment; as one senior banker framed the issue, 'The big banks are like pawnshops: they demand real collateral from borrowers and lots of it.' Instead, China's financial system lubricates the large, the established, and the well connected, like the state-owned enterprises that in 2006 still accounted for nearly half of the assets of China's industrial enterprises.[39] Nonstate enterprises, therefore, must obtain their financing from informal sources – either from people they know or from informal financial institutions.

One expert who helps to train bank staff in the hot new area of risk evaluation and risk management finds that, even after receiving training in risk modeling and techniques for appraising risks of potential SME borrowers, bank staff and managers continue to be motivated by what they understand best: acquiring market share. Banks' loan-pricing patterns continue to cluster around the official benchmark lending rates, even though regulators have left them room to price at higher rates that reflect borrowers' risk.[40]

Once SMEs have obtained informal financing and become established, they must rely on retained earnings. To make a leap in growth, however, instead of going to a bank, they must go to private credit agencies, which cover a wide range of institutions from credit associations and shareholding cooperatives to underground money houses that charge high interest rates.[41] Moreover, bank loans still depend on whom you know, as businesses owned by Party members are more likely to obtain them.[42]

The central bank recently drafted a regulation that would allow individuals and companies to extend loans as long as they do not have bad credit or a criminal record. Legalizing private credit agencies, which thrive in coastal provinces such as Zhejiang despite their underground status, would increase competition for the state-owned banks and eventually bring such credit channels for SMEs under central bank oversight if they are permitted to accept deposits. The number of small-scale private lenders is also increasing. In 2008, about thirty private banks, mostly in the less urbanized areas, opened their doors, and the Zhejiang provincial government has set a target to charter a hundred private lending institutions – which are permitted to lend but not to take deposits – within one year.

These developments signal a shift that is consistent with China's overall rebalancing strategy. Increasing the availability of loans to capital-starved SMEs will help to stimulate the growth of labor-intensive light manufacturing and the creation of more jobs.

SME Finance in India

India's challenge is framed by a recent report on financing the unorganized sector, which estimates that the sector contributes 30 percent of GDP but receives only 5 to 6 percent of institutional credit. These enterprises, whose size is restricted by India's labor laws, also face restrictions on their access to bank financing because of the quantitative requirements of priority lending policies and government-mandated interest rate caps. Microcredit financial institutions are often celebrated as the solution to this access problem, yet these are relatively few in number (about eight hundred in total), small in size (only ten have more than a hundred thousand clients), and located mostly in the southern part of the country. Most borrowing from these institutions is for large, one-time consumption expenditures, such as weddings, rather than for investment.[43]

Solutions to this funding puzzle include suggestions for a national fund to support such enterprises and expanding formal bank lending to such enterprises by allowing banks to use local agents rather than expensive branches to service them. The use of no-frills bank accounts, not least by governments using these accounts to make transfers under the National Rural Employment Guarantee Act, is one means to this end. So is allowing more competition for the banks from informal institutions and small private banks. If they work, such approaches could reduce directed lending pressures on banks.

India's stock markets provide another alternative, but most of the few thousand listed enterprises are small and little traded. Instead, although SMEs tend to grow more than twice as fast as the economy, they rely on family, friends, trade credits, and loans from government development finance institutions for startup and growth finance.[44] Indeed, half the respondents to a 2004 survey said they faced an acute shortage of capital and difficulties in obtaining credit.[45] Another survey, in Uttar Pradesh, found that banks took thirty-three weeks to process loan applications and required bribes (which were larger if the loan came from a government scheme); money lenders were much more willing to make loans, even for consumption purposes, but, of course, these loans were much more expensive.[46]

The Challenge Ahead

In both China and India, restrictive government policies account for the inability of financial institutions to finance future engines of economic growth. The two countries' governments apparently believe that growth is sufficiently robust to cover the costs of the political objectives they impose on their financial systems. Yet, the leader of the Expert Group on Mumbai as an International Financial Center warns, 'The "go-slow-at-any-cost" strategy (of financial reform) has had the unintended consequence of India's financial system now lagging too far behind the real economy. It is not meeting India's needs for efficient, cost-effective domestic or global financial intermediation. That is why corporate India and high-net-worth individuals look abroad for their financial needs … with India and Indian finance losing out permanently.'[47]

In India, however, the issue is not only corporations and high-

net-worth individuals but the continued marginalization of Second India, which can be addressed in part by making finance
more readily available for SMEs. In China, the shift toward greater
reliance on domestic consumption can be accomplished in part
by freeing up market forces in the financial system, offering higher interest rates on deposits, and permitting the exchange rate to
appreciate (to reduce heavy reliance on capital-intensive, export-
oriented manufacturing), which would raise household incomes
and create more jobs in light industry.

Neither country is yet meeting the financing needs of their host
of small private enterprises because their banks and capital market institutions cannot or will not manage the risks. Relying on
government intervention – and, in China, on lending to large enterprises – is safer, but more costly in terms of foregone long-term
growth. What more can be done to improve the risk-management
capabilities of financial institutions? Could technology help small
entrepreneurs access modern financial services in market-friendly
ways that are also sustainable business models for financial institutions? Or, to compensate for shortcomings in their labor markets and, particularly in China, for the weaknesses of state-owned
banks, should the two countries rely more heavily on technology
and innovation as drivers of growth? We will see evidence in the
next chapter that ambitious governments and dynamic enterprises are in the game but neither country is a technology titan.

chapter four

From Latecomers to Technology Titans?

The opening up of new markets, foreign or domestic, and the organizational development from the craft shop and factory to such concerns as US Steel illustrate the same process of industrial mutation ... that incessantly revolutionizes the economic structure from within, incessantly destroying the old one, incessantly creating a new one.

– Joseph Schumpeter, *Capitalism Socialism and Democracy*

At times over the past two millennia, China and India have led the world in science and technology. The opening ceremonies of the 2008 Beijing Olympics boldly illustrated China's inventions of gunpowder, the compass, paper, and moveable type, and its understanding of hydraulics, iron smelting, and ship building long exceeded Europe's. As long ago as the fifth century, India's mathematicians devised the decimal system, realized the unique significance of zero, and calculated π to multiple decimal places.[1]

As the two countries reemerge into global prominence, science and technology again will influence their growth prospects. So far, each has reached its high-growth trajectory by increasing the capital available to labor and by adapting and imitating foreign ideas and technology. Their future growth prospects, however, will depend on their ability to commercialize and apply both existing and new technologies. In short, if they are to sustain their competitiveness, they will have to sustain innovation,[2] and if they are to sustain their current high levels of growth, they will have to diffuse innovation to compensate for weaknesses in their labor and financial markets.

Both countries rely on foreign technology, but are they making the transition from imported technology and ideas to domestic innovation? U.S. economist Richard Nelson's view of how technological advance has occurred in the modern world provides a framework for thinking about this transition.[3] He argues that no single factor promotes technical advance or encourages firms to learn new capabilities and bring new products to market or create new technologies. Rather, the process involves problem solving and trial and error. He focuses on firms' strategies and decision-making, and emphasizes the importance of supportive institutions in a country's 'national innovation system,' which includes government agencies and policies, education and training institutions, financial institutions, and governance at all levels. Outdated institutions, inappropriate technologies and incentives, and obsolete technologies can hamper innovation and the more efficient use of resources. Further, Nelson views innovation as a continuum that begins with imitation but evolves to adaptation of products and processes and, later, to original innovations.

This chapter looks at the national innovation systems of China and India and how their firms – large and small, foreign and locally owned – learn and improve their productive capabilities. It turns out that, although China's national innovation system is more top-down and its policies interventionist, which creates problems and distortions, intense market competition is now driving impressive productivity gains in manufacturing. And although India's celebrated successes in IT services portray the country as more innovative, it cannot escape the significant disconnect between the outward orientation of this sector and its techno-manufacturing industries on the one hand, and the marginalization of Second India on the other. Far from defining India's future prospects as gloomy, however, this disconnection offers significant opportunities for future growth if the gap can be closed.

To see things in context, consider internationally comparable indicators of technological capability (Table 4), which show that China has eight times more researchers than India has, two and a

Table 4: Indicators of Technology and Innovation, India and China, 2003–04

Indicator	India	China
Researchers in R&D, 2003 *(number)*	117,528	926,252
R&D researchers per million population, 2004	119	708
Spending on R&D, 2004 *(US$ billions)*	5.9	27.8
Spending on R&D, 2004 *(% of GDP)*	0.85	1.44
Scientific and technical journal articles, 2003 *(number)*	12,774	29,186
R&D spending per scientific and technical article *(US$)*	460,000	953,000
Patents granted by U.S. Patent Office, 2004 *(number)*	376	597
R&D spending per patent granted *(US$ millions)*	15.6	46.6

Source: World Bank, *Unleashing India's Innovation: Towards Sustainable and Inclusive Growth* (Washington, DC: World Bank, 2007), p. 31.

half times the number of technical publications, and spends five times as much on R&D. Looking at R&D spending as a percentage of a country's GDP – what economists refer to as 'R&D intensity' – we see that, in 2004, the figure was 3.2 percent for Japan, 2.7 percent for the United States, and an average of 2.3 percent for the industrialized countries as a whole – that is, for the members of the Organisation for Economic Co-operation and Development. By contrast, R&D intensity was 1.6 percent for China and 1.0 percent for India. Yet, these numbers hide a significant development: by 2006, China's absolute amount of spending on R&D had overtaken that of Japan.[4]

Still, developing trained manpower and increasing spending on R&D, in themselves, do not assure economic growth. In both China and India, the number of patents granted – the internationally recognized measure of the production of new ideas and products – is modest. The U.S. Patent Office has granted more patents to China than to India, but China's spending per patent is three times India's. And neither country has yet produced its own world-renowned brand names. India's high-tech producers are world-class enterprises but their products are hidden in back-office operations and business processes. The famous brands owned by China's Lenovo (IBM's ThinkPad personal computer business) and India's Tata Motors (Jaguar and Land Rover) were bought from western companies.

The National Innovation Systems of China and India

A country's national innovation system, to use Richard Nelson's framework, includes government institutions that support R&D, as well as educational and training institutions and trade and FDI policies that determine its openness and receptiveness to learn from abroad. Both China and India have ambitious technology plans: China intends to be spending 2.5 percent of its GDP on R&D by 2020, and India 2 percent by 2012.[5] China's innovation system is dominated by ambitious R&D megaprojects and long-range targets carried forward by supportive government spending, and policies that promote infrastructure, education, and FDI inflows. India's system is more reliant on market institutions; it also has large public research institutions and at least one world-class private research institution, the Indian Institute of Science, founded by the Tata family in Bangalore in 1909.

China emphasizes the strategic importance of 'an innovation-oriented nation,' a goal elaborated in its National Medium and Long-Term Science and Technology Development Plan (2006–20), which aims to reduce the country's reliance on foreign technology. President Hu Jintao emphasized this goal in 2006 when he visited Microsoft in Seattle, where it was evident that the value of a few successful patents far outweighed the revenue China earns from the exports from the many factories set up through joint ventures between Chinese and foreign enterprises (known as 'foreign-invested enterprises').[6]

Science and technology has long been a cornerstone of China's development strategy. During the period when central planning dominated the economy, R&D centers were organized around the products for which ministries were responsible, a structure that effectively prevented communication between producers and users of R&D. In the 1980s, when science and technology was revived, the emphasis shifted to a more commercially driven, decentralized, and networked architecture of R&D clusters and science parks. Various levels of government now encourage enterprises to increase their own industrial R&D, and have spent heavily on modern infrastructure and research and commercialization facilities. Examples include Beijing's Zhongguancun Science Park, a biotechnology park in Pudong, and a particle physics center in Guangdong.[7] Large investments in telecommunications and information infrastructure have also transformed information flows, and foreign enterprises are encouraged to enter the market in recognition of their value in diffusing modern knowledge and skills.

This 'techno-nationalist' approach to innovation does not assure success, however, for a number of reasons. First, ambitious targets for national projects can create unrealistic pressure to perform – witness South Korea's experience in stem cell research, where such pressure led to claims, subsequently exposed as fabrications, that researchers had created the world's first stem cells from cloned human embryos.[8]

Second, a techno-nationalist approach can create incentives that are inappropriate. For example, although China's economy is increasingly market-based, as competition intensifies in most industries, its Science and Technology Development Plan ignores market forces, as well as the implication that innovation depends mostly on small, incremental changes in response to market signals from competitors and customers. As a result, the Plan also essentially ignores the need to protect intellectual property rights. China's laws in this area are largely consistent with those of the World Trade Organization (WTO), but they are not enforced, which reduces the incentives of the owners of such rights to take risks with new products or processes that respond to intensifying competition.[9]

The effects of this lack of enforcement of property rights were evident in a study I and a colleague undertook of privately owned high-tech enterprises in market-friendly Zhejiang province.[10] One dynamic private enterprise in the electronics industry, for example, complained that it had no way to enforce its rights when competitors imitated its products and violated its Chinese patents. A private telecommunications equipment supplier also complained that large, well-connected state-owned enterprises were outcompeting small private firms because they had the inside edge on standards setting, which affects decisions on future product development. For small private firms that are driven by the bottom line, such decisions can be key to their success or failure. State-owned enterprises also create financial difficulties when they are slow to pay their equipment suppliers, and military connections give them an edge in supplying military products.[11]

The third drawback of China's national innovation system is its orientation largely toward international markets rather than local and domestic ones. Since foreign firms dominate the country's export sectors, they inevitably develop linkages among themselves, which the Chinese government encourages and supports – to the detriment of local firms that lack similar linkages.[12] There are, however, exceptions. When deciding where to locate state-owned enterprises, China's central planners initially shunned coastal provinces such as Zhejiang, viewing them as strategically vulnerable. Left to their own devices, then, light industries grew up in such provinces, requiring little capital or few skills and clustered together in intense competition and with a high degree of division of labor. Despite the national commitment to central planning, provincial and local governments tolerated and understood such markets.[13] Linkages grew up among provincial educational institutions and local firms, and university administrators and professors were permitted to serve as consultants and board members – and often as owners. Provincial and local governments also collaborated with universities in creating industry standards.

India's national innovation system reflects its historical self-sufficiency policy framework. Its public research institutions account for 70 to 80 percent of total R&D spending, with 80 percent of those funds allocated to defense, space, and nuclear research. The remaining 20 percent is channeled through four large public organizations: the Council of Scientific and Industrial Research, the Indian Council for Agricultural Research, the Department of Science and Technology, and the Indian Council of Medical Research. The Indian Planning Commission, however, has signaled its willingness to encourage a more supportive public environment for private enterprises, more competition, new entrants, and new sources of finance, such as FDI, to help successful enterprises expand.[14] Still, linkages between public institutions and the private sector, and spillovers from one to the other, are limited. This segmentation matters, as we will see, because it ignores the needs of smaller enterprises in the unorganized sector.

Both China and India have relied heavily on foreign investors to transfer technology. The presence of foreign firms diffuses technical and marketing knowledge and other skills among local employees, and affects domestic competition. Particularly in the information and communications technologies, automotive, consumer durables, aerospace, chemicals, biotechnology, and agriculture sectors, the two countries have attracted large investments by multinationals in local R&D centers,[15] some of which now engage in basic research. Both Microsoft and IBM, for example, have R&D centers in Beijing that are linked to other centers located around the world, while IBM India has the largest number of local employees of any multinational in the country.

The effects of these investments on the domestic economies, however, are mixed. Although multinationals are attracted by India's low-cost, English-speaking technical manpower, which give them a cost advantage in their global operations, there is little spillover of these investments into the domestic economy. India's export-oriented high-tech industry has embraced foreign firms and excelled in foreign markets, but its technical and managerial successes have yet to diffuse among domestic industries or to reach many in the general population. The limited penetration of the Internet, for example, is evident in India's low use of computers – India's twenty-four personal computers and three broadband connections per thousand population is only about one-thirtieth the rate in China.[16] In China there is more diffusion into the domestic economy but language and institutional differences hinder the pace and extent of such diffusion.

One area in which the effect of foreign investment is particularly evident in both countries is the fast-evolving auto sector.[17] In China, the government originally intended to use the clout and expertise of foreign partners as a quick way to build a domestic industry. In 1976, China's largest producers were state-owned enterprises First Automobile Works (FAW) and Shanghai Tractor and Automotive, now known as SAIC. Volkswagen, the first foreign auto company to invest in China, was required to enter into a joint venture with a local firm, and chose to team up with both SAIC and China FAW Group. But Chinese companies have been quick to learn: by 2007, five domestic companies had emerged in this intensely competitive market, accounting for nearly a third of total sales.

India has also relied on joint ventures to supply the domestic market. In the 1980s Suzuki, the Japanese car and motorcycle maker, was the first foreign entrant, teaming up with local car maker Maruti to produce a cheap car that was more modern than the venerable Ambassador that alone supplied the market. Today, Maruti-Suzuki holds the top market position followed by Tata Motors, India's largest domestic producer. Most of the global brands are also located there, with some, like Hyundai, using India as a global production base for one of its models.[18]

In the pharmaceuticals industry, India became one of the fastest-growing markets in the world after India adopted WTO rules for protecting intellectual property in 2005. Once the multinationals were reassured that their proprietary assets would be protected, they expanded their clinical trials and contract research activities in the country and entered into alliances with Indian drug firms. In contrast, in China, where domestic drug companies focus on traditional medicine and perform some generic manufacturing, intellectual property rights remain a contentious issue, although the central government has countered with tax and procurement incentives to encourage foreign investment in drug innovation and technology.[19] Illustrating the lengths to which some Chinese companies go to reassure foreign patent holders, one contract research organization reportedly forbids its scientists from noting down the formula of a chemical compound when they are in the central facilities; instead, they are required to write in code so that colleagues who do contract work for other clients cannot copy their work.[20]

Another key dimension of a country's national innovation system is its education and training institutions. China's education system is far ahead of India's in producing basic literacy and skills and, as we saw in Table 4, researchers and technical publications. India does produce world-class technical manpower, skilled researchers, and knowledge creators, but not nearly enough of them, the effects of which are showing up in the declining quality of its research. Indeed, in 2006, the prime minister's scientific advisor, C.N.R. Rao, criticized research from Indian universities as 'hitting an all time low. They are unable to perform and compete.'[21]

In summary, the Chinese and Indian national innovation systems are still works in progress. China's techno-nationalist policies and institutions are impressive in ambition and size but are oriented to international markets, rather than local ones. Incremental market-based innovation occurs largely on its own, despite slow progress on the supportive institutional 'software' such as enforcement of property rights and an independent judiciary, which are needed to support the growing dynamism of small, nonstate enterprises. In India, where market institutions are taken for granted, the segmentation of the economy is exacerbated by public research institutions that ignore the private sector and the country's small and medium-sized enterprises. These weaknesses hamper the ability of such firms to learn how to be competitive in world markets and to develop greater industrial capabilities.

Enterprises and Their Capabilities

A ranking of the twenty largest enterprises in China and India by market capitalization (see Table 5) reflects the multiple roles of the state in production, regulation, and finance. In both countries, the list is dominated by huge energy companies, utilities, heavy industry, and financial institutions. In China, nine of the twenty are banks, three of which now rank in the top thirty in the world. All of China's largest enterprises are state owned, while about a fifth of India's are.

India has a number of large family conglomerates – with well-known names such as Tata, Birla, Godrej, and Ambani – that date back to the days of the British raj. They survived and prospered after independence, in part, because they were not nationalized; instead, the government chose to regulate them heavily, a decision

Table 5: The Top Twenty Enterprises in China and India, 2009

	China				India		
Global 2000 Rank	Enterprise	Industry	Ownership	Global 2000 Rank	Enterprise	Industry	Ownership
12	ICBC	Banking	SOCB	121	Reliance Industries	Oil & gas operations	Private
14	PetroChina	Oil & gas operations	SOE	150	State Bank of India Group	Banking	SOCB
23	China Construction Bank	Banking	SOCB	152	Oil & Natural Gas	Oil & gas operations	SOE
30	Bank of China	Banking	SOCB	207	Indian Oil	Oil & Gas Operations	SOE
33	Sinopec-China Petroleum	Oil & gas operations	SOE	317	National Thermal Power	Utilities	SOE
72	China Life Insurance	Insurance	SOE	329	ICICI Bank	Banking	Private
139	China Telecom	Telecom services	SOE	463	Tata Steel	Materials	Private
141	Ping An Insurance Group	Insurance	SOE	508	Bharti Airtel	Telecom services	Private
143	Bank of Communications	Banking	SOCB	582	Steel Authority of India	Materials	SOE
221	China Merchants Bank	Banking	SOCB	689	Reliance Communications	Telecom services	Private
235	China Shenhua Energy	Materials	SOE	773	Larsen & Toubro	Capital goods	Private
263	Baoshan Iron & Steel	Materials	SOE	795	Bharat Petroleum	Oil & gas operations	SOE
326	China Pacific Insurance	Insurance	SOE	769	Bharat Heavy Electricals	Capital goods	SOE
345	China Citic Bank	Banking	SOCB	808	HDFC-Housing Development	Real estate / financial services	Private
353	CCCC-China Communications Construction	Construction	SOE	834	Tata Consultancy Svcs	Business services & supplies	Private
356	China Cosco Holdings	Transportation	SOE	848	Hindalco Industries	Materials	Private
389	Industrial Bank China	Banking	SOCB	864	HDFC Bank	Banking	Private
412	China Minsheng Banking	Banking	SOCB	883	DLF	Real estate / financial services	Private
443	Shanghai Pudong Dev Bk	Banking	SOCB	891	Infosys Technologies	Software & services	Private
453	China Railway Group	Construction	SOE	946	Punjab National Bank	Banking	SOCB

SOE = state-owned enterprise; SOCB = state-owned commercial bank.
Source: 'The Global 2000,' *Forbes Magazine*, special report, 8 April 2009. Reprinted by permission of Forbes Magazine © 2009 Forbes LLC.

that led to close government-business ties. More recently, India's high-tech enterprises have transformed the corporate landscape; indeed, India's experienced private entrepreneurs have their firms on the map *despite* the government. World-class enterprises such as Infosys, Wipro, and Sasken entered the IT back office and software businesses in reaction to the costly restrictions and delays imposed by India's so-called license raj, which, until it was abolished in 1991, tightly controlled trade in goods such as computers and computer parts. The entrepreneurs realized, however, that computer services and software were beyond the reach of bureaucrats – what they did not understand they could not control – so these could be traded freely.

In China, all enterprises were nationalized after the founding of the People's Republic in 1949. Well-known nonstate enterprises such as Huawei, Datang, and Lenovo originated as public institutions. Lenovo, for example, was a public R&D institution that was hived off into an enterprise group known as Legend, and has since evolved into an internationally known commercial enterprise. It is also an excellent example of the important role that state R&D institutions and state-owned enterprises have played in reallocating resources to the private sector. Private firms have also had considerable success in recruiting professionals as the state sector has been restructured – sometimes hiring entire teams of R&D personnel.[22] These enterprises are the ones that attract attention, but each country also has a host of small enterprises that, in how they learn and grow, are the more interesting stories. By one estimate, China has around forty million small and medium-sized enterprises, many of them located in the coastal provinces.[23] Entrepreneurs in Wenzhou – a city that supplies most of the world's cigarette lighters, zippers, and light switches – have prospered despite one set of institutions, bureaucrats and the Party, by relying on another set of institutions, informal networks and clusters, that supply ideas, markets, and private informal credit associations. Indeed, the latter, for ideological reasons, were dismissed until recently as 'underground' and illegal.[24]

India's small enterprises have different constraints, relating more to weaknesses in their ability to access and absorb new knowl-

edge. A 2006 survey found that small firms in the organized sector
not only had lower productivity – their value added was less than
Rs 500, or about US$10 per worker – compared with larger firms;
they also lacked the channels through which they might access
knowledge to improve their performance. A tiny number of firms
in the survey, most of them large in size, had value added of more
than Rs 1,000 per worker. Based on this difference in value added
per worker, it was estimated that output might be increased nearly
fivefold if the smaller enterprises were able to apply knowledge
that already exists in the Indian economy. Moreover, since the organized sector accounts for less than 10 percent of India's work
force, the myriad small enterprises in the unorganized sector are
likely to be even less productive and, therefore, would stand to
gain significantly from access to the technologies and knowledge
available to larger firms.[25]

Enterprises learn and improve their technical capabilities in
a variety of ways: through knowledge spillovers from other local
firms, through interactions and joint ventures with foreign firms
and supply chains, and though their own efforts to raise productivity. In response to competitive pressures, they learn how to
change the way they produce, finance, and market their products,
and improve product quality. They also learn how to engage in
product and process innovation in cooperation with, or response
to, the suggestions or demands of their customers. All of this takes
place within the larger context of their country's national innovation system and the role the state chooses to play.

The Experience of Chinese Enterprises

Cheap capital, a stable exchange rate, and rapid growth in domestic and foreign demand have encouraged Chinese nonstate
enterprises to start up or expand. Productivity increases are being
driven by intensifying market competition and an increasing willingness to defer to the principle of 'creative destruction' – that is,
to let less competitive firms fold and new firms enter. The presence
of foreign firms provides further stimulus. Yet China's exports of
high-tech products still depend on imported technologies, sug-

gesting that enterprises are largely adapting existing technologies rather than creating new ones.

Outsiders are frequently surprised to learn how politics and business interface in China. Large enterprises have Party cells, which are involved in high-level human resource and other strategic issues. State involvement ensures political control and a homogeneous business culture, but it inhibits incentives to innovate in a number of ways. At all levels, enterprises must hedge against the difficulties posed by a tightly controlled political system that lacks checks and balances and by local officials who have considerable discretion in how policies and rules are applied. It has been suggested that Chinese businesses have developed a distinctive industrial strategic culture to cope with this environment by focusing on relationships with key bureaucrats and political figures that will help them gain exception from arbitrary rules. Collaboration with other firms becomes secondary, even risky, unless they have similar political arrangements. The result is an undermining of trust and encouragement of short-term profit taking over long-term investments. With short-term focus, almost by default, the more productive higher-technology industries and exports that depend on interregional supply chains are heavily weighted to foreign-invested enterprises.[26]

Others, however, question such skepticism about the investment implications of these arrangements, pointing out that foreign-invested enterprises are not leading China's R&D effort – in fact, their share of total R&D spending is small. Rather, their impact is to motivate domestic firms to spend on R&D and to enhance the efficiency of local Chinese firms through their interaction in technology markets.[27] The implications for collaboration between firms, however, are valid: collaboration suffers if entrepreneurs fear their partners will violate their intellectual property or if the state fails to enforce intellectual property laws. A study of firms in China's preeminent Zhongguancun Science Park in Beijing illustrates the park's 'incapacity to ensure accountability, protection of intellectual rights [sic], or legal conduct of enterprises. Not only is there no information source to check the references of potential partners, there is also little recourse for illegal or unethical conduct. If contracts are violated or firms are cheated, the victim has to assume full costs to right the wrongs. The high risk of external transactions discourages flexible network arrangements.'[28]

Significantly, direct government intervention in production is declining as firms learn to compete. In the past, local governments often intervened to protect local industries, but as nonstate firms have become more competitive and profitable, they have expanded geographically using their own internal funding or by acquiring other firms, and taken up the production and employment slack of state-owned enterprises that have closed or merged.[29] Large state-owned enterprises, too, are investing in R&D, mainly in large-scale, capital-intensive industries such as telecommunications equipment, machine manufacturing, and pharmaceuticals.[30] And even small but fast-growing electronics firms are investing in process development and speculative 'long shots.'[31] Color television is one industry where China has become a leading global producer through trial and error, whereby some firms have succeeded and others have failed. Cement and textiles and apparel producers have also successfully adjusted to market forces. The auto parts industry demonstrates that production capabilities can be effectively transferred through supply chains from international automakers to first-tier local parts suppliers, although quality declines rapidly in second-tier suppliers.[32] More recent anecdotal evidence shows that even this is changing as second-tier suppliers improve their capabilities.

Some governments of Chinese coastal provinces are not just reducing their intervention as market forces take over, but standing back and allowing the process to unfold. When demand for toys, jewelry, textiles, and apparel plummeted as the 2008 global recession got under way, the government in Beijing expressed dismay at the rise in factory closures and unemployment in Guangdong province that followed. Provincial officials were sanguine, however, indicating they preferred a strategy of 'emptying the cage for new birds' that would see polluting, labor-intensive enterprises replaced by high-tech and environmentally friendly enterprises.[33]

Enterprises in China also rely on trade and FDI as sources of learning – indeed, China is now the most open of the emerging markets, with total goods trade (exports plus imports) accounting for 67 percent of GDP in 2006 (compared with 33 percent in India).[34] Beginning in the late 1970s, China cautiously opened its economy, first on an experimental basis in special economic zones and then more widely in the 1990s. Its exporters learned to penetrate new markets and achieve scale economies beyond what was possible in the domestic market. Imports have been an important channel of learning because they carry new knowledge that can be added to the capital stock, either directly or through imitation or reverse engineering.

More significant, however, is the role of FDI, strategic alliances, and joint ventures, which impart new skills and knowledge to local employees and suppliers, which then diffuses into the economy as they change jobs or start their own enterprises. This increased openness has intensified competition in Chinese markets, particularly as foreign producers gradually have gained permission to operate wholly owned enterprises, putting pressure on all but the most efficient firms.[35]

Foreign technology diffuses through FDI and joint ventures in several ways. In the auto industry, one channel is through the migration of talent from foreign to domestic enterprises. For example, faced with intensifying competition, leading domestic firms Chery and Geely developed their production and design capabilities by recruiting talented people from abroad or luring them from joint ventures. Chery's success has been largely driven by its hiring of ethnic Chinese returnees, who then harnessed local talent to push forward on research and design. Geely, another fast-growing local car company, was unable to recruit the best and brightest from abroad, but managed to lure talented people from local automotive joint ventures to staff positions at all levels.

Foreign-invested enterprises, however, still play a key role in China's exports.[36] In 2003, they produced 77 percent of China's exports of industrial machinery; 90 percent of its exports of computers, components, and peripherals, and 71 percent of exports of electronics and telecommunications equipment.[37] In addition, the *domestic* value added in China's exports is still low – a share estimated at just 15 percent in the case of electronic and IT products, with the rest coming from imported components.[38] But this is changing; in the intensely competitive domestic markets, sourcing components within China is a way to reduce costs. Increasingly, domestic suppliers are not only foreign-invested enterprises but other domestic firms capable of producing such components as tools and dies and covers for laptop computers.

Finally, prodded in part by intense domestic competition, Chinese entrepreneurs are learning to be responsive to customer demand, as evidenced by data showing that Chinese firms obtain more design patents than invention patents.[39] One strategy has been to capture rural markets before taking on foreign competition from multinational firms in city markets. Alibaba, a well-known Chinese counterpart to eBay, started up in a small city targeting small businesses and individuals and teaching them through its Alicollege how to make their transactions on the Internet. It also runs an annual Alifest, a Berkshire-Hathaway–style gathering of its customers at Zhejiang's Great Hall of the People, where successful customers share their experiences.[40]

The Experience of Indian Enterprises

India's story, in contrast, is about enterprises in enclaves of excellence that are well managed by experienced entrepreneurs, export oriented, rapidly growing, and well financed. They exist alongside the rest of the economy, which is riddled with bureaucratic restrictions and still industrializing, and where innovation is more likely to be improvisations by individual farmers and small businesses aiming to circumvent bureaucratic restrictions. Technologies are diffusing only slowly through the domestic economy as some of the country's largest enterprises develop new business models to serve the vast market of low-income consumers.

In India, foreign knowledge has been suspect, and the country has not taken advantage either of internationally available knowledge or knowledge generated by its public research institutions. Despite the liberalization of trade and FDI that has occurred since 1991, access to foreign knowledge is still relatively restricted. Compared with Brazil, Russia, and China (the other so-called BRIC countries), Mexico, and South Korea, India's inflows of FDI are much smaller (although they grew rapidly in 2007 and 2008), its shares of imports and exports of knowledge-intensive capital goods in total trade are much smaller, its trade barriers are higher (though Russia is an exception), and its administrative requirements, such as the time needed to enforce contracts, are far higher.[41]

Among Indian enterprises, however, there are lots of exceptions. For example, Wipro has leveraged India's openness to transform itself from a vegetable oil producer into, first, an IT manufacturer, and then a global IT services firm with forty thousand employees. Its first partner/customer in a software contract was GE; together they produced designs for the Indian market until 1991, when global worries about the Y2K software glitch stimulated demand for Indian software skills and resulted in a steep increase in revenues. Today, Wipro has a product design and development niche in the global market for R&D services.[42]

Small, rapidly growing private firms in such industries as auto parts and pharmaceuticals have also transformed themselves by leveraging ties with foreign firms. One such example is the ambitious pharmaceutical producer based in Noida, an enclave outside New Delhi, introduced in the first chapter. Another is an auto parts producer located in Gurgaon, another industrial enclave near New Delhi, which began in the early 1970s making sewing machines. Realizing sewing machines were a sunset industry, the owners shifted into auto parts production in the early 1980s and, on a visit to Japan, convinced Honda to accept their company as a supplier to its Indian motorbike business. In 1985, the company launched an initial public offering to raise funds for its transformation, and by 2005 it had become a first-tier parts supplier with sales of US$154 million. It hopes to have become a billion-dollar company by 2010.[43] In both examples, public infrastructure investments in industrial parks made them attractive locations for these fast-growing firms, while economic liberalization opened their horizons beyond satisfying local markets, and, in the case of the auto parts producer, a foreign partner helped the firm raise its productivity and opened opportunities for customer-driven innovations.

Business investments in employees and on-the-job training are often overlooked as innovation drivers. Yet, even very small Indian enterprises share knowledge with their employees and, more informally, with other firms. Many also reward employees for new ideas in the form of bonuses, stock options, or promotions. The World Bank is critical of India because of the failure of its government to deliver quality primary schooling, which hampers the ability of many workers to upgrade their skills. Yet, Indian manufacturing and IT enterprises in the organized sector are keenly concerned with human capital development. One equipment producer in New Delhi told me that the value management attaches to employee skills is sufficiently high that, during a cyclical downturn, employees were not laid off but given intensive on-the-job training.[44] The IT sector has also been pushed into supplying its own skills training, not only because of the skills shortages that emerged during the boom of 2006 and 2007, but also because of the inability of any but the most elite technical training institutions to supply the necessary advanced skills.

Furthermore, just as Chinese firms have become more productive by cutting costs and developing new processes in response to intense market competition, so India's large enterprises spend heavily on R&D, mainly in pharmaceutical, transportation, electronics, and IT. Among their successful innovations are the 'global delivery model' in IT services and the pharmaceutical industry's generic drug molecules. The IT services industry is also finding ways to move beyond the low-cost advantage that provided the basis for its export successes. Anticipating that countries such as the Philippines and China will be able to replicate these cost advantages, Indian service providers are acquiring deeper knowledge of their customers' businesses in order to develop more sophisticated methodologies and the tools to serve them.[45]

More than in China, customers are the other significant drivers of innovation for Indian firms.[46] Like China, India has a huge number of potential consumers of modest means whom Indian entrepreneurs are beginning to target by determining what prices they can afford to pay and then re-engineering their supply chains accordingly. Mobile phone companies such as Bharti Airtel and

Reliance Communications, for example, have determined what an Indian farmer would be willing to pay for a mobile call – it turns out be the price of a stamp for a postcard – and have re-engineered their value chains to reduce costs to meet that modest price. A similar effort has produced a low-cost phone.[47] The potential for cheap phones and phone calls to revolutionize the information available to rural Indians is demonstrated by the case of fishermen in Kerala. Traditionally, after returning to their home port from a night's fishing, they had to accept whatever price was offered for their catch. Mobile phones now allow them to call around to different ports to find out which one will give them the best price and then head there instead.

Other commercial innovations include the "Simputer" developed by Amida to provide word processing and e-mail services in villages regardless of language. Low-cost Internet connectivity pioneered by the Indian Tobacco Company (ITC) through its e-Choupal initiative has equipped thousands of villages with computers and satellite connections as part of its agricultural procurement program. Farmers use the computers to check prices and sell their products online, cutting out the middlemen and their expensive commissions. Reliance Industries is developing a network of supermarkets based on integrated 'farm to fork' supply chains that also open up wider product choices for farmers and replace the middlemen. Reliance plans to become the 'off-taker of last resort,' transferring market risk away from the farmer and into its own system. Another innovation, by SKS Microfinance, provides smart cards to microfinance organizations that make small loans to small farmers and landless labor and co-locates ICICI Bank's automatic teller machines at rural Internet kiosks to provide affordable banking services to rural customers.[48]

An innovation aimed at low-income consumers which has fired the world's imagination is Tata Motors' Nano. After determining that the average Indian driver could afford no more than 100,000 rupees (about US$2,500 at 2008 exchange rates) for a car, Tata Motors reduced its costs to that level by re-examining the basic necessities – one windshield wiper instead of two, three bolts per wheel instead of four, a hollow steering column, cheap replaceable head lights – and re-engineering parts of the value chain to achieve its 'frugal' target. Robert Bosch, the world's largest auto parts company, agreed to supply a low-cost, simplified version of its Motronic engine-management system.[49] The first Tata Nano displayed in 2008 generated worldwide interest in the market potential for such small basic cars. While it is too early to tell, Tata may have created a new global brand.

Not Yet Titans

Neither China nor India has yet become a technology titan, but each has made significant progress by adapting the technologies and applying the skills of others. For China, reducing its dependence on foreign technology is the first step toward achieving its global ambitions; restoring its historical capabilities as an inventor is another. Yet, its techno-nationalist targets for R&D investments in, say, nanotechnology could turn out to be a costly exercise in 'picking winners.' Instead, a major driver of China's economic growth for some time to come is likely to continue to be its comparative advantage in low-cost skilled labor. The big story is the intense competition under way among the many small nonstate enterprises, which drives adaptations consistent with that comparative advantage. To survive, to keep ahead of the domestic competition, and to catch up with foreign firms, these enterprises are highly motivated to invest in innovation. Their successes, based on independent thinking, incremental learning, and relatively labor-intensive technologies, could frustrate or delay the leadership's global ambitions. This creative destruction has a social cost, however, and China needs to have a progressive social safety net in place to help smooth the fallout from this process.

In India, the notion of creative destruction is far less acceptable than in China – indeed, it is considered anathema. Experimentation is seen as wasteful in a resource-scarce business environment, and failure is not an acceptable price of success in a society that prides itself on a millennium of continuity. It is also a lesser issue than in China, since the Indian economy has yet to experience the widespread dynamism that is now characteristic of the Chinese. Moreover, the disconnect in India between the organized and unorganized sectors seems to have carried through to disconnects between the high-tech and industrial exporters and the rest of the economy, and between public research institutions and the private sector. Existing knowledge is not yet being sufficiently diffused, but initiatives built on IT innovations to connect small and medium-sized enterprises and rural users with financial institutions, to generate solar energy, and to produce affordable transportation show promise to leap frog – or at least to circumvent – India's restrictive labor policies and interventionist financial regulation, which retard the full development of its human capital and waste financial capital. At the end of the previous chapter, I asked whether innovations can be used to address the failure of India's financial system to reach small, productive firms. The answer seems to be yes, but progress is slow – IT is only just beginning to connect Second India.

The shortcomings of India's labor market institutions, which perpetuate unequal opportunities, of China's financial system, which favors state-owned enterprises, and of the two countries' national innovation systems, which have ignored small enterprises for too long are examples of market failures and institutional weaknesses that only governments can correct. Are they up to the job? If not, what are the likely consequences? In the next chapter we will see that China's growth sprint could be cut short and India's more recent spurt could slow.

chapter five

Sprints, Spurts, and Stumbling Blocks

This miracle will end soon because the environment can no longer
keep pace.
– Pan Yue, China's deputy minister of the environment,
7 March 2005

Failure to reform a bloated public service is putting the country's
[India's] huge economic achievements at risk.
– *The Economist,* 8 March 2008

Rapid growth is not an end in itself but the means to raise living standards and pursue societal goals such as education, skills
training, and the reduction of inequality. In China, the Communist Party, facing the failure of central planning, unambigu-
ously chose to dash for growth by freeing market forces in large
swathes of the economy. But some regions have advanced faster
than others and polluting industries are degrading the environment. The central government aims to address these market failures in its Eleventh Plan (2006–10), but success is not assured:
if growth is to be sustained, the autocratic government institutions that have been effective in delivering rapid growth need to
change course and loosen up. In India, the leaders of the ruling
Congress Party, also facing the failure of central planning, preferred to be poor but pure and chose inclusiveness over growth; it

arguably achieved neither. Instead, regulation, bureaucracy, and direct government intervention to raise living standards hindered growth and divided the labor force into those who have benefited from economic growth and those who have not. Many obstacles have been removed since the 1991 financial crisis, but significant ones remain.

In both China and India, moreover, growth strategies and sheer numbers have collided with the physical limits to industrial growth. Now, governments must align producers' incentives with the full costs of polluting, emitting, and consuming finite natural resources. Both countries subsidize fuel, electricity, and water as adjuncts of both growth and equity. These subsidies are politically popular, but the longer they persist, the larger will be the demands on treasuries and the longer the eventual transition to market prices. Without greater conservation efforts and the adoption of clean technologies and practices, neither country will be able to sustain growth, since, as China's deputy minister of the environment has warned, 'the environment can no longer keep pace.'

What policies and institutional choices created these stumbling blocks of rising inequality and environmental strain and how can they be removed? Clearly, neither country can continue with business as usual. Modern communications make it difficult to hide environmental degradation and allow those left out of the benefits of growth to see what they are missing, leading to social and political tensions that could challenge the Communist Party's legitimacy in China and fracture India's democracy. As these two giants assume a more prominent role in the world economy, their 'soft power' increasingly will be determined by their success in meeting these challenges.

The Stumbling Block of Inequality

When markets work efficiently, accelerating growth is like the proverbial rising tide that lifts all boats. Some boats rise higher than others, however, as improvements concentrate in certain regions and benefit particular groups of people. The issue is no longer the alleviation of absolute poverty, at least in China, where living conditions have improved for hundreds of millions as material shortages have disappeared, although 16.6 percent of Chinese were still living below the dollar-a-day poverty line in 2006. By comparison, 34.7 percent of Indians were still mired in that degree of poverty.[1] The two countries show other stark differences as well: as of 2006, 43 percent of children in India under age five were underweight, compared with 7 percent in China, while the mortality rate of Indian children under age five was three times that of Chinese children (76 versus 24 per thousand live births) – and India's maternal mortality ratio was ten times higher than China's (450 versus 45 per hundred thousand live births).[2]

At the same time, income inequality is increasing more quickly in China than in India.[3] Moreover, inequality between rural and urban incomes in China is widening: urban incomes are now 60 to 75 percent higher than rural incomes, on average. The big gap, however, is between incomes in the coastal provinces and those in the interior. State-owned enterprises are still major employers in the interior provinces, while, in the coastal provinces, increasingly dynamic nonstate enterprises, many of them outside urban areas, are driving rapid growth.[4] In India, virtually no poverty reduction occurred between 1951 and 1981. Only when Rajiv Gandhi began his market reforms in the early 1980s did the percentage of the population below the official poverty line begin to decline. Income inequality, however, changed little in the 1990s: in rural areas it remained unchanged or declined marginally, while in urban areas it increased by around 10 percent.[5]

China has relied on rapid growth to reduce poverty by drawing people out of agriculture into modern industries. Investment spending in manufacturing and on infrastructure, as much as 45 percent of GDP in recent years, has been the main driver of growth along with foreign demand for China's manufactured exports. Such high rates of investment have exceeded consumer spending, which accounted for only 35 percent of GDP in 2006, down from 47 percent in the early 1990s.[6] In the words of Chinese economist Justin Lin, who is now the World Bank's chief economist, China's growth strategy has 'defied' the country's comparative advantage in low-cost labor and encouraged heavy investment in capital-intensive manufacturing, which produces many fewer jobs.[7] Saving by individuals has also been declining because wages, government transfers, and investment income have been held down by competitive pressures from the country's huge labor supply and by the low return to individual savings offered by its banks, among other reasons.[8]

To rectify matters, the Eleventh Plan aims to rebalance China's pattern of growth away from investment toward consumption. Reducing the emphasis on investment will reduce the capital intensity of industry and shift it toward services and labor-intensive production such as light industry. These are also the industries that will be less intensive in their use of inputs of energy, raw materials, and capital. With a less capital-intensive industrial structure, the economy could continue to grow with less saving and rely more on increases in efficiency and improvements in human capital as sources of growth.

But how to increase consumption when one of the reasons individuals save rather than spend their wages and other income is because they must cover the costs of schooling, health care, and old age by themselves? One way is for government to pick up these costs and spend more on an improved social safety net, leaving more income in people's pockets. Further reform of financial markets to increase the efficiency with which savings are used and household savers are rewarded would also boost their incomes.[9] In the countryside, this means better access to income-earning opportunities off the farms and beyond family-operated businesses; in the cities, it means providing an adequate social safety net to put a floor under incomes.[10] Channeling credit to small and medium-sized enterprises would help to create jobs in labor-intensive light industries.

A number of institutional and policy changes have also been identified to change the manufacturing and investment bias in production. These include allowing the exchange rate more flexibility to appreciate, allowing the market to determine the prices of inputs, removing tax subsidies for manufacturing, requiring state-owned enterprises to pay dividends to the government to reduce their investment bias, and removing restrictions that hamper the development of services industries. Finally, the remaining *hukou* restrictions on rural-urban migration could be eliminated, which would help to reduce rural poverty and encourage local officials to carry out the Eleventh Plan's rebalancing strategy.[11]

None of this rebalancing will happen overnight; even with less emphasis on saving and investment, the Chinese economy's trend toward a gradual slowing of growth over time is unlikely to change, but at least growth would become sustainable as changes in institutions shift its drivers away from investment in capital and toward investment in people, knowledge, and improved efficiency.

India's strategy, in contrast, shows continued ambivalence about growth and mistrust of the effect of free markets on economic outcomes. When the Congress Party–led UPA coalition took power in 2004 it responded to voter dissatisfaction with the previous government by re-emphasizing its longstanding commitment to inclusiveness, a policy that has been criticized as both anti-poor and anti-growth. Industrial licensing and investment restrictions, bank nationalization, rules on labor redundancies, and ceilings on urban land holdings have all restricted jobs and growth.[12]

The government's current economic plan focuses on restoring growth momentum to the stagnant agricultural sector. There is little public support, however, for a 'big bang' restructuring that would increase agricultural productivity and open up opportunities for the rural population to move to urban areas. Farmers question why their subsidies should be reduced while urban subsidies and living allowances for government employees remain secure. Others note that the small size of the average farm, the large number of farmers' dependents, and the low-return, high-risk nature of village agriculture all argue for continued subsidies.[13] In my interviews with Indian elites, retired public servants, and senior private sector figures, however, most stressed the need to raise agricultural productivity, rather than to ease constraints on industrial growth. One view among this group reflects Gandhi's vision of rural life and stresses India's comparative advantage in agriculture. Many of these individuals also believe that the country's vast rural population cannot be absorbed into cities whose infrastructure is already groaning under the weight of newcomers. There seems, in fact, to be an implicit acceptance that the unorganized sector is pro-poor.

These views may help to explain the focus of the 2007 report of the National Commission for Enterprises in the Unorganised Sector, whose preface states that one of its major highlights is the 'existence and quantification of the unorganised or informal workers.' One would have thought that a more significant highlight would expose the reasons that most of the labor force is in Casual India. Instead, the report makes no reference to the policy restrictions that have created the unorganized sector, but focuses on the second-order consideration of improving its management. Prime Minister Manmohan Singh recognized this anti-labor, anti-poor framework in a December 2005 address to the 40th Indian Labour Conference when he talked about a new deal for India's working people. In referring to the textile sector, for example, he stated, 'The jobs that were driven out of the organised industrial sector into the unorganised sector can be regained. New employment can be created in this potentially labor-intensive industry. It will, however, require some reform of our labor laws and in our urban land utilization laws. We must think ahead and think creatively, so that thousands of new blue-collar jobs are created in this major segment of our domestic industry.'[14] Yet little progress has been made because of a political stalemate between those who see reform as pro-poor and those who see the status quo as pro-poor. They cannot both be right, and the statistics on maternal and child mortality and poverty, even though they have declined from even higher levels, clearly show the challenge that remains.

Rising Expectations, Rising Violence

Along with rising inequality in China and India are rising expectations. In China, the central government has begun to channel resources to equalize opportunities by providing primary health care and basic education and social programs, but will these resources reach the intended targets? India is poorer but purer: average incomes are lower than in China but so is inequality. Abysmal public services have failed to equalize opportunities. India's long tradition of direct intervention to equalize outcomes continues, however, with programs such as the National Rural Employment Guarantee Act and a debt-waiver scheme for farmers. These are having some positive effect, but excessive and outdated laws and regulations and poor quality basic services continue to frustrate expectations.

Many people are willing to accept the inequalities caused by rapid growth and development if they believe their children will have better opportunities and outcomes. Left unaddressed, however, these inequalities will become concentrated in areas and among groups least able to deal with them. In India, for example, the poorest states are also those with large agricultural populations, low literacy rates, poor infrastructure, and poor institutions of governance, while in China, as we have seen, whole provinces and regions have failed to benefit from the country's rapid growth.

At the same time, those dislocated or left behind by rapid, urban-based growth know what they are missing. Most Indian community centers now have televisions. So do Party offices in China's villages. Heightened expectations for a better life and more economic opportunities create unprecedented pressures for change from the bottom up. There are signs of growing impatience in China, with increasing reports of ad hoc protests over land, environmental degradation, and the heavy handedness of the police. In India, violent protest increasingly is orchestrated. Urban violence appears to be motivated by ideological and communal factors, as Islamist groups from within and outside the country target major political and economic locations, such as the Parliament Buildings in New Delhi in 2001 and Mumbai's tourist hotels and railways in November 2008. Rural violence is also spreading and has support from the poor and marginalized. By some estimates, the Naxalites – a Mao-inspired rebel movement founded in 1967 in West Bengal – are active in 185 districts in 17 of India's 28 states. More recently, these groups have also focused on vulnerable points in the infrastructure necessary to support India's rapid urbanization.[15]

China's Demographic Stumbling Block

One stumbling block to future growth that China faces but India does not, at least in the medium term, is the demographic structure of the population: India's population is youthful, but China's is aging, which raises questions about the potential concentration of poverty and inequality in the older population. China is aging because of the one-child policy introduced in the late 1970s, when declining fertility finally caught up with declining mortality but the overall population was still growing faster than economic output. The policy was introduced as an emergency measure but has remained in place. Its strict enforcement in urban areas (rural families were allowed a second child) has led to underreporting of births since the 1990s. Despite the policy, China enjoyed its own demographic dividend between 1982 and 2000 as the population of productive age grew faster than the total population.[16] Demographers argue that, as the size of the total population has begun to stabilize, China could enjoy a second demographic dividend if aging leads to capital accumulation, but it is too early in the transition to predict whether this will be the outcome.

The International Labor Organization, however, describes China's aging as a 'demographic cliff' over which the proportion of prime-age working people (those ages 25 to 54) is falling as the birth rate slows and the proportion of the elderly (those over age 65).[17] As China's population growth slows, the ratio of workers to retirees will rise from 10 to 1 today to 2.5 to 1 in 2050.[18] Such a ratio would not be unusual in the advanced industrial countries – by 2040, Japan will have just over 1 worker per dependent – but China is unique in that the shift is occurring at a much lower level of per capita income.

As a result of this demographic shift, China faces slowing growth and rising pension costs. As labor force growth slows, economic growth will slow unless it is offset by rising productivity, which, is happening to some extent: between 2003 and 2006, productivity and efficiency improvements in manufacturing offset cost increases in inputs, including wages.[19] Wages will continue to rise, however, as the number of 15-to-24-year-olds shrinks and the flow

of youthful rural migrants slows. Growth will slow first in the manufacturing, construction, and commercial services that rely on
that age group, and China's low-cost advantage in manufacturing
will erode.[20] In the longer term, suitable investments in upgrading
people's skills and lengthening their working life will offset some
of the demographic change; already China is investing heavily in
college education as one response to this challenge.

The other major challenge arising from demographic change
relates to pensions. Will the rising number of elderly receive publicly funded pensions or will they face inequality and poverty because they will have had to fund their old age using their own
savings or those of their families? China's urban social security system is now relatively well developed for a developing country, but
it faces rising liabilities that will be a drain on the public purse unless, as other countries have done, contribution rates are raised,
payout rates are reduced, or the urban retirement age is raised
to 65 (from the usual ages 55 for women and 60 for men). Moreover, the rural population will age faster than the urban as parents
remain in the villages while their children migrate. The central
government has responded by expanding rural health insurance
to nearly 90 percent of China's counties and setting up a rural
medical assistance scheme and a transfer program to provide minimum income support. These programs provide some assurance
that the demographic problem is manageable.

The Stumbling Block of Finite Resources and
Environmental Challenges

The other major stumbling block that China and India face is
more absolute. The size and speed of the increase in their industrial and residential demand are straining the carrying capacities
of the world's natural resources and the global commons. This
does not mean China and India should not industrialize; rather,
the issue is how to accommodate their added demand within
global supply constraints. Clearly, new technologies are required
to increase efficiency and reduce their environmental footprint.
Indeed, all countries need to reform institutions and policies to

encourage efficient energy use and reduce pollution. What, then, are the linkages in the two giants between their public policies and institutions and these external challenges?

Between 1995 and 2005, China and India together accounted for a third of the global growth in oil demand. As they fuel their growing industrial production and vehicle usage over the next two decades, their demand for energy is expected to rise at a faster rate than that for the world as a whole.[21] China is less energy efficient than India: during the period 2005–08, China's GDP and energy consumption grew at 11 percent rates (which would double consumption every seven years if they were to continue) while the increase in India's energy consumption, at 4 percent, lagged its GDP growth (9 percent). The difference is explained not by superior energy efficiency in India but by the fact that half its population does not yet have electricity, and subsidies for power and petroleum products favor farmers at the expense of manufacturers. To sustain recent growth rates, however, India will have to increase electricity production sixfold by 2030.[22] Even as living standards increase and energy consumption grows in both countries, however, their per capita energy use is still quite low: China's per capita energy use is 20 percent of that in the United States, and India's is lower still.

Rising energy consumption pushes up prices and causes worries about security of supply. Both countries have generous endowments of coal, but must rely on imports of oil and natural gas. China feels greater vulnerability to supply disruptions because its imports come from unstable countries and must be transported through sea lanes under the control of other nations.[23] India also worries about supply disruptions, but for a different reason: its power sector is inefficient and its energy infrastructure inadequate, and supply has been unable to keep up with demand.[24]

The environmental costs of energy consumption are also rising. Coal-fired power plants produced 67 percent of China's primary energy needs in 2003. Its carbon dioxide emissions, which track coal usage quite closely, were four times larger than India's.[25] Energy-efficiency and anti-pollution campaigns are having an impact – plants built since 2001 have access to more efficient combustion and scrubber technologies. But producers, squeezed between rising coal prices and government-imposed caps on what they can charge for their electricity, cut costs by idling scrubbing equipment when possible and using cheaper low-grade coal, thus undermining the policy objective.[26]

Water is another potentially binding constraint on growth in both countries, because of uncertain rainfall, pollution, and inadequate infrastructure. In China, seasonal rainfall causes flooding in the south and west and drought in the north and east. Most of the land-intensive crops are growth north of the Yangtze River, in an area with only 20 percent of the nation's water resources. Forty-five percent of China's water is used for agriculture, which produces just 2 percent of GDP. In 1998, the flooding Yangtze River displaced 223 million people and killed more than 3,000. In India, flooding of northern rivers regularly displaces large numbers of the poor in the populous affected states.[27] Environmental critics in China charge that most of the rivers in the northern plain are 'open sewers'; the World Bank argues the same is true of rivers in India.[28]

In the past 150 years, India has made large investments in water infrastructure, but these have not been well maintained or extended, so large expenditures now are required to rebuild. Storage capacity is only 200 cubic meters per capita; in China, it is 1,000 cubic meters.[29] India has harnessed only 20 percent of its hydro power (in developed countries it is 80 percent) because most potential dam sites are in heavily populated areas and acquisition of land from rural owners is fraught with conflict. In Rajasthan, for example, the Narmada Dam, built in the 1940s to supply irrigation water and hydroelectric power, has attracted protests and controversy over its effects since the 1980s. In 2003, groups who feared displacement if the height of the dam were raised five meters sought a Supreme Court ruling on the issue.

Both China and India subsidize irrigation. Indeed, in China, it is one of the Party's preferred methods of raising rural incomes since nearly half of the country's cultivated land is irrigated – compared with a third in India and 6 percent in the United States. The Indian government also relies on water and electricity subsidies to help low-income farmers access irrigation. India's Eleventh Plan emphasizes more equitable distribution of water and greater efficiency of use by encouraging rural water use associations that are elected and empowered to set water charges. To alleviate shortages, both countries have turned to groundwater, China for the first time just 25 years ago. Groundwater now accounts for 20 percent of China's total supplies and 50 percent of India's irrigation supplies. India's middle classes increasingly use it for their domestic water supply instead of poor-quality public water, which is left to the poor.

As China's industrial complex expands, so will its reliance on fossil fuels, much of them imported. Adding to demand is China's growing fleet of cars – projected to number 573 million by 2050; India, too, is become a nation of automobiles, and will have an estimated 367 million on the road by 2050, compared with 237 million in the United States.[30] How will they cope? Fossil-fuels-intensive technologies have delivered jobs, but at what cost in congestion and pollution? Acid rain now falls on a third of China and is increasing in India. Each country has two of the world's ten most-polluted cities. The health costs of environmental degradation are also climbing: air pollution is associated with 400,000 excess deaths every year in China and 170,000 in India. Indeed, the long-term cost of the dash for growth may be higher than anticipated. In 2006, China's deputy environment minister, Pan Yue, reported that 70 percent of the more than two million deaths a year from cancer were pollution related. He also estimated the annual cost of environmental damage at 8-to-13 percent of GDP and said levels of pollution could double in thirteen years.[31] A Chinese Academy of Science study estimates that, between 1980 and 2000, if the price of water had taken into account the cost of pollution, China's GDP growth rate would have been 6.8 percent instead of 9.6 percent.[32]

Governments in both countries face increasing popular pressure to find new ways to produce and consume energy that are both more reliable and more environmentally friendly. This means reducing the share of electricity that comes from conventional coal and increasing the share of renewable sources. It means improving the efficiency of heavy industry and enforcing environmental regulations. It also means pricing energy at market prices to reduce consumption, encourage the use of cleaner, more efficient energy sources, and increase energy production.

Efforts to account for the cost of water pollution by requiring enterprises to invest in waste treatment have been slow to bear fruit. Firms with such facilities must be forced to use them, because the process consumes a lot of power and is expensive to operate and maintain. Pollution control is also lax in China: just 22 percent of urban waste water is treated and a third of the population lacks access to clean drinking water, a higher proportion than in India.

In the face of these environmental challenges, China began to develop a policy response in 2005; India's approach has been more haphazard. Growing international criticism of China's rising impact on global energy supplies caused the Chinese government to worry about its growing dependence on imports. Energy security was made a goal in the Eleventh Plan, with a compulsory target of a 20 percent decline in energy consumption per unit of GDP by 2010, to be met by conservation and substitution, among other means. The Plan also calls for a 10 percent reduction in pollution, with a toxic waste spill near Harbin, which polluted the city's water supply, shining a spotlight on China's deteriorating environment. The energy efficiency target, however, has been difficult to achieve. At first, the problem was weak enforcement, a failure publicly admitted by Premier Wen Jiabao. More detailed planning and targets followed, including the imposition of energy-efficiency programs on the largest industrial users, the elimination of tax rebates on energy-intensive exports, and widespread closure of inefficient plants.[33] In 2008, petroleum and electricity prices were raised, and the government department responsible for environmental protection was upgraded to a full-fledged ministry, able to engage in Beijing's turf battles as an equal. Now, laws on water pollution are being enforced, penalties imposed on waste water, and new construction projects assessed on their environmental impact. But disputes remain between the laws and regulations of the environment ministry and those of the water resources ministry. In any case, the laws do not define pollution clearly. And, among eight ministries and commissions – with mandates as varied as long-range planning, the budget, water and waste water, flood control, irrigation, treatment plants, groundwater extraction, water-borne disease control, and watersheds – who is in charge? In fact, protecting the nation's rivers is effectively the charge of a network of ten thousand local environmental protection bureaus that do not focus on the national interest.[34]

Clean energy use is also beginning to make progress in both countries. China is reported to have invested US$12 billion in clean energy in 2007 and could be the world's leading producer of electricity from renewable sources. Part of the US$586 billion stimulus package is also reported to be directed to low-carbon investments in conjunction with a target to shift 20 percent of total energy consumption to renewables by 2020. Enterprises such as Suntech Solar are emerging as major producers of solar panels; wind turbine production has reached 4 gigawatts, with capacity split half-and-half between Chinese and foreign enterprises. In India, enterprises such as Suzlon are also active in wind power generation, and solar panels are widely used throughout the country. Both countries also have big plans for nuclear as a source of clean energy. In 2005, nuclear energy accounted for just 3 percent of India's and 2 percent of China's power generation.[35] In India, eight new reactors will soon double capacity, and there are plans for 20,000 megawatts of capacity by 2020. China plans to increase nuclear energy's share of power generation to 4 percent by that year.

China is beginning to acknowledge that it must address these market failures in the planning period, by empowering the relevant ministries to enforce the regulations and by funding research. India has encouraged energy efficiency, but has undertaken little follow through, partly because the country is less industrialized. A more effective response will be necessary if India is to break bottlenecks in energy supply, industrial growth, and employment.

Each of these stumbling blocks raises the larger question: is a state that tolerates market failures up to the challenges of correcting them?

Can They Address Market Failures in Time?

Governments do not cause growth; entrepreneurs, investors, and firms operating in markets do that. Governments establish the policies and institutions that affect their production and investment decisions by signaling prices, providing information, and defining property rights. The 2008 report of the World Bank's Commission on Growth and Development highlights how governments matter. Committed, capable, and credible governments and free markets are strongly correlated with growth.[36] Such governments also attempt to correct the failure of markets to allocate resources efficiently. Sometimes they do this well; at other times, government failure replaces market failure. How are the governments of China and India addressing inequality and the environment?

China's Attempts to Address Market Failure

In China, business-as-usual has deep historical roots. Emperors once occupied the paramount positions Party leaders now fill. The Party's overriding political objective is to maintain public order and its own grip on power. It has done this by delivering jobs and economic growth and by pursuing gradual, controlled change. The elite bureaucracy has existed for a thousand years, deteriorating during the decline of the Manchu dynasty but rebuilt by the communists. Today, promotions are based on regular performance evaluations whose criteria reflect the Party's political and economic priorities. The Party relies heavily on administrative measures to advance its economic goals. Incentives encourage rapid growth at any cost. With grey areas around traditional practices of *guanxi* and informal networks, official corruption persists and the central government has not yet found a way to control it.

Most of the prices of industrial inputs are administered; those of capital, land, energy, and water are subsidized. The exchange rate is managed to provide stability for exporters and to protect farmers from cheap imports. Lax enforcement of labor and environmental regulations favor enterprises' bottom lines. All these send powerful signals to expand production, with its implications for resource allocation, industrial structure, and employment. Despite attempts by bank regulators to ration lending and by bureaucrats to halt expansion of steel and aluminum plants,[37] a heavy industry 'gold rush' has been under way in China. The growth of capital-intensive heavy industry, moreover, has come at the cost of job losses elsewhere in the economy, exacerbating income inequality, and severe industrial pollution.

The administrative approach produced a thirty-year dash for growth that was spectacularly successful – and spectacularly wasteful. Official corruption is one of the most troubling side effects of administrative discretion and decentralization. Internet usage is censored, and Party members are becoming increasingly sophisticated at projecting Party views in Internet discussions.[38] At the same time, the Internet and text messaging on China's half-billion mobile devices have revolutionized the spread of information about alleged abuses of power and citizens' protests. In June 2008, for example, it was widely reported that ten thousand people had rioted in Guizhou province to protest the handling of a girl's death, which had been ruled a suicide by the Public Security Bureau. A month later, thirty thousand people reportedly mobilized over claims of a police cover-up of her alleged murder. In the same month, migrant workers in Zhejiang province demonstrated after one of their number was arrested by police; around the same time, a police station and local administrative offices in Guangdong province were attacked by people responding to rumors that a motorcyclist had been beaten by police.[39]

Land transactions are another focus of public concern. In the absence of clear property rights enforced by an independent legal system, citizens turn to traditional modes of redress through petitions to Beijing and local protests. By 2005, by official estimates, there were 87,000 local protests against official corruption. Local officials regularly take a share of government infrastructure investments and receive cuts from land transfers to developers. By some estimates, corruption costs as much as 3 or 4 percent of GDP.[40] The urban housing market has been effectively privatized since the late 1990s, but the land is state owned, while leases are tradable. Nonurban land is still collectively owned, and farmers are granted thirty-year leases. Land around urban areas is routinely requisitioned from farmers by local governments, which then engage in murky but lucrative transactions with real estate developers.

The closed, centralized industrial structure of thirty years ago has been transformed into a dynamic, decentralized capitalist economy, with diverse interest groups, a growing urban middle class, and entrepreneurs mixed with large state-owned oligopolies and traditional officialdom. Beyond is the large population in the countryside. The central government has moved to combat abuses of power with a range of measures. In 1994 came a major recentralization of public finance that reduced opportunities for local corruption, a significant downsizing of the bureaucracy, and attempts to create a civil service system. The National Bureau of Corruption Prevention, which reports directly to the State Council, supervises the Party's anticorruption efforts. Discretionary powers of local officials have been reduced, accountability and disclosure standards for state-owned enterprises have been raised, and a State Audit Administration now has investigative powers. As well, the Party undertakes internal disciplinary measures. Intentional or not, these administrative reforms fall short of the justice and accountability provided by an independent legal system because they continue to hold the Party outside the law.

Legislative changes have also been made, but with unclear intent and enforcement. Rural land use legislation and an antimonopoly law adopted in 2008 are two examples. Land use legislation has been interpreted as allowing farmers to lease or transfer land allocated them. The policy specifies that such transactions should be voluntary and involve adequate compensation. An experiment in Guangdong province is reported to allow farmers to trade nonarable 'construction' land without going through local governments.[41] Few details are available, which suggests that the policy might be controversial among interest groups within the Party. The purpose of the antimonopoly law is also uncertain. Its ultimate aim presumably is to increase efficiency and protect the public interest against monopolistic behavior and abuses of economic power. Yet it is not clear that state-owned enterprises will be subject to the law or that it will be used to curb abuses of administrative or regulatory power by government departments. The commerce ministry's decision in March 2009 to block Coca-Cola's bid to take over juice maker Huiyuan was widely seen as protecting a Chinese brand, rather than as preventing the concentration of market power.

If the rebalancing strategy is to succeed, however, the government will have to increase its efforts to encourage local officials to carry it forward. Presumably, the center will administer medical insurance reform that ensures access to primary health care throughout the country, for reasons similar to those that led to the public finance reforms of a decade ago. Delivery of social programs and education will have to rely on changes in the performance evaluations of local officials since the monetary rewards from promoting service industries and delivering health care and education will pale in comparison to those realized in the past from land transactions and industrial investments.

Going forward, the challenge is for the government to move further toward a strategy that is more open, provides appropriate signals for a complex economy, and competently corrects market failures.

Insights into the top leadership's views of 'democracy,' a term frequently used in their speeches, were provided in 2006 by Premier Wen Jiabao to a visiting US delegation. A later interpretation by the Brookings Institution's John Thornton indicated that, when Chinese leaders talk about democracy, they are referring to 'elections, judicial independence, and supervision based on checks and balances.[42] Mandatory elections now occur in almost one million villages. Experiments with elections at urban residential and township committees are also under discussion. Elections for positions within the Party are contested; independent candidates have stood for election to People's Congresses in Beijing and Shenzhen. In the run-up to the Seventeenth Party Congress in October 2007, policy debates within the Party were publicly aired in the press by those espousing a variety of positions.

But these experiments are limited by the actions of Party members who seek to retain control.[43] To prevent loss of Party influence in village elections, candidates for village chief must be drawn from the local Party branches. Corrupt local leaders intimidate citizens who attempt to assert their rights. There is also evidence of innovations, however, such as county-level 'democratic consultation meetings,' in which Party cadres encourage people to express their concerns about policies and programs. In Sichuan, non-Party members have participated in nominating candidates for township elections. NGOs still receive only limited recognition by government officials, but an initiative in Wenzhou, Zhejiang province, opened linkages between officials and entrepreneurs through local chambers of commerce – horizontal networks whose initial purpose was to promote product standards and enforce intellectual property rights in various industries; they have now extended their activities to include more open channels for business-government relations.

Also, local officials have initiated channels of communications with citizens using the Internet. As long ago as 1986, the mayor of Nanjing introduced a 'mayor's mailbox,' which has since expanded to include citizen commentary and complaints about officials and levels of service. The city of Hangzhou started a similar program in 1998.[44] In May 2007, the Shanghai municipal government suspended construction of the Maglev high-speed train slated to connect Shanghai and Hangzhou in response to publicly expressed citizen concerns about potential radiation levels in adjacent neighborhoods.[45] The Party is also using other channels, such as public opinion polling and independent evaluations by consultants. Civil society experienced a huge boost in 2008 around the unprecedented outpouring of donations and spontaneous group and individual initiatives to rescue victims of the Sichuan earthquake.

A free press is the other major check and balance on power in democracies. China's press has learned that investigative journalism sells papers. Yet, as a recent commentary on the relationship between the press and government observes, 'government-business collusion has provided an endless stream of material for the media [but both government and business] ... continue to exercise an uncanny ability to restrict the media.'[46] While informal

techniques of 'media oversight' of governance and power relationships are being practiced, this occurs in the absence of a legal
framework defining both media rights and obligations.

The rule of law and judicial independence will take longer to
achieve. Chinese institutions are moving away from traditional
reliance on justice rendered by the educated bureaucratic elite
toward a more independent legal system. Until the mid-1980s, the
legal system was staffed by former military personnel with no legal
training. Lawyers were state employees until the 1990s, when the
system was professionalized. Since 1989, citizens have been permitted to sue the state, and in 1999 an amendment to the constitution declared China is 'governed according to law.' Judges are still
appointed by local officials, however, rather than by the central
government, leaving them vulnerable to political connections and
pressures when it comes to law enforcement.

Examples abound of flaws in the system. In one instance, a foreign joint venture partner sued its Chinese partner for violation
of intellectual property rights. Both parties stated their cases before a judge; later, when they were called to hear the ruling, the
foreign partner turned up, the judge turned up, and several thugs
appeared who threatened both. The case was never settled.[47] Another example illustrates how a government that enforces some
rules, such as crushing dissent, fails to enforce others. A journalist
in Beijing seeking to renew his auto registration was informed by
the traffic police of his accumulated violations, all recorded by
cameras on Beijing roads, that would cause his license to be revoked if they were not cleared. Instead of lifting his license, however, the police advised him to find drivers with clean licenses who
would (for a fee) clear his record. An auto dealer later obliged.[48]

Countries that have made the transition to good institutions exhibit strong correlations among growth and political stability, governance by the rule of law, an absence of corruption, and credible
competent government. In World Bank surveys, China ranks below India on measures of voice and accountability, the rule of law,
and control of corruption, but much higher on political stability,
government effectiveness, and the quality of its regulations. There
is little evidence that China's experiments with more open gover-

nance and the rule of law have had much effect on corruption. The Party faces the dilemma of trying to reduce opportunities and incentives for corruption while retaining the loyalties of those on whom it must rely to govern. Its own overweening emphasis on rapid growth is one of the incentives for growth-compatible corruption. But as the economy shifts toward higher-value-added and less-energy-intensive activities, current practices will obstruct growth. As long as the Party polices itself, lifting members above the rule of law, how can this change? Behind the answer to all these questions is the role of the Party. The way forward is being intensely debated, but the taboo on challenging Party supremacy remains unbroken.

Published studies and news reports provide some insight into these debates. In early 2008, as an important example, senior researchers at the Central Party School in Beijing published a study with a foreword written by the school's deputy head. *Gong jian,* the characters in its title, broadly refer to the need to conquer the toughest road blocks on the way to political reform – the implication being that the gradualist approach to reform has tackled the easiest reforms first. The Party researchers do not advocate national elections or a multiparty system, but in their review of thirty years of political reform they imply that, without further reforms, the Party will fall behind public expectations and economic realities. The researchers note that the increasing monopolization of government and administrative power to serve bureaucratic interests while simultaneously reforming the economy has released 'civic power,' which they argue could be destabilizing. The decentralized market economy, the authors observe, is congruent with an appropriately centralized political system, one that has Party leadership and controls but whose functioning will be much improved by better definition and division of powers among the People's Congress, the People's Political Consultative Conference (a channel to incorporate social and corporate groups and individuals), the government, and the judiciary – all of which should work together and yet balance each other. The Party researchers recommend that the National People's Congress be turned into a fully representative body, with government officials removed from its ranks; that the administrative elite be better trained and evaluated; and that intra-Party democracy be developed. They further recommend a more open, transparent, and democratic legislative process, with a hearing system used for important legislation. They suggest that government departments should no longer be permitted to initiate legislation. Significantly, they warn that, without significant political reform, China's economy will become less efficient and productive.[49]

Experiments with on-the-ground reforms apparently are under way in Shenzhen, the site of the first experiments with Special Economic Zones three decades ago. These include direct elections of candidates to the local Party congresses and a system of permanent representatives. The Shenzhen administration is also reported to be experimenting with special legislation to expand media autonomy in exposing corruption and with an independent anticorruption agency along the lines of Hong Kong's Independent Commission Against Corruption. It is reasonable to expect that such experiments will be closely monitored, as were earlier economic reforms, and that what works will be kept and encouraged to spread.

Will this transition lead to good institutions? With economic openness, high educational levels, and the demonstration effect of the rapid growth of its east Asian neighbors, China has several of the catalysts need for a successful transition. Missing, most critically, is accountability. Persistent corruption is a mounting official concern, as suggested by reports of an investigation into a fire that destroyed the Television Center skyscraper in the new CCTV complex in Beijing during New Year's celebrations in January 2009. Financial deals have been uncovered involving the construction manager, who was also the legal representative of both a construction company involved in the project and the company that supplied the fireworks that started the fire.[50] There is much China could learn from anticorruption institutions in Hong Kong and Singapore. Moreover, no laws yet spell out free speech or the role of the press, although tolerance of greater press freedom and investigative scrutiny seems to be reflected in the Shenzhen special political zone. The Party's dilemma has been summarized

as, 'Fight corruption too little and destroy the country; fight it
too much and destroy the Party.' As corruption becomes a major
constraint on growth, an independent legal system will become
more important. Significantly, debate on the form of democratization appropriate to China is under way, with most intellectuals
supporting continued Party-led incremental reforms, while some
have called for a kind of Nordic-style democratic socialism.

Charter 08, a document signed initially by two thousand Chinese citizens and released on UN Human Rights Day in December
2008, includes a nineteen-point blueprint for democratization. It
acknowledges the material progress since reform and opening began and the Party's partial acknowledgement of rights since then.
But it laments the fact that China has many laws but no rule of law,
endemic official corruption, decaying public ethics, weak human
rights, growing inequality, and sharpening animosity between
officials and the people. Its blueprint would radically change incentive structures and transfer power, through elections, to the
people. Authorities promptly banned the document and detained
its authors for questioning.[51]

Charter 08 charts the future but does not address how that
might come about. China watchers in the West have ventured a
number of political scenarios. In one, China remains authoritarian for the foreseeable future, but succumbs to the ailments of
crony capitalism and is unable to renew itself. In another scenario,
as in other modernizing states, the middle class eventually pushes
for more political rights, which will lead to either Party reform
or regime change. A third scenario sees China following its east
Asian neighbors by softening its authoritarianism over time and
becoming essentially a one-party democracy on the model of Singapore or Japan, preferably the former – Japan, South Korea, and
Taiwan have strong public institutions and governance and the
rule of law, but have failed to find democratic ways to finance their
political parties, leaving them open to corruption and crony capitalism from close ties with business.[52]

How might ordinary Chinese react to Charter 08 and the other
transition scenarios? Reports of popular views suggest that many
are uncomfortable with the western idea of multiparty contested

elections, an institution with little precedent in China. Who would win and who would lose from the implied increase in individual freedom and from holding the powerful to account in this way? Would the transition be peaceful, and orderly? Ordinary Chinese emphasize that the remarkable improvements in their material lives over the past thirty years have greatly increased their personal freedom.[53] If they had to give up these material gains in exchange for more freedom, most would choose to avoid the uncertainties of a transition. They are uncertain that democracy and the transition to democracy are consistent with the peace and order they value so highly. There are strong popular memories of the chaos of the Cultural Revolution and of the instability that followed attempts to introduce democratic reforms early in the twentieth century. The comment one often hears is to the effect that, 'We Chinese are willing to put up with a certain amount of corruption and top-down direction as long as order is maintained in our daily lives.'

A 2004 U.S. summary of Chinese public opinion surveys revealed that both the potential winners and losers from political liberalization prefer the status quo to the risks of change. Workers in declining sectors, such as state-owned enterprises, have incentives to support the Party since they rely on its socialist promises. But the winners, too, such as entrepreneurs, fear that reforms might threaten their prospects and privileges.[54] Further, the growth of the urban middle class has created large, relatively affluent interest groups whose values and interests are very different from the more conservative and ideological views of those in rural areas who outnumber them. This awareness colors the attitudes of urbanites to free elections in which the outcome might not necessarily reflect their interests.

China's autocratic institutions deliver fast growth, initially guided by governments, but now largely by market forces. Its increasingly complex market economy and diverse interest groups require softer authoritarianism, a change that is widely recognized and debated by the elites. If China were to adopt 'good' institutions, it would reduce the incentives for corruption and arbitrary actions by local officials and increase accountability. Whether the

many rhetorical references to 'democracy' will produce these results is not yet clear, but China's chances of sustained long-term
growth will depend on achieving them.

India's Attempts to Address Market Failures

India seems to have all the public institutions China lacks. Its multiparty democracy was prominently on display in the month-long
general election in early 2009. It has an independent press, checks
and balances written into the constitution, and a large and vocal
civil society that monitors policy and often leads the way in social
experimentation. Newspapers flourish in India's many languages,
and the independent judiciary is increasingly activist in the face of
political paralysis on key issues.

The dark side of democracy in India lies in the failures of these
public institutions to function effectively. Interest-group competition creates policy gridlock and corruption goes unchecked.
Some elected representatives have criminal records. The civil service, one of the world's largest and once one of its best, has lost
its professionalism and accountability. As in other parliamentary
democracies, the career civil service was originally intended to be
apolitical, providing its political masters with objective advice that
reflected the national interest rather than narrow special interests. A huge bureaucracy that includes government ministries, the
police, and railways is considered unaccountable and unable to
deliver the simplest public goods. A mere 5,600 in the elite Indian
Administrative Service (IAS) 'run the country.' India's constitution prohibits politicians from firing IAS officers; they may only
suspend or transfer them. A public sector hiring freeze that began in 2001 continued for much of the subsequent decade and
by 2008 three-quarters of a million positions were vacant.[55] Half
of all IAS positions are reserved for tribal people, *dalits*, and low-
caste Hindus. When the UPA coalition took power in 2004, Prime
Minister Singh identified administrative reform as his top priority,
but little was accomplished during the five-year mandate beyond
shrinking employment.

Economic reform in India is a messy process, frequently para-

lyzed by competing interest groups. Compromises on many policies tend to take the lowest-common-denominator approach, and
change is so incremental as to be barely discernible at times. Political authority is diffused among competing political parties with
electoral bases in the states – which have constitutional authority
for education, agrarian reform, and land revenues, among others. Political parties representing caste and regional interests have
proliferated to such a degree that the center is now ruled by multiparty coalitions with varying goals and interests.

Malfunctioning institutions and gridlocked politics, in turn,
prevent India's using fully its considerable resources to reach
its economic potential. When the UPA coalition entered office
in 2004, it believed it had received a clear message from the vast
rural electorate for inclusion – implying more government intervention. But the message could also be interpreted as a call for
faster delivery of economic reforms. In the five ensuing years, the
coalition, unable or unwilling to spend political capital to obtain
agreement on reforming restrictive labor laws, defaulted to direct
intervention through the National Rural Employment Guarantee
Act. This costly, subsidized rural employment program provides
up to one hundred days of paid work a year for rural households,
and is rife with opportunities for corruption by local officials. Its
critics charge that 'paying villagers to dig holes and break stones
is easier than undertaking reforms that create sustainable jobs.'[56]
In some of the poorest areas, program funds now appear to be
monitored and distributed with fewer leakages than in previous
years, but corruption remains a problem. Nationally, the program
provided rural households with an average of 17 work days in fiscal year 2006/07, with higher participation in the poorer states.[57]
In its interim fiscal year 2009/10 budget, the central government
reported that 35 million households participated the previous
year, and it allocated a further 3 billion rupees (US$0.6 billion)
to the program.

In another direct intervention, the equivalent of more than
US$15 billion (twice the size of the education budget) was chan-
neled to indebted small farmers in the wake of press reports of
thousands of suicides. The program bypassed the bureaucracy by

putting money directly into farmers' pockets – and wooed their
votes in the upcoming national election. Whether these funds
reach the poorest farmers, who still rely on money lenders, is another matter.

Why have India's governments failed to change its restrictive
labor laws? No one seems willing to shoulder the task of reform
because it would mean taking on the unions, political ideologues,
state governments, and businesses that find it convenient to rely
on low-cost, informal arrangements. Reforming labor laws would
increase efficiency in the manufacturing sector as production
achieves scale economies. Both competition and costs would increase since, presumably, new labor legislation would address
legitimate issues of job security, pensions, and minimum wages.
Most important, the creation of large numbers of productive jobs
with decent working conditions and competitive compensation
would be possible in India at last.

Inadequacies in India's financial system compound the problem. Job-creating small businesses must rely on their own internal
resources because they cannot obtain bank loans. Capital is wasted
because financial institutions are compelled to purchase riskless
public sector bonds that are then used to subsidize public consumption, which leaves less capital available for riskier, but more
productive, private sector borrowers. Business in India is fraught
with difficulties – a 2007 World Bank survey ranked India one hundred and thirty-fourth out of one hundred and seventy-five countries on 'overall ease of doing business' (China came ninety-third)
and sixty-fifth on 'the ease of obtaining credit' (China ranked one
hundred and first). Bureaucratic detail consumes much more of
Indian business people's time than is the case in the industrialized
and other east Asian countries.

Columbia Business School economist Amar Bhidé makes the
useful distinction between government interventions that block
economic activity and those that add value. He concludes, from a
study of the costs of doing business in Bangalore, that, although
governments at various levels have removed some of the most
counterproductive interventions in markets such as small-scale industry reservations, they have failed to upgrade public institutions.

A prominent example is the way governments protect property rights, particularly land. Laws protect land ownership rights, but governments fail to provide even the most basic support in terms of accessible and accurate ownership records and the means to settle disputes. Bhidé also emphasizes Indian governments' lack of focus on fixing problems of inadequate physical infrastructure, unreliable electricity supply, and inefficient tax collection, which are the truly binding constraints to growth.[58]

The delivery of public sector services, particularly health, is generally agreed to be abysmal. Despite an extensive network of facilities, rural health facilities are used by only 20 percent of those seeking outpatient services and 45 percent of those seeking treatment. The rural poor have shunned these facilities since a forced sterilization campaign sponsored by Sanjeev Gandhi, one of Indira Gandhi's sons, was pressed on them in the early 1970s. Expectations of public health institutions are also low because of high rates of employee absenteeism (around 40 percent nation-wide), crumbling facilities, and inadequate supplies of drugs and equipment. Public funding is also distributed unfairly: in 2001, the poorest 20 percent of the population receive only 10 percent of public health subsidies, while the richest 20 percent received a 30 percent share.[59] Solutions, unfortunately, are not easy to come by and progress is slow. One suggestion is to provide the poor with vouchers that they could use to access either public or private care. The idea has merit, but many rural areas lack service providers of any kind.

Electric power generation and distribution is also still largely a public sector activity, with authority belonging to the states. Although power generation can be decentralized and possibly privatized, power grids, necessary to transmit and distribute the power, are natural monopolies that cannot be privatized without market failure and therefore remain publicly owned. In many rural areas, customers are not metered and do not pay bills, and electricity theft is common. Prices are subsidized because politicians promise free electricity to gain votes. Households must cope with daily power interruptions, while businesses usually install their own backup generators. Despite these problems, affected interest groups have slowed reforms that would introduce more efficiency and capacity into the sector. Still, in 2003, the central government set out performance criteria for the states to meet to qualify for financial assistance, including replacing underperforming state electricity boards with generation utilities, transmission companies, and distribution licensees that operate with transparency. Gujarat state's government then embarked on an ambitious program to replace its monopoly with modern facilities and more decentralized entities run by professionals. Subsequent press reports praised the Gujarat government for demonstrating how electricity could be efficiently produced and reliably delivered to rural areas, and other states are now following Gujarat's lead.[60]

Reforms, then, are possible when a determined effort is made to focus on binding constraints rather than on second-order issues, and when interest groups coalesce around common goals such as connectedness and productivity growth. So, why do fatalistic acceptance and the incremental approach prevail? The frequently cited excuse is India's fractious democracy. But the evidence suggests that India's politicians have chosen to reduce poverty through direct intervention rather than to allow market forces to work.

Limits to Growth?

Correcting market failures and replacing outmoded policies and institutions are not easy and can be expensive. In China, some catalysts for good institutions exist: intense competition, openness, rising education levels. But the binding constraint is lack of political accountability through regular elections, an independent judiciary, and a free press. The Party's experiments may soften its authoritarianism, but members frequently remain above the law. Still, the Party does realize that it is held accountable for maintaining growth, reducing inequality, and cleaning up the environment.

The challenges of the institutional and policy changes required to rebalance China's growth pattern are formidable because of their wider implications. Suppose, for example, that market prices were introduced for key inputs. If the cost of capital reflected true market scarcity, the financial system would have to be reformed and interest rates deregulated, which would require that the exchange rate be allowed to move more freely. Monetary policy, by definition, would be freer. Could an independent central bank be far behind?

Or suppose regulations and laws already on the books were more widely enforced. Enforcing the law that state-owned industrial enterprises pay dividends to their owners would trim their profit margins and reduce the earnings available for reinvestment.[61] Enforcing the Labor Contract Law would put upward pressure on labor costs, as would higher agricultural incomes. Lower profits would bankrupt small commodity-like producers with razor-thin margins, shrinking China's vaunted export machine.[62]

Increasing consumption and reducing precautionary savings will take time to deliver. The public health care system was dismantled with the demise of communes in the late 1970s and most state-owned enterprises in the 1990s. The government now intends to provide medical insurance to cover primary care, rebuild the rural health care system, and raise rural incomes. These are desirable initiatives on which tangible progress is being made, but it will take time to restore citizens' trust in these public services sufficiently to make a difference to the goal of increasing consumer spending.

And what about the response of local officials to a central government rebalancing strategy that would reduce their revenues and incomes? Premier Wen Jiabao roundly criticized the officials in Guangdong province who would 'empty the cage for new birds,' and demanded the provincial government support the challenged industries. Intellectuals, too, called on the province to change its institutions and improve its business environment to attract new industries.

In short, China has an impressive agenda of policies and institutions to rebalance growth toward services and greater reliance on consumer spending. But the broader implications of this agenda for entrenched interests raise the question of whether the changes now in the works will be sufficiently rapid and effective to satisfy rising expectations. How will the Party manage both the market economy and the well-informed and diverse interest groups it creates?

In India the catalysts for good institutions are improving as protectionist policies are removed, the economy is opened to the winds of international competition and education reforms take hold. The May 2009 general election was an additional and unexpected catalyst which delivered a strong pro-growth message by giving the Congress Party-led coalition a working majority in Parliament.

How will Prime Minister Manmohan Singh, who has been freed from the black hole of coalition management he occupied since 2004, use this mandate? By continuing to subsidize the poor through increasingly expensive programs such as the National Rural Employment Guarantee Scheme? This would be an easy and popular course, but it is a short-term fix. It would increase deficit spending and leave little for other urgent initiatives, such as infrastructure and electricity, which are truly binding constraints on future growth of industry and employment.

There are tough political choices to be made. Deficit control and focused spending on infrastructure and an overhaul of the entire education system could have payoffs down the road comparable to the telecommunications reforms of a decade ago. Reform of land administration and labor laws could unleash growth in agriculture and manufacturing that could put India's economy onto a 10 percent a year growth trajectory. Continuing on the steady-as-she-goes, pro-poor path of incremental change of the past half-decade will not banish the poverty of Second India, and the Congress Party would have only itself to blame in the 2014 general election.

In both countries, the stakes are high. By 2030, unless there are major technological innovations, they will face critical energy shortages and deteriorating climatic conditions that will profoundly affect economic growth – and inequality.[63] There is an organized insurgency in India's more remote rural areas, and organized threats to its urban infrastructure are on the rise. In China, less organized protests are a standard feature. Failure to address rising economic inequality would only magnify the potential for explosions.

The stakes are high in the rest of the world as well. Increasing interdependence means that government failures and successes have effects far beyond national borders. What are the implications of China's successfully rebalancing its economy so that Chinese consumers save less and spend more? And what if India takes full advantage of its potential in labor-intensive manufacturing? Such changes would only shift the center of economic gravity to Asia more quickly. In the next chapter, we examine the threats this shift poses and the opportunities it might create as the two giants continue their economic transformations.

chapter six

As Gravity Shifts

Let us not be dainty of leave-taking but shift away ...
– Shakespeare, *Macbeth*, II.iii

Nothing has quite matched the global financial crisis in highlighting the possibility that the gravity shift might accelerate. The International Monetary Fund's frequently revised forecasts beyond September 2008 showed global growth slowing, stopping, and then contracting. In the fourth quarter of 2008, U.S. GDP dropped by 6 percent, as that country entered a deep and possibly prolonged recession. But China and India continued to grow, although at slower rates than a year earlier. Geopolitical analysts look at these trends and see a zero-sum game: they win, we lose. Economists see it differently. By the principle of comparative advantage, when all countries specialize in what they produce most efficiently and then trade, everyone wins.

The gravity shift that is occurring with the rise of China and India has obvious economic implications. One, of course, is microeconomic. The shifting economic dynamism is opening new opportunities for international business, but also more competition. The other implication is macroeconomic: governments must manage the growing interdependence in good times and avoid protectionism when growth slows.

At the microeconomic level, global supply chain innovations are facilitating international business, opening up production on a global scale, and presenting new opportunities for specialization, especially in manufacturing. For the past decade, we have read about how the production of a single good – say, a computer – can be 'unbundled' into thousands of parts and components, each of which is produced at the location where it can be done most efficiently, then shipped to another location with abundant supplies of cheap skilled labor for final assembly. Merchandise trade volumes have expanded as parts and components cross borders numerous times before final assembly. Nowhere are these supply chains more widely used than in east Asia, where they have developed over the past three decades following Japanese just-in-time innovations in the auto and electronics industries. Suppliers cluster together to cut costs and share information. Governments facilitate clustering with tax breaks and infrastructure investment in now-ubiquitous export-processing zones, industrial and science parks, and special economic zones.

As they integrate into global supply chains, China and India are major beneficiaries of the opportunities for specialization, in that they access capital and knowledge that flow through these chains and leverage their own strengths within global markets. China's cheap but educated labor has particularly benefited from this revolution in production by moving from agricultural jobs into higher-productivity and higher-paying jobs in enterprises that participate in these global supply chains.

The rest of the world also benefits from the openness that made these innovations possible. India's IT services, which have driven that country's exports and much of its growth, assist businesses in the English-speaking world to reduce their operating costs. The world's consumers benefit from China's low-cost exports by paying less for clothing, footwear, furniture, and consumer electronics and having a wider range of choice. China's neighbors benefit from the growth in their exports of components to China, while China's growing demand for oil, aluminum, steel, copper, and coal benefits raw materials producers in Australia, Brazil, Canada, and South Africa.

From the macroeconomic perspective, the gravity shift has at least two significant implications. One is that it is changing the

nature of the China-India economic relationship, as business decisions and government facilitation deepen economic ties and bilateral integration. Further progress over the next twenty years could
transform the Asian region, with global consequences. The other
implication is for the imbalance between the Chinese and U.S.
economies and how that might be resolved. China's rebalancing
strategy is intended to increase domestic consumption. But will
China spend more at the same time that the United States spends
less? While the U.S. consumer, in the wake of the housing and
financial crises and severe recession, is saving more and spending
less, public spending has temporarily filled the gap. How to manage this imbalance is a key issue as growth is restored in the world
economy.

Business Strategies

Business strategists are beginning to change their perspective
of the two giants as low-cost supply bases and large, but homog-
enous, consumer markets. Now, they are realizing the potential
of tapping into a diversity of local markets for huge numbers of
low-, middle-, and high-income consumers. But they are also awak-
ening to the implications of China and India as the home bases
of new international competitors and as locations from which to
serve global markets. For international business, the implications
of the shift in economic gravity are two-way. As the two economies
restore their high growth rates after the global recession, they will
expand the size of global markets, creating more opportunities
for large-scale production and specialization. In turn, scale and
specialization help to raise global productivity – the means by
which more is produced from the same resources. As total production grows, so does employment.

As industrialization and urbanization in China and India proceed, the number of middle-class households in those countries is
expected to grow rapidly: a fifteenfold increase in China between
2000 and 2025 and an eightfold increase in India (see Figure 3).[1]
Still, many millions more will be low-income people living in rural
areas. Tapping into the diverse markets for these groups should

Figure 3: The Growth of the Middle Class, China and India, 2005–25

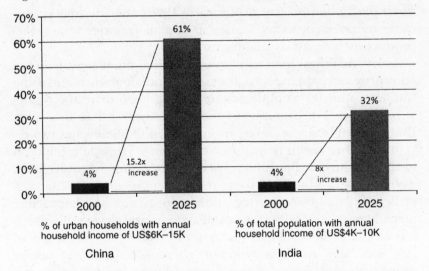

Source: Anil K. Gupta and Wang Haiyan, *Getting China and India Right: Strategies for Leveraging the World's Fastest Growing Economies for Global Advantage* (New York: Jossey-Bass/Wiley, 2009), pp. 80–81.

become a core business strategy. Nokia, the Finnish phone producer, has taken this innovative route in India, where it has more than 50 percent of the market share in mobile phones. Its success is based on a range of products from high-end, hi-tech devices to simple, cheap models for rural users in harsh environments. Nokia also distributes its products in a wide variety of ways, including through its own urban stores, electronics outlets, and vendors in villages and towns. The company's strategy has given it scale economies in R&D, a dominant market share, and brand loyalty.[2]

Auto producers will also flourish in the large markets – as we saw in the last chapter, by 2050 there could be 573 million vehicles in China and 367 million in India. Today, Volkswagen sells more cars in China than in Germany, and General Motors sells twice as many Buicks in China as in the United States, having made design adaptations to suit the Chinese market. In India, the Maruti-Suzuki joint venture holds the top market position, followed by

Tata Motors, India's largest indigenous producer. Hyundai entered the Indian market in the early 1990s after the market became more open; today, it uses its Indian factories as a global production base for its 1.5 liter cars.[3]

As Hyundai has done with autos in India, other multinational enterprises are tapping the Chinese and Indian markets and using the two countries' complementary strengths to drive their global businesses. For example, of the eight research labs that serve IBM's global business, three are in the United States but two recent additions are in Bangalore and Beijing. These labs build on local strengths: in Bangalore, speech recognition, e-governance, e-commerce, and software research and engineering; in the larger Beijing lab, business integration, information and knowledge management, and certain types of systems and devices. Each lab has inbuilt redundancy to manage the risks of serving a global customer base, and if one encounters problems another can be called into play. Together, they answer the question of where the company can find the best resources to deliver value to its global customers.

Multinational pharmaceuticals firms are also changing their business strategies to take account of Asia's rising market potential and abundant lower-cost technical talent. India's pharmaceuticals market is one of the world's fastest growing (17.5 percent in 2006), with much activity in clinical trials and contract manufacturing. It is seen as less risky than China's because of changes to India's laws and regulations to protect intellectual property. Not only is the local market growing fast, but R&D alliances are being struck with Indian firms – such as Ranbaxy, to identify new drug targets, and Nicholas Piramal, for drug development. The Chinese market is seen as attractive to serve, but joint ventures and alliances are deemed risky because of China's different practices and culture.[4]

The characteristics and strengths of local markets provide a variety of opportunities for leveraging products into international markets. For example, GE Healthcare China built its business by focusing first on the underserved nonurban market, where it sold used diagnostic equipment, and built its credibility by creating jobs and training people. It then leveraged these advantages into a global business based in China. In India in the late 1980s, GE, along with Nortel, pioneered relationships with Indian enterprises to build outsourcing businesses. GE initially tried to build a global manufacturing business, which proved disastrous because of quality problems. These were fixed after eight years of working with suppliers to raise their standards, first in producing generics, and then working up to critical parts. In 2000, GE chose India for its first R&D center outside the United States. While Indian manufacturing standards were still lacking, GE found that their software products *were* reliable and entered into a joint venture with Wipro. Today, using the strengths of both operations, GE produces a radiology system sold internationally that relies on software algorithms from Bangalore and final assembly in Beijing. Significantly, in both its Chinese and Indian businesses, GE began by working with local talent, rather than by building conventional distribution systems for imported products.[5]

Local initiatives, such as India's 'bottom of the pyramid' products aimed at low-income customers, could also seed innovative applications in other countries. Currently, most of these innovations – the Tata Nano car, low-cost computers, solar energy applications for basic energy needs – are aimed primarily at local markets, yet these technologies easily could find markets in other developing economies and even in advanced economies. For example, despite a forty-year government emphasis on brick-and-mortar bank branches, rural India still lacks access to basic banking services. With the rapid diffusion of mobile phones and data services, however, secure and efficient mobile banking for low-income Indians should not be far behind. In China, Alibaba.com, the successful online marketplace, attributes its success to starting out in smaller cities, where it was forced to focus on individuals and small businesses, rather than on the large state-owned enterprises and multinationals located in the larger cities.[6] Nobel Peace Prize winner Mohamed Yunus, from Bangladesh, is blazing a trail outside the developing countries by demonstrating the potential of his microfinance operations for low-income Americans. His organization plans to offer US$176 million in loans in the poorer sections of

New York City and then expand the business to the rest of the United States.[7]

China's and India's enterprises are also investing in each other's country, to extend their reach internationally and to learn from the other's market. In 2006, Bharat Forge, India's largest automotive forging enterprise, entered into a joint venture with China FAW Group, an automotive manufacturing giant, to supply auto parts to Chinese assemblers. Indian outsourcing companies in IT and BPO have also invested in China, both to follow their global customers there and to use China as a base from which to serve third countries – for offshore design centers to service the Japanese market, for example. Bharti Airtel uses China as a sourcing base for low-cost appliances and telephones. In the other direction, Huawei Technologies, China's top telecommunications equipment maker, has a significant presence in India, having invested US$100 million in a research lab in Bangalore that draws on the software skills of two thousand Indian engineers for its global business. Huawei and ZTE, another Chinese telecommunications equipment maker, are major suppliers to Reliance Communications, one of India's largest mobile telephone operators, which is pushing its low-cost mobile phone network deep into underserved rural India. And Delhi Metro is using Chinese engineering and construction companies in its second phase of construction.

These are *big* deals, but just a taste of the economies of scale and potential competitiveness opportunities that are open to companies that tap both markets.

Chinese and Indian companies are also investing abroad to service world markets. Lenovo, the Chinese computer firm, was one of the first to turn itself into a global player when it acquired IBM's PC business in 2004. Since 2007, Bharat Forge has spent US$250 million on overseas acquisitions to diversify beyond its Indian automotive roots. With operations in the United States, Germany, Sweden, China, and elsewhere, the company seeks proximity to its major markets because its success depends on face-to-face interactions, rather than on Internet exchanges, with the customers for its sophisticated and specialized designs.

U.S. state governments are wooing Chinese and Indian producers large and small to locate in their jurisdictions. South Carolina alone has Hailun, a Chinese piano maker; Haier, a household appliance maker; and Shanxi Yuncheng, which makes printing plates. Chinese IT firm ISoftstone has acquired a Seattle-based R&D firm, while Minsheng Bank and the China Investment Corporation have invested in U.S. financial institutions.

Chinese enterprises have also spearheaded the hunt to secure supplies of natural resources and to diversify China's holdings of foreign assets. Using government-to-government deals in Africa, they have acquired rights to exploit natural resources in exchange for concessional loans and Chinese assistance in building infrastructure or providing social services. China National Petroleum Corporation owns much of Sudan's largest oil venture. China has accessed oil reserves in Nigeria and Angola and mineral deposits in the Democratic Republic of the Congo and Zambia. In these deals, a Chinese construction company is mandated to carry out the project, often with assistance from China's Ex-Im Bank, in exchange for obtaining oil or mineral rights. As latecomers in the acquisition of sources of supply, the Chinese have been willing to close deals with states that western governments deem pariahs. China's dealings with these states have been facilitated by its belief in noninterference in other countries' affairs – a policy that resonates in African countries that have suffered from colonialism. China's continuing involvement in Africa, however, has also led it to lessen its indifference toward governance failures and civil rights abuses. After years of unqualified support for the Khartoum government, China now condemns Sudan's actions against rebels in Darfur and contributes to the African Union's peacekeeping force there. Chinese officials have also distanced themselves from the government in Zimbabwe.

Other deals have been initiated by both the Chinese government and by state-owned enterprises with help from state-owned banks. In 2009, the Chinese government loaned Brazilian state oil company Petrobras US$10 billion in return for a long-term oil supply contract. Further, the government has pursued a 'going out' policy that encourages state enterprises to make large foreign investments and acquisitions to increase capital outflows. The largest-ever commercial investment, a US$20 billion investment by Chinese metals group Chinalco in the Australian mining company Rio Tinto, fell apart for commercial reasons in 2009 but not before it was subjected to close scrutiny by the Australian authorities for its strategic implications. The Australian government had earlier blocked a bid by China Minmetals Corporation, a trading company, for Australian Minerals on national security grounds.

India's largest entrepreneurs have sought to extend their successful business models beyond the subcontinent, with the Tata family's Corus and Jaguar and Rover acquisitions heading the list.[8] Since 2004, other Indian enterprises, many of which are now well known in their industries, have made a number of acquisitions in the steel, automotive, pharmaceuticals, engineering services, and IT services industries. India's state-owned oil companies have secured natural resources through investments and acquisitions. Part of the strategy was to target marginal areas where China is absent, such as Cuba, Libya, and central Asia, where India is welcomed as a counterbalance to China. They have competed head on with the Chinese for some assets, such as those of PetroKazakhstan, but they have also cooperated to increase their bidding power and avoid competitive effects on price. India's Oil and Natural Gas Company joined with China National Petroleum Corporation and Sinopec in successful joint bids for assets in Syria and Colombia.

China's acquisitions meet with more suspicion than India's because most of the former are by state-owned companies, whose managers, experienced only in the near-monopoly market power of their home environment, often lack familiarity with international business. Moreover, their close government connections raise questions about their long-term intentions and whether their business decisions will be based on market forces. So far, the evidence suggests that Chinese investors are seeking through their investments to secure supplies of natural resources and to diversify the investments of China's foreign exchange reserves beyond low-yielding financial assets like US government bonds. India's entrepreneurs do not generate such suspicions because they are privately owned and more familiar with international business.

Will They Produce Everything?

China also makes people nervous because it is shifting 'up the value chain' to produce goods that previously only developed countries exported. India's success in IT services and business process outsourcing also causes worry because the economic future of developed countries supposedly lies in these more sophisticated service-based industries. Inspection of both the theory and the evidence suggests these concerns are overblown. A country will be better off if it specializes in products in which it has comparative advantage and imports other products from countries that produce them more efficiently. China's biggest cost advantage is in labor-intensive industries, because of its abundant low-cost skilled labor relative to capital and natural resources. Given its comparative advantage, it should export light manufactured goods and import capital-intensive goods and natural resources. This pattern might change over time as China builds its own production capacity and its firms increase their technical capabilities. India's source of comparative advantage, in theory, is also low-cost labor, but its bias in education spending toward technical and postsecondary schooling has produced abundant supplies of technical graduates in the services industries. At the same time, levels of basic education in India lag those in China, which means that much of India's low-cost labor cannot find work the modern sector without substantial skills training.

The pattern of both countries' exports is what we would expect. Since 1992, China has become a net exporter of a long list of labor-intensive goods – including toys, textiles and apparel, sports equipment, furniture, telecommunications and electrical equipment. In return, it purchases heavy industrial goods, machinery and equipment, and natural resources. For its part, India exports business services, petroleum products, engineering goods (machinery, instruments, transportation equipment, and metals), and gems and jewelry. It is also shifting toward the export of telecommunications and electrical equipment and office machines and away from textiles, apparel, footwear, and other light manufactures.

Looking behind the shift, however, it is apparent that, in China, many of these exports are finished goods simply assembled in that country for export. Moreover, studies of the skill content of finished telecommunications and electrical equipment show an interesting result: although Chinese production technologies are becoming more sophisticated, if one excludes assembly operations – known as the 'processing trade' – from comparisons of the ratio of production workers to total employment by industry, the skill content of exports in 2002 was no higher than a decade earlier.[9] In other words, the skills embodied in the sophisticated components assembled in China are not located in China.

The use of inputs produced in China itself is also increasing, presumably at the expense of foreign ones,[10] but who is producing these domestic inputs? Are Chinese or foreign firms responsible for the value added? Foreign producers, who still rely heavily on imported components, accounted for more than half of China's manufactured exports in 2004.

India's exports of commercial services owe their prominence to their size relative to the Indian economy and to their role as a driver of domestic growth. In 2006, these services exports were a smaller share (2.7 percent) of the world total than China's (3.3 percent), but India's were growing faster. Services dominate goods in India's overall trade, its merchandise exports accounting for a mere 1 percent of the world total, compared with China's 8.6 percent).[11] Low-cost manufacturing should be part of India's story, but its labor laws and institutions have caused India to miss out on the shift of global supply chains to China and other low-cost countries such as Thailand and Malaysia. Instead, its exports of capital-intensive manufactured goods are growing – in fiscal year 2006/07, India's exports of machinery, instruments, transportation equipment, and manufactured metals increased by 38 percent.

A related question is how quickly China and India are improving the skills of their work forces. China has built its preeminent position in global supply chains by combining foreign capital and knowhow with educated, low-cost labor. Both countries produce large numbers of postsecondary graduates each year: in 2005, India produced two and a half million new university graduates; by 2008, China was graduating six million a year. Behind the numbers, however, factors such as quality of skills, language abilities, and willingness to move influence the employability of graduates in international businesses. On those criteria, only 10 percent of Chinese and 25 percent of Indian engineers are deemed suitable; the percentages are lower still for categories such as financial professionals and generalists, with Indian graduates considered more suitable than Chinese. India's pool of suitable talent includes 130,000 engineers; China's has 160,000 engineers, but could have had many more if its suitability rate matched that of India.[12]

The emergence of China and India, then, is benefiting consumers and businesses in countries that import from them, by providing a wider choice of goods at lower prices, opportunities for specialization and scale in production and trade, a wider range of investment opportunities, and new sources of capital. These, however, are opportunities for exchange *between* one industry and another; in fact, many of the gains come from trade *within* industries. Much of the trade in global supply chains is a form of this 'intra-industry trade'; for example, China imports electronic components that are then assembled and exported as finished goods, all within the same industry. Intra-industry trade tends to occurs where there are only a few producers but their level of technological and other sophistication varies. Thus, China exports low-end household appliances, consumer electronics, and apparel to European markets, while European producers of high-end household appliances, luxury electronics, and designer apparel export to China. Indeed, the growth of intra-industry trade has been a key element in promoting the integration of European economies over the past fifty years. Today, this specialization in manufacturing is increasingly found, not just in final goods, but in parts.

The Opportunities in Our Own Comparative Advantages

For the rest of us, there are opportunities in what China and India cannot do as well. China has abundant supplies of labor, but its financial system relies mainly on banks that use capital inefficiently, and it is only beginning to address the contradictions between state-driven R&D targets and the free-wheeling creativity of firms outside state-owned enterprises and science parks. India also has abundant labor, but misuses its savings in a different way and its entrepreneurial innovation dominates that of China. In their future growth, both countries share the physical constraints of the lack of natural resources and too much pollution.

In these weaknesses and constraints lie opportunities for the rest of the world. Countries well endowed with natural resources find ready markets in China and India, and suppliers benefit from rising commodity prices. As long as huge numbers of Chinese and Indians continue to join the middle class and aspire to middle-class lifestyles, demand for commodities will only increase. Yet, the huge size of the Chinese and Indian populations and rapid industrial development of their economies is accompanied by rising local and international concerns about the effects on the environment and on the global commons. Already, two-thirds of China's major cities and many of India's face water shortages – half of China's major lakes are severely polluted and a quarter of its population has access only to polluted water to drink. India's problems are less severe only because of its lower levels of industrialization and urbanization. Air pollution is closely linked with excess deaths in both countries. Energy efficiency is also low, although China's is improving.

For firms in more advanced countries, used to stricter regulatory regimes and having the technological ability to increase energy efficiency, treat industrial wastes, and produce and distribute clean water, opportunities abound if China makes a determined effort to tackle these problems. At the moment, many regard weak environmental compliance in China as a source of its low-cost advantage: as younger Chinese observe, 'Not being able to see the sun is a cost of job creation and rapid growth.' But pollution and waste of resources could well jeopardize growth. If China's own environmental laws were enforced, much of its low-cost advantage in manufacturing would erode, although the higher costs that would result probably would not slow its momentum of growth.[13]

Public demand for cleanup is beginning to pressure the Party to realign incentives. Evidence of this change of heart is in the Eleventh Plan. which sets compulsory targets for energy conservation, emissions reduction, and renewable energy – which is to account for 15 percent of total primary energy consumption and 8 percent of total power generation by 2020. Ten major energy conservation projects have been identified, a goal of 100 percent collection and treatment of sewage in thirty-six large cities by 2010 has been advanced, building standards are being upgraded, and key river valleys are targeted for cleanup. Conservation will be rewarded and wastage penalized, and monitoring will be stepped up now that, as we have seen, a full-fledged ministry has responsibility for the environment.

As these changes take place, sooner in the coastal regions than in the interior, opportunities will increase for foreign expertise in designing and producing environmental and energy-efficient services and products. Chinese cities are already turning to foreign enterprises to build new water plants or buy existing facilities, but regulatory, legal, and pricing problems exist – including the typically low price of water and low wastewater treatment levies.[14] Workplace safety is another area where Chinese firms will face higher costs as new laws are phased in; as this happens, western firms able to achieve safety at much lower costs will have a competitive advantage.

Similar changes can be expected in manufacturing. American strategist Daniel Rosen emphasizes how governments continue to interfere in market decisionmaking.[15] China's myriad nonstate enterprises compete on an uneven playing field with state-owned enterprises that wield monopoly power and use their connections to get growth-obsessed local administrators to look the other way on environmental and labor laws, and banks that dismiss nonstate firms as high risk because they lack government contracts or connections as collateral. All these obstacles prevent them from growing and achieving efficient economies of scale to compete. Rosen notes that intense competition is compressing the margins of low-cost manufacturers, forcing them to become more innovative and to find new customers abroad. Surveys, including my own, of private firms consistently note that the speed of the expansion of their customer base is challenging their management capabilities, and they have yet to apply information technology to increase their efficiency. Moreover, they are resisting the transparency that would make financial data available to management, joint venture partners, and the tax authorities because they mistrust the discretionary powers of local officials. When they seek international customers by moving abroad, they find themselves at a severe disadvantage because they lack experience of strong regulatory and legal regimes and sophisticated transparent financial systems and must rely on foreign expertise to correct these deficiencies. As well, China's inefficient financial markets prevent them from using capital efficiently, creating another competitive advantage for foreigners with such knowhow.

As China's low-cost manufacturers develop their capabilities, however, it is the middle- and low-income countries of east Asia and beyond that will feel the direct and indirect effects most strongly. They currently benefit from China's demands for their parts and components; however, as Chinese suppliers develop their capabilities, foreign sourcing will decline and firms in neighboring countries will have to adjust their production to specialize in goods that are complementary to or differentiated from those available in China.

India could follow China into low-cost manufacturing if it reduced domestic regulatory barriers and infrastructure constraints. But progress likely would be slow. For some time, employment growth in Indian manufacturing will be limited to 'techno-manufacturing,' the production of engineering products that leverage local technical skills. This part of its economy will be competitive with similar activities in the advanced countries.

The challenge for the advanced countries is to adjust to the changing global division of labor that these mobile companies and ambitious governments are driving – just as they had to adjust to the Industrial Revolution's shifting patterns of industries and employment in the eighteenth and nineteenth centuries. It seems clear that the advanced countries will continue to dominate advanced manufacturing, where labor is not a major cost factor.

They will win in the production of complex goods and design- and research-intensive products and components.

In the auto industry, for example, jobs in standard auto parts are moving to China, India, and Vietnam, where labor is cheaper. Yet suppliers such as Bharat Forge are moving closer to their European and U.S. customers and creating sophisticated jobs in design and customization as they do so. The auto industry will not leave North America or Europe: design and R&D activities will remain close to customers, as will distribution and servicing activities. Generalizations about the futures of whole industries must be made with care. While less sophisticated *segments* of industries are moving to lower-cost locations, more complex segments will remain.

How far will this process go? Princeton University professor Alan Blinder suggests that, at the extreme, over the next twenty-five years every good that can be packed in a box will be outsourced if it can be produced more cheaply somewhere else. Any service that can be digitized and delivered electronically without a decline in value will be outsourced as well. This leads Blinder to argue that we must think in terms of what foreigners cannot do more cheaply and computers cannot do faster. His answer lies in what economists call 'nontradables' such as services that require a personal presence – divorce lawyers, say, but not contract lawyers.[16]

Others say this view ignores comparative advantage. Bradford Jensen and Lori Kletzer do not dispute the trend but question both theory and evidence, arguing that the numbers of jobs actually being transferred abroad is much smaller than is claimed and that comparative advantage is working. The United States imports low-wage, low-skill goods and services and exports high-wage, high-skill goods and services. The structure of U.S. exports of manufactured goods has shifted toward capital- and knowledge-intensive exports in such industries as chemicals, computers and electronic products, transportation equipment, and machinery. Services exports are also shifting toward business services, motion picture and video production and distribution, and sophisticated communications such as software publishers and satellite telecommunications.[17] Amar Bhidé argues that China and India are nowhere near to catching up with U.S. capabilities to develop and use technologies – indeed, they lag Japan, South Korea, and Taiwan, which have been chasing the United States much longer.[18] The foreign R&D centers of U.S. companies such as IBM focus on meeting their customers' global business requirements; they leverage local capabilities as part of their global offerings, not to replicate their R&D capabilities abroad.

MIT globalization expert Suzanne Berger has surveyed enterprises in what are commonly regarded as sunset industries in the industrialized countries – textiles, apparel and footwear producers, among others – and finds that a firm's capabilities and strategies determine how and where it produces. Some firms manage successfully by offshoring all their manufacturing; others keep many functions at home and remain profitable – even tee shirts are still produced in the United States by American Apparel. Others, like Geox in the shoe industry, leverage proximity to the customer, design expertise, and supplies of highly skilled labor. Berger concludes that the only lasting sources of advantage are the strengths that allow a company to detect new opportunities and develop its capabilities in a constant forward march toward novel products and processes. Innovation and productivity growth are not a story of individual prowess alone, but of individuals combining their talents with societal capital – the stock of infrastructure, financial institutions, legal system, business practices, bureaucracy, research institutions, and public culture.[19] A country's policy and institutional environment for labor matters as well. Of workers who became unemployed when their jobs moved to China, India, and other low-wage countries, about 70 percent in the United States found new work within six months, but only 40 percent did in Germany.[20] One of the main reasons for the difference is Germany's generous unemployment benefits and strict hiring and firing laws, which reduce the incentives to find an alternative job.

Managing the Gravity Shift

The story is not one of competition between 'them and us,' but of benefits for all. China's and India's integration into the world economy promises substantial gains for advanced countries that invest in the human capital required to become knowledge economies – indeed, it is difficult to overestimate the importance of investment in education, at every level. The advanced economies also need to become more flexible by facilitating, rather than restricting, the mobility of labor and capital, both geographically and among sectors. And they should rethink systems of human capital development and support – in a world of increasingly intense global competition and rich, but aging, populations in the advanced countries, skill and agility will command a premium. Also in need of elimination are bureaucratic obstacles and tax burdens that raise the costs of production and of doing international business, relative to those of our competitors, The checklist of what needs to be done is well known, but includes policies to promote investment, greater emphasis on enterprise learning through clustering, and changes in business taxation to remove obstacles to productivity-enhancing capital investments.

The fear of change is not misplaced. Workers are at risk of losing their jobs because of technological change, import competition, and outsourcing. They are at risk because their jobs are in labor-intensive industries that require low levels of skill, and whose workforces are aging and relatively immobile. It is also the case that women bear a disproportionate share of the burden of job loss due to import competition.[21] Foreign competition does destroy human capital as people with specific skills lose their jobs; and governments in advanced countries need to respond appropriately by encouraging workers to invest in themselves over their entire lifecycle and by making sure adequate social safety nets are in place to help workers cope with the shift.

An unexpected lesson of the 2008–09 global economic crisis was that global supply chains are a double-edged sword. Asian economies benefited from exporting components to China when exports of final products to the advanced industrial economies were booming. The disappearance of that external demand cascaded at remarkable speed through global supply chains: Japan's output dropped 13 percent in the last quarter of 2008 and in January 2009 its exports fell by nearly 50 percent, the largest drop on record; U.S. and Chinese exports (cars and electronics) dropped by 58 percent and 40 percent, respectively. Other Asian economies were hit in similar ways. The vertical integration in supply chains helps explain the speed and magnitude of the declines. When demand declines for a final product like a computer, countries that specialize in producing particular components or processes for the computer are affected immediately. As these components are shipped across borders, often several times as the computer is being built, each shipment is counted as a separate transaction in the trade statistics. As demand booms, trade flows rise dramatically. And, as we saw, when demand contracts, trade contracts even faster.

U.S. consumers were a major driver of the most recent demand boom. Unfortunately, they were also living beyond their means. They felt wealthy because of strong equity markets and rising house values, pushed along by government policies that encouraged home ownership. They also used their rising home equity to borrow and consume even more. Imports, many sourced in China, far exceeded exports, contributing to the U.S. trade deficit, which reached historic levels before it began to decline during the crisis. Conveniently, China's earnings of foreign exchange from its exports and inflows of FDI were also growing as the Chinese authorities intervened in the market to prevent the currency from appreciating beyond what they saw as a gradual and sustainable rate. U.S. government bonds were an attractive, low-risk asset, which they acquired in large amounts. When the U.S. economy began to slow down and housing prices did the unthinkable by falling, the stage was set for a global contraction; its magnitude was exacerbated by the effect of mortgage defaults in the vastly overleveraged U.S. financial system.

Thus, another cause of the gravity shift is the marked change in the external financial positions of the United States and China. It might be convenient to trace the source of China's large foreign-exchange reserves back to an under-valued currency, but the real issue is the imbalances in the two economies. The United States is now the world's largest debtor nation, China the largest creditor. The Chinese government has anticipated the need to reduce its reliance on exports by rebalancing the economy. The Obama administration, for its part, has acknowledged its dependence on continued Chinese holdings of government bonds.

The Chinese are increasingly anxious that the capital value of their large holdings of U.S. securities could drop if the U.S. dollar depreciates. A longer-term concern is the possibility that future U.S. inflation will erode the real value of these holdings. The Chinese and the Americans are in the same boat. The United States repeatedly has urged China to allow the yuan-dollar exchange rate to appreciate, which would slow the accumulation of foreign reserves. The Chinese do not show any signs of moving in this direction, particularly since the 2008 recession, which took them by surprise, leaving millions of laid-off workers without the safety net envisaged in the Eleventh Plan. They prefer to rely on rebalancing, but it is unlikely that domestic consumption will replace savings in the short run. What is clearer is that the postrecession U.S. economy will grow more slowly and from a smaller size as sectors adjust to restore their balance sheets. Competition among foreign producers will intensify as U.S. demand for imports slows, and protectionist sentiment likely will grow in the U.S. Congress if unemployment stays high for a protracted period. Heading off these tensions will require care, skill, and, at least in China's case, a larger view of the international consequences of the conduct of domestic economic policy. Is China ready and willing to take on the added responsibilities that attend its rise within global institutions that manage global crises? Is India? Or will they plead their right as developing nations, as India has done, to move slowly in the collective effort to improve stewardship of the global commons? The answers to these questions will shape the next two decades and are central to the final chapter.

chapter seven

The New Asian Powerhouses and the World Economy in 2030

That which cannot be avoided, welcome.

– Chinese proverb

In a matter of two decades or so, Asia will dominate the world economy. By 2030, the Chinese and Indian economies combined will be nearly twice the size of the U.S. economy, with China itself larger than the United States and India fast closing the gap. Some projections have this happening as soon as 2020; others see China overtaking the United States by as late as 2035, with India following by 2040.[1]

Many observers look at the new Asian powerhouses and predict that their rising economic prominence will reshape the world order. Such predictions may prove correct, but they are unlikely to be borne out in the next decade, or even two. The translation of economic clout into political power depends on a number of factors, beginning with China's and India's immediate ability to weather the global recession. They will also have to sustain their fast economic growth rates, which will require continued adjustment of their domestic institutions and policies. Another important factor is their ability and willingness to cooperate with each other and with their Asian neighbors and to take on more responsibility in global institutions. The evolution of China's relationship with the United States will be particularly significant now that China is the world's largest creditor and the United States its largest debtor.

In 2009, as the world economy contracted, the Chinese and Indian economies continued to grow.[2] They are likely to weather the global crisis better than most countries because their households and businesses have healthy balance sheets and their governments responded quickly to declining external demand. Certain sectors were hit harder than others, however – in China, between seven and eight million workers in manufacturing and another two to three million in related services sectors lost their jobs in late 2008 and early 2009; a further five to ten million construction workers were affected by the decline in housing and infrastructure construction.[3] In India, the effect on trade was smaller because of the country's still-modest involvement in global supply chains. But its more open financial markets meant that, when Indian companies found themselves frozen out of foreign credit markets, they turned to the domestic market and pushed up interest rates, creating a liquidity squeeze.

Both China and India adopted robust domestic policy responses to the global crisis. China introduced a US$586 billion fiscal stimulus package, shared among the central and local governments, and stepped up commercial bank lending. The package had an immediate effect on infrastructure and building construction and materials-related industries, and Chinese economic growth began to rebound in the first quarter of 2009 at a pace sufficient to prompt the government to call on the banks to moderate their lending. Indian fiscal policy was constrained by persistent deficits and a public debt amounting to 80 percent of GDP (compared with 20 percent for China); nevertheless, the central government injected US$40 billion in additional fiscal stimulus in the February 2009 budget. Lower commodity prices helped offset some of the negative effects on trade, current account balances, and inflation, while good weather helped cushion rural consumption (which accounts for 57 percent of total consumption).

Significantly, both governments channeled part of their fiscal stimuli into projects to sustain long-term growth: infrastructure projects in India, and the planned rebalancing aimed at boosting household incomes and encouraging domestic consumption in China. The Chinese government placed laws on social insurance and medical care reforms before the National People's Congress in March 2009 and budgeted more than US$100 billion to carry them out.[4]

The Growth of China and India to 2030

Looking further ahead, China's growth will slow by 2030, while India's growth will accelerate. Why such different trends and what do they imply?

China's slowdown is predictable. As Japan, South Korea, and Taiwan industrialized, each initially grew at high rates similar to China's; after several decades, growth declined to permanently lower levels. Growth also slowed down as income per capita reached around the equivalent of US$13,000 (accounting for differences in price levels from one country to another),[5] suggesting they had reached the limit of returns to reallocating labor to more productive jobs. China may cross that threshold by 2030 (see Figure 4).[6] Indeed, China's challenge to sustain long-term growth could be greater than India's because it must rely heavily on using existing resources more efficiently and creating new industries and even new knowledge. India's task is easier in that it still has the option to move labor out of agriculture into labor-intensive manufacturing, which has worked in other successful, fast-growing economies.

A closer look at the factors that affect China's economic growth reveals that, in the decade from 1996 to 2006, it was driven mainly by investment, which amounted to as much as 45 percent of GDP. To compensate for the slowdown in labor force growth that is expected after 2012 for demographic reasons, investment in China would have to increase to at least 60 percent of GDP – a proportion that cannot be sustained. Investment at lower levels, however – whether at the current 45 percent of GDP or the historical average of 33 percent – could see China's economic growth rate decline to below 8 percent by 2025.[7] Sinologists Dwight Perkins and Thomas Rawski back up this scenario. They are optimistic about the positive effects of increasing education, but they suggest that if China relied on labor and capital alone over the next two decades,

Figure 4: The Rise in Living Standards, Selected Economies, 1820–2030

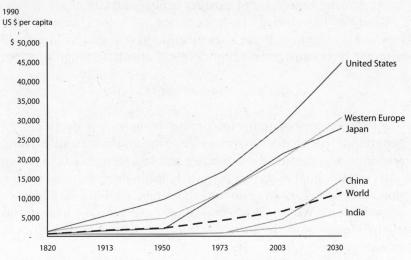

Source: Angus Maddison, 'Asia in the World Economy 1500–2030 AD,' *Asian-Pacific Economic Literature* 20 (2, 2006): 33.

it would manage only 5 percent growth. If this startling projection is correct, the onus for China's future growth is heavily on productivity improvements and getting more 'bang for the yuan.' Yet, to sustain growth at 9 percent over the next couple of decades, China would have to push productivity growth above 4 percent – a gargantuan task and probably unachievable. At best, Perkins and Rawski suggest, China's future growth is likely to decline to between 6 and 8 percent.[8]

In contrast, India will grow over the next two decades because it has room to raise investment rates and because its labor force will continue to grow. If India can raise annual net investment somewhat, from 7.4 percent to 8 percent, it should be able to maintain the 8 percent rate achieved between 2003 and 2008. If it could raise the annual investment rate still more, to 8.4 percent, the growth rate would reach nearly 10 percent by 2011. Unfortunately, India's saving rate is too low to sustain this rate of investment, and persistent government deficits divert savings into public subsidies and spending. Instead, the country's future room for maneuver lies in making better use of existing capital and labor.

What do these broad-brush scenarios imply for changing policies and institutions? What is the likelihood that such changes will sustain China's and India's high levels of growth through to 2030?

Can China Sustain Rapid Growth?

Can China compensate for its coming demographic decline? The general view is that China must get more output from existing resources and create new industries and knowledge. To the casual observer, this goal might seem quite feasible since political leadership successions are in train and the long-term policy framework is established. What is less clear, however, is how key institutions might change and, in so doing, sustain or undermine China's growth prospects.

In the near term, the broad outlines of policy are surprisingly clear: barring a catastrophe, change will be gradual and controlled. Current practice suggests three transitions at the top are likely between now and 2030. In 2012, President Hu Jintao and Premier Wen Jiabao are expected to turn over the leadership to two newcomers to the Politburo Standing Committee, Xi Jinping from Shanghai and Li Keqiang from Liaoning province. These two men, who likely will hold power until 2020, are of the generation that was sent to the countryside during the Cultural Revolution and that has matured during the reform period. Their Party, regional, and economic backgrounds, however, are quite different. Xi is described as supporting continued rapid growth, with further economic liberalization and reliance on the private sector. Li is said to be more concerned with equity and redistribution – with addressing disparities and developing a social safety net. The stage is thus set for China to carry forward its rebalancing strategy; time will tell whether differing interests will be the catalyst for a healthy rebalancing of power or for political tension.[9]

The 2030 economic framework is also discernible. It is already evolving toward greater reliance on domestic demand by encouraging consumption and spending; that will allow it to improve social services and develop a social safety net and to rely less on the industrial, investment-driven model of recent years. The two leadership successors are expected to continue the focus on rebalancing by diffusing the fruits of growth beyond the coast into the inland provinces to the north and west.

The outlook for China's political institutions by 2030 is more uncertain. Political scientists argue that rising incomes and greater economic security unleash a yearning for a greater say in how one's taxes are spent and how one is governed. Citizens in South Korea and Taiwan have demanded, and achieved, more political freedom, but Singapore's long experience with one-party democracy, a highly competent bureaucracy, and controls on the press and civil society is of interest. Chinese politics already involves increasingly well-informed intra-Party debates. Civil society could be included through controlled consultative mechanisms. If the economy continues to perform well, strong pressure for national elections is unlikely, if only because many feel the Party is serving their interests. The 2008 economic slowdown showed that China's leaders were acutely aware of being held to account. If things go badly wrong and China has a serious economic crisis, however, all bets are off. It is when things go wrong that democratic institutions show resilience by providing accountability to the populace through regular elections.

Will experiments with pragmatic change suffice? The basic challenge of rebalancing must be met through the public institutions that will channel government spending to the poorer and slower-growing provinces, where employment and productivity growth lag because of their dependence on state-owned enterprises. The central government's dilemma is to ensure that it achieves redistribution in transparent and accountable ways while retaining the loyalty of local officials. As important, success in steering drivers of growth toward technology and innovation and greater efficiency will require more transparency, checks and balances, and accountability. China's current leaders are responsive to public opinion, and quiet discussions are taking place among elites about possible changes. My own expectation is that China's politics will remain authoritarian, but with room for a wider range of views and voices of corporate and social groups – if not necessarily for individuals – to provide informal modes of accountability.

China's population will become more urban as it ages in the years ahead. As many as a billion people (between 60 and 70 percent of the population) will live in the coastal megalopolises and in towns all over the country that have grown suddenly into cities – already, China has more than two hundred cities of over a million people each. By 2020, as per capita income passes the US$13,000 level, the population will be increasingly middle class. At the same time, the labor force will be shrinking: by 2030, the number of 15-to-24-year-olds entering the labor force (178 million) will be nearly 30 percent smaller than in 2010 (229 million). The effects of this shrinkage will be felt in a number of ways. Wages will rise because of growing scarcity and pro-labor laws such as the new Contract Labor Law. Employers will attempt to offset these higher labor costs by, for example, increasing productivity or moving labor-intensive operations to lower-wage locations, whether to inland Chinese provinces or offshore. To increase productivity, manufacturing operations would have to move up the 'value chain' by producing their own sophisticated components instead of importing them. But China lacks the skilled labor needed for such operations – most migrant workers have only nine years of schooling; as Minxin Pei at the Carnegie Endowment has noted, 'emptying the cage for new birds' will not work without skills upgrading. While the global slowdown continues, China would benefit by providing free continuing education programs to migrant labor to upgrade their skills, with monthly stipends as an added incentive.[10]

China's Achilles' heel, however, could be its financial system. The result of directed lending, a heavily managed exchange rate, and administered interest rates is that capital is priced too cheaply, which encourages its wasteful use and the direction of too much of it to unproductive borrowers in the state sector. This means China cannot sustain the investment rates that have driven its recent rapid growth unless it allows the cost of capital to be determined more by market forces. This will require China to allow the yuan to float freely on foreign exchange markets, something not seen as a priority as long as the global financial crisis continues but a likely monetary policy change by 2020.

Increased monetary independence would have several significant consequences. Market-determined interest rates likely would rise and, as deposit rates rose in response, there would be a positive effect on the wealth of China's long-suffering small savers. As banks compete for borrowers, loan rates would come under pressure, which would reduce the spreads on which the banks rely for riskless income (as much as 85 percent of their operating income comes from spreads). The banks best equipped to assess and monitor risk will be the ones that succeed and grow. There could also be bank failures among the new, small private banks that were attracted initially into finance by the generous spreads. Unless they attracted low-risk borrowers and manage risk, they would suffer from nonperforming loans as interest rates rose with deregulation in the years ahead.

The banks could be a drag on future growth if the government continues to direct their lending. In November 2008, for example, the government called on the banks to help stimulate domestic demand in response to the global slowdown. The central bank cut the amount of money banks were required to have on hand and established loan guarantee schemes to share any new credit risk. For its part, the central government encouraged banks to step up consumer and rural credit, and changed tax policy to help them to deal with any new nonperforming loans that might result.[11] And lending rose rapidly as the banks matched public spending on infrastructure, with most loans going to large, well-connected corporate borrowers rather than to smaller nonstate enterprises. It will take some time for these loans to mature. Will they be repaid on time? Or will the banks simply have been used to support favored enterprises that otherwise might have failed because of excess capacity and declining demand?

Continued government ownership and intervention in markets also inhibits the transparency required for markets to function efficiently. State-owned enterprises continue to enjoy privileged positions vis-à-vis the regulatory authorities and to occupy the commanding heights of the economy, dominating rail and air transport, finance, energy, telecommunications, utilities, heavy machinery, and defense industries. Compared with nonstate enterprises, moreover, the state sector is still a large and inefficient user of capital – its share of industrial production is less than a third of the total but it still received a third of investment funds in 2005. The government owners of state enterprises are becoming more demanding, as are market analysts and their minority shareholders. Those that fail to produce global brands are being sold off or merged.[12] In contrast, many parts suppliers in the electronics and electrical equipment and other industries are private, as is most retail and much wholesale commerce; official estimates put the number of private enterprises employing more than eight people at 658,000.[13] But private and foreign firms have a return to capital that is as much as fifty percent higher than for wholly state-owned firms;[14] clearly, industrial output could be significantly higher if all enterprises, regardless of ownership, used capital and labor equally efficiently.

A further problem is that Chinese governments have not yet overcome their ambivalence about protecting property rights, which are a key factor in sustaining long-term growth because they ensure that innovators are rewarded for their efforts.[15] True, governments in leading localities such as Beijing and Guangdong use promises to protect intellectual property to differentiate themselves from jurisdictions that do nor offer such protection, and enforcement of existing intellectual property laws likely will improve in response to demands from Chinese enterprises. But, as Premier Wen Jiabao has signaled, an independent judiciary and the rule of law are unlikely to emerge in the immediate future. China has managed to grow so far without such protection or enforcement of contracts, probably because of alternative channels, such as extensive trust-based networks, the disciplines and protocols of global supply chains, and access to Hong Kong's sophisticated business services.[16]

In addition, while laws intended to encourage competition are on the books, their enforcement is problematic. The widespread failure of labor-intensive manufacturing enterprises in the 2008 downturn raised questions about the effectiveness of China's nascent laws on bankruptcy and mergers and acquisitions.[17] Bankruptcy laws were introduced in June 2007, but it is not yet known if market forces are replacing government preferences as to the timing of bankruptcies. Questions also remain about the intent of the 2008 Anti-Monopoly Law. The ruling on Coca-Cola's proposed takeover of Huiyan, the Chinese juice maker, has left questions about whether its intent was to increase domestic competition or to protect the interests of Chinese firms over those of foreign firms.

As China relies more heavily for its future growth on technological advance and innovation than on cheap labor and capital, tensions will increase between political control and an increasingly market-based economy. New technologies will be internally generated in innovative enterprises run by people who think independently, who even disagree with the prevailing science or government directives. In turn, the enterprises they run will be willing to take risks to develop new ideas and products. Public institutions that tolerate failure and financial institutions that can manage risk will be important elements in this business environment. Yet, China's political institutions are still primarily preoccupied with control. Productivity in many industries is driven by intense market competition and demanding customers, but the incremental, market-driven innovations that could become transformational are not yet apparent. Innovation is still driven from the top through large, conservative institutions, dependence on foreign technology is widespread, and market signals are frequently distorted as powerful political interests bend the rules. The result of these institutional obstacles is that China's growth will continue to be driven by adapting and diffusing the technology of others.

China will find it difficult to compensate for its demographic decline unless it reduces the administrative discretion of local officials, makes Party members accountable, and protects property rights. Continued government intervention in the banking system could be a drag on long-term growth as bad loans pile up, and skills shortages in the shrinking labor force could be a drag on productivity growth. One would be wise to hedge these conclusions, though. The leadership is pragmatic and willing to encourage what works. China's size and diversity allows for informal experimentation with more open forms of governance and greater accountability – such as those reportedly taking place in

Shenzhen. Unique Chinese institutions that tolerate diversity and protect and reward risk taking could yet surprise.

Can India Sustain Rapid Growth?

The prospects for India in 2030 make an interesting story because of the obvious potential for gains simply from making better use of existing resources of labor, capital, and knowledge. To the casual observer, this task should be straightforward in a democracy, especially when the gains would accrue to Second India's millions of voters. Yet India's fractious bottom-up democratic processes have so far failed to overcome the legacy rigidities of its top-down socialist past.

Four general elections are likely in the next twenty years, and each probably will deliver another coalition government. Which coalition governs, however, is becoming a question of declining economic importance as successive coalitions try different combinations of inclusiveness and growth. Perhaps by 2030 a generational change will have led younger voters and political candidates to shed the ideology of poor and pure. As many observers argue, in a democracy like India's, reforms that enhance and sustain high growth rates eventually can diffuse throughout the country as voters in states that are left behind push to achieve what faster-growing states have done. But if India fails to overhaul its educational institutions and connect Second India to finance and information, its youthful and still-growing population will become a threat rather than an asset. With progress in these areas, India's economy could outgrow China's by 2030.

In 2030, income inequality in India will be higher than it was in 2010, but lower than in the China of 2030. It will also be more urban: 40 percent of the population will live in its growing towns and cities, and many will have middle-class incomes. Overall, however, India will still be well below the US$13,000 income threshold at which growth typically slowed in the east Asian economies, suggesting continuing room for rapid growth. India's growing middle class will be well educated and will benefit from the higher wages that result from the country's shortages of skilled labor. But the other 60 percent of the population will still depend on the farm or on casual, low-quality service jobs that generate very low incomes. Perhaps by then, private sector initiatives, such as the Reliance Industries Fresh project, will have created supply chains that raise agricultural productivity and help farmers to market their produce competitively and transport it to urban markets.

India's number one challenge is to make Second India employable in the modern sector. In 2030, the population will still be youthful, and nearly a billion people will be of labor force age. Illiteracy among India's youth is not as high today because their parents voted for budgets for private schooling and NGOs have improved the quality of basic education. Governments could build on these popular preferences by allowing private sector providers to deliver education at all levels, from primary school to postgraduate university studies, and by giving parents vouchers to spend on education as they choose. As well, an estimated 80 million workers in the unorganized sector need vocational training to repair or build up their skills.

But from where will the jobs come? India's restrictive labor laws are anti-labor in that the regulations they impose in effect "protect" unskilled labor from permanent jobs by raising the costs to employers of hiring them. The perception among India's elite, however, is the opposite – that these laws are pro-labor and to oppose them would be anti-labor – which helps to explain why the UPA coalition elected in 2004 shied away from modifying them. Although Prime Minister Singh recognized the need to remove constraints, at least in the textile industry, the government compromised by appointing a commission on the unorganized sector and continuing to freeze public sector hiring. Strangely, labor unions seem not to realize that their membership is shrinking because the organized sector is shrinking, and that changes that allow the organized sector to grow would better serve their interests.

The task of shrinking Second India may have to await a change of elite attitudes and a determined political effort to recruit those who would gain from changing the laws, but this seems unlikely until a new generation of politicians and voters takes over. Technology could speed the transition. Deregulation of the telecommunications sector is India's most successful effort to correct government failures to date. IT connectedness has taken off like a rocket: in 2007 alone, a hundred million new mobile users signed up, and by 2016 that could grow to include half the population, or seven hundred and fifty million people. This connectedness is already revolutionizing the primary sector, as fishermen and farmers find more attractive markets and prices for their produce than those available through government-controlled channels. Internet connectivity has been slower to catch on. Illiteracy is undoubtedly a constraint, but bottom-of-the-pyramid innovations such as ITC's e-choupals are enlarging the options of farmers and small and medium-sized enterprises and allowing them to enter larger markets. Internet innovations are also making it easier for small firms to access banks and even venture capitalists and equity markets; new ideas and jobs are bound to follow as finance becomes easier to obtain.

India's connections abroad are also growing. Commercial services exports, which have driven export growth for more than a decade, grew by 36 percent in 2006, while merchandise exports are growing at a 21 percent annual rate. India's entrepreneurs – among them Tata Consulting Services, Tata Motors, Tata Steel, Infosys, Biocon (a pharmaceutical company), and ICICI Bank – are adopting global strategies. India's global presence will remain smaller than China's, reflecting its smaller capital stock, but India's entrepreneurs will inject more creativity abroad and productivity at home.

India's other big policy challenge is to restore fiscal balance to government accounts. State governments may provide the answer, as illustrated by an example from Orissa, next door to West Bengal in the northeast and one of India's poorest states. In the 1990s, the state government ran a deficit equal to 6 percent of its total state product and poverty was rife, particularly among its large tribal population. Since 2000, the deficit has been turned into a surplus, and poverty reduction has been faster in rural than in urban areas and faster than the national average. Strong political leadership and changes in institutions both played a role. Political leaders built public support for fiscal reforms; corruption was reduced and investments made in physical infrastructure.[18]

One would like to think that India will free financial institutions from the requirement to invest in government bonds. But the immediate official reaction to the 2008 global financial crisis was to increase deficit spending and to delay reforms scheduled for 2009 that would have reduced government ownership of banks and allowed more foreign participation. The financing requirements of the huge planned spending on infrastructure, however, could be the catalyst for bond financing and more FDI, since they emphasize public-private partnerships, which require such instruments.

Indian governments are involved in the economy through both ownership and intervention. Half of the public sector enterprises owned by the central government are in heavy manufacturing, including steel, cement, chemicals, and capital goods; in the 2005/06 fiscal year, they accounted for 85 percent of the assets of all Indian public sector enterprises and more than 11 percent of India's GDP (by comparison, China's industrial state-owned enterprises contributed 15 percent of GDP in 2005).[19] In 1992, the central government embarked on a 'disinvestment' program that privatized some of the more successful enterprises but made little more progress. By fiscal year 2005/06, when the program was abandoned, only 12.5 percent of the value of government assets had been sold.[20]

Outside the IT services sector, the many government interventions from the mid-1960s to the early 1980s left a thick overburden of restrictions that still hobble private enterprise, segment the economy, and prevent efficient use of resources. Bankruptcy laws exist, but the judicial process is protracted, and efforts to streamline it fall short of delivering the speed and flexibility of Chapter 11 procedures in the United States. The World Bank ranks India at 140 out of 178 countries in its 2009 report on the ease with which businesses can be closed. Urban land restrictions add to the difficulty of freeing up the resources of failing businesses. These restrictions were intended to prevent land from concentrating in a few hands; instead, bankrupt firms cling to their businesses rather than move on because it is so difficult to realize the value of their land, which is often their most valuable asset.[21]

What are the prospects that these obstacles to growth will be removed? Governments have deregulated telecommunications, are upgrading the transportation infrastructure, and have reduced the administrative burden in the special economic zones, while private sector innovations are diffusing IT capabilities into the domestic economy. Important obstacles remain, though, and are on the wish list for action now that the Congress Party–led coalition has been given a strong mandate to govern.

As this manuscript went to press, however, there were signs that the government might waste its mandate by continuing to subsidize the poor, rather than opening doors for them. The debt waiver for farmers and the National Rural Employment Guarantee Scheme were popular in the election campaign and, as noted earlier, Mrs. Sonia Gandhi has been outspoken in her support for continued government ownership of the financial institutions. But these are short-term fixes and the products of bad institutions and bad policies. The recent election afforded India an opportunity to adapt them further to encourage growth; with good institutions, the country could reach a 10 percent growth trajectory over the coming decade. That would require Indian governments to reduce deficits and redirect savings toward productivity-enhancing investments in electricity, transportation, and rural infrastructure. The long-delayed liberalization of the financial sector should also be on the agenda, as should labor market and education reforms, to release the full potential of the labor force. Further improvement in the quality of basic education and an overhaul of the rigid structures in higher education would have long-term payoffs in higher productivity and be politically popular. Liberalizing restrictive labor and land laws would be more controversial, and would require boldness – or stealth – but it would also have dramatic long-term payoffs by creating labor-intensive manufacturing and services that open avenues for workers to leave agriculture and could herald a new dawn for Second India.

This is the agenda on which India's leaders should be evaluated in the coming months and years. It is likely, however, that continued incrementalism will triumph over bold change and that the Indian economy will grow, as in the recent past, despite bad institutions. But it will not be at the hoped-for 10 percent rate; neither will it generate the numbers of good jobs India needs.

What China and India Could Do Together

China and India have a shared history, now largely forgotten, of exchange and mutual learning that came to an end when Turkic and Afghan invaders arrived from the northwest around a thousand years ago. In the twentieth century, the two countries have been deeply mistrustful of each other and the bitter border war in 1962 still scars Indians' memories. The bilateral economic relationship warmed after the Cold War ended, when both governments began to see the potential mutual benefits of growing economic interdependence. Rajiv Gandhi visited China in 1988 as uncertainties increased about India's relationship with the Soviet empire. Further visits followed in 1992 and 1993. In 1996 President Jiang Zemin made the first visit by a Chinese head of state to independent India. In 2003 Prime Minister Vajpayee visited Beijing and Premier Wen visited New Delhi. Since then, leaders have engaged in annual meetings.

These warming ties are also efforts to offset mutual suspicions of each other's strategic intents. China resists India's permanent membership in the UN Security Council and in regional forums, such as the East Asia Summit and trans-Pacific and Europe-Asia forums, that might elevate India to peer or rival status in the region.[22] China's nuclear capabilities and its patronage of Pakistan have been a source of major anxiety for India and were the catalyst for the latter's decision to embark on its own costly nuclear weapons program in the 1990s and to seek closer cooperation with Japan and the United States. The United States and China have clashed repeatedly over China's assistance to Pakistan's strategic programs, which some see as the central obstacle to better relations between China and India.[23] China has also sought warmer ties to prevent India's aligning itself too closely with U.S. efforts to contain China, something Indians themselves resist. A free trade proposal by Pakistan's president in late 2008 signaled a potential watershed for the troubled bilateral relationship. But the Mumbai massacre a few days later set off a new round of bilateral tension and recrimination that not only short circuited the initiative but also sharpened the focus on the threat to the entire region from extremist elements within Pakistan. Islamic extremism – in Kashmir, Delhi, Mumbai, and Xinjiang – has affected both governments and has led to modest intelligence sharing.[24]

India's improving economic performance has had a major effect on its elite's aspirations to be global players. It sees itself as an emerging economic power that will become the world's most populous country, a founding member of such global institutions as the United Nations, the WTO, and the IMF, and one of the world's great democracies. China's opposition to the formalization of these aspirations with a permanent seat on the UN Security Council and quiet rivalry between the two countries within Asia will affect the tone of the relationship for many years to come. At the same time, however, their proximity as next door neighbors and their common domestic challenges are driving a new rapprochement, to promote economic exchange and minimize military rivalry.

Within this strategic context, economic cooperation is gaining momentum – a joint working group already oversees the bureaucratic planning and implementation of closer cooperation. India's IT successes have impressed the Chinese, and its growing success in curbing population growth using voluntary family planning has attracted interest. India's increasingly liberal economic policies and liberal politics provide a potential counterexample to China's liberal economic policies and autocratic politics. Other governments expect that China-India relations will be a significant factor in the Asian region and that cooperation and competition, but not confrontation, will characterize the bilateral relationship.[25]

One of the most interesting future economic possibilities is a bilateral free trade agreement – indeed, the two countries have been studying the possibility since 2005. Two-way trade has been growing since then at annual rates of about 46 percent, reaching US$25 billion in 2007 and US$38 billion in 2008. If growth continues at that rate, total trade between the two countries could reach US$200 billion by 2015, roughly the size of China and Japan's total trade in 2005. The problem is that the balance of this trade is strongly in China's favor; in 2007, for example, India imported nearly three times as much from China as it exported.[26]

Economic ties are also deepening through the activities of the two countries' international firms, which are seeking out investment and other opportunities in each country. Indian software companies such as Wipro, TCS, and Infosys are investing in China to serve their global clients there. Others are marketing software solutions to increase the efficiency of Chinese manufacturers and to take advantage of Chinese skills in chip design. Still others are using China as an offshore design center for business in Japan. Indian manufacturers have also invested in China: Bharat Forge's 52 percent investment in auto giant China FAW Group in 2006 was the largest Indian joint venture at the time. Meanwhile, Chinese multinationals such as Huawei Technologies are investing in India. In 2007 India's Reliance Communications outsourced to Huawei the expansion of its huge, next-generation mobile phone network deep into rural India. U.S.-based multinationals such as IBM and GE are also locating business units in both countries, where they are developing the complementary talents of Chinese and Indian workers and knitting them closely together.

Ties of these kinds are part of the context for the study of a possible free trade agreement in goods that Premier Wen Jiabao first suggested in 2005. Progress, however, has been slow. In a 2007 conversation, a captain of Indian industry asserted to me that Indian businesses cannot assess their competitiveness against Chinese counterparts because of the many subsidies the latter receive. The trade imbalance is seen as another reason to proceed with caution. Still, the fast growth of two-way trade despite numerous obstacles on both sides suggests there are large potential gains from removing them. As well, both countries trade less with each other than they do with the rest of the world, which means there is room for two-way trade to grow and for each to exploit its comparative advantage.

In 2005, an official Joint Study Group concluded that a free trade agreement would provide benefits similar to those realized by European nations many years earlier and by the North American Free Trade Agreement.[27] There are, for example, potential gains from growing trade *within* industries that export to the other country – already, the two countries export chemicals and manufactured goods to each other. Bringing down trade barriers would allow enterprises in each industry to specialize in producing those goods in which they are most efficient and to import goods they produce less efficiently. If the two trading partners merely exchanged totally different goods, there would be little case for a free trade agreement. But free trade in Europe and North America demonstrates that major industries, such as autos and steel, become more productive by rationalizing operations to place business segments in locations that offer the greatest production efficiency. Gains from free trade would also be realized through access to each other's large market, enabling producers in both countries to exploit the greater potential for economies of scale. Reducing barriers to direct investment flows would enhance this effect, since industrial restructuring would encourage more investment. Another gain from free trade would come from access to the other market in order to produce for third markets, as Indian software producers are doing by locating in China to serve the Japanese market. The certainty of rules and regulations under a trade agreement would also reduce market risk and encourage enterprises from third countries to locate in the free trade area to serve both markets.

As tariffs and nontariff barriers were removed over time and enterprises were able more easily to access markets in the other country, stiffer competition would induce greater efficiency and new opportunities for specialization, particularly if each country produced different products. India, as the smaller partner, stands to gain more from access to the larger Chinese market if it were willing to cut its higher industrial and agricultural tariffs – just as Canada and Mexico have gained from access to the much-larger U.S. market. Additionally, to meet competition from Chinese manufacturers, Indian governments finally would have to address restrictive regulations that limit firm size, thus providing a much-needed stimulus to Indian manufacturing and jobs. Free trade proposals make little mention of agriculture, however, since India still protects its millions of small farmers in the belief that they will be uncompetitive against foreign producers. Both the Joint Study Group and Indian economic expert Arvind

Panagariya of Columbia University argue that Indian agriculture, which is protected by tariffs that are higher than in China, should be liberalized in any bilateral free trade agreement. The Indian government sees it differently, however, insisting that any reduction in tariff protection occur only within the broader context of multilateral trade negotiations.[28]

What are the prospects for such a big step toward deeper integration? In light of the shifting patterns of bilateral competition and cooperation, a strong case can be made for trade liberalization as the Indian economy becomes more flexible and open. Both India and China have pursued trade-liberalizing talks with the Association of Southeast Asian Nations (ASEAN), Japan, and South Korea: India is negotiating economic partnerships with South Korea and Japan, while China, South Korea, and Japan are discussing a three-way free trade agreement. Some trade-liberalizing agreements are already in place: China's are with other Asian countries, while India's are with both Asian and non-Asian countries, such as Chile. Most of these agreements, however, are riddled with exceptions, and discriminate against third (usually smaller) countries. This is particularly true of the South Asian Free Trade Agreement, in which India and its partners have insisted on hundreds of exceptions.

Looking to the future, this flawed record suggests an opportunity. A comprehensive free trade agreement between China and India – one that has a robust period in which to phase in the reduction of barriers and few sectoral exceptions – would set an important example that an Asian free trade agreement can have economic, not just foreign policy, benefits. Reducing the list of exceptions likely would require a concerted effort that could last until 2015 to develop the necessary confidence and political support in India. A decade-long phase-in period would also be required to allow import-competing industries to adjust.

A full-fledged China-India free trade agreement is possible by 2030. The strategic potential of such an agreement would reach far beyond its obvious bilateral benefits if it allowed other countries in the neighborhood to join. This would solve a conundrum that faces the Asian region.

Asia at a Crossroads

Asians are 'thinking Asian.' For the first time in modern history, they are thinking about the region rather than about their immediate neighbors or foreign powers. In contrast to Europe, where countries have common histories, values, and political systems, Asia has been three subregions separated by diverse cultures and economies and politics. As well, although Germany and France resolved their historical animosity after World War II, mistrust and competition between Japan and China lingers on. As a result, there is little support in Asia for pulling together into a United States of Asia and speaking with a single voice. Even so, a regional framework is in the making. The oldest institution in the region is ASEAN, founded in 1967, which has allowed new powers to emerge peacefully, avoiding a balkanized southeast Asia.[29] Also, since the end of World War II, the U.S.-Japan alliance has provided a double peace guarantee to China and Japan and a security umbrella under which countries in the region have been free to focus primarily on their own economic development. Market-driven trade and investment ties within the region also have proliferated, tying their economies ever-closer together.

U.S. interest in the region is motivated primarily by geopolitical concerns. The U.S. government reacted strongly in the 1990s to former Malaysian prime minister Mahathir's East Asian Economic Caucus initiative as one that would draw a line down the center of the Pacific to create an inward-looking Asian bloc. For a time, the United States threw its weight behind the Asia Pacific Economic Cooperation (APEC) forum, which included countries bordering the Pacific in North and South America as well as Asia. Since 2001, however, the United States has been distracted, first by the Middle East and terrorism and more recently by the financial crisis.

Asians nevertheless have pushed ahead with their own regional institutions for security, trade, and finance to manage the region's growing economic dynamism and to fill perceived gaps in global institutions. Neither the WTO nor the IMF is perceived to serve their interests as well as it once did – rightly or wrongly, they regard the IMF as having failed them in the 1997–98 Asian financial crisis. Yet, Asians recognize they have been major beneficiaries of open markets and trade liberalization in the postwar period, and the difficulties of the current round of multilateral trade negotiations and the increasing reliance of other countries on preferential trade agreements have encouraged them to pursue similar avenues.

Prominent Asians see their region as at a crossroads. Already, it contains the world's two largest populations, living side by side, and twenty years from now, three of the world's four largest economies will be located there. By 2020, China will be producing 44 percent of Asia's economic output, while India and Japan will account for 17 percent and 15 percent, respectively.[30] Together, the economies of the three will be 20 percent larger than that of the United States. As China and India emerge as economic powerhouses, they will compete with Japan and each other for influence and leadership in the region – unless a serious commitment to community building creates common goals and channels for closer cooperation.[31] Evolving regional institutions have ASEAN at the core and other countries joining extensions that depend on the purposes of the group. This 'ASEAN-plus' architecture expanded after the Asian financial crisis of the late 1990s, when the heads of the ASEAN economies plus those of Japan, China, and South Korea formed 'ASEAN + 3' to draw lessons and prevent such a calamity from happening again. Since then, ASEAN + 3 has taken both finance and trade initiatives, most of which are bilateral.[32] Later, to counter China's influence, Japan pushed the East Asia Summit – which organizers see as the kernel of a future east Asian community – to expand to include Australia, New Zealand, and India. As a latecomer, however, India does not fit easily into the prevailing 'east' Asian institutional model, although it is a member of the Asian Regional (security) Forum, where it also helps to counterbalance China. Each of these groups is better known in Asia by the acronyms that appear in Figure 5.

Financial cooperation within the region deepened after the financial crisis of the late 1990s when it became evident that, as long as the region lacked modern capital market institutions such as bond markets, much of its substantial savings were interme-

Figure 5: Asia's Regional and Trans-Pacific Institutions

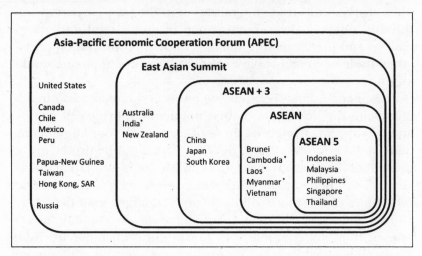

*India has applied to join APEC. Cambodia, Laos, and Myanmar are not members.

diated in international financial centers such as New York and London. In response, in 2000 finance ministers and central bank governors from ASEAN + 3 set up the so-called Chiang Mai Initiative to provide an emergency financing facility for its members. An Asian Bond Market Initiative followed in 2003, assisted by an Asian Bond Fund that pooled foreign-exchange reserves from member central banks to invest in bonds issued by members in their own currencies. The Chiang Mai Initiative started as a series of bilateral currency swap agreements among members' central banks; by 2009, those currency swaps totaled US$120 billion. The long term plan is to pool these arrangements into a common fund run by members, which will have voting power according to their weight in the fund (China, Japan, and South Korea are the largest contributors). Since their own funds are on the line, members will engage in regular surveillance of each other's economic performance and policies.[33]

Trading arrangements have also proliferated within the region. By December 2007, governments (and ASEAN) had initiated 134 such arrangements, with China, India, South Korea, and Singapore heading the list with the most initiatives.[34] These trade agreements, however, are riddled with exceptions and inconsistent rules of origin (which specify the amount of value added in a duty-free product that must originate within the trading partners), raising questions about whether governments' intentions are to pursue foreign policy objectives, rather than economic liberalization, and about the net benefits to businesses – which wonder why they do not simply pay the tariff and avoid the transactions costs of documenting the origins of a product's components. Efforts to develop a road map for a pan-Asian free trade agreement have been ongoing since the late 1990s. One route is negotiations among the ASEAN + 3 countries; another is a series of ASEAN + 1 negotiations (with China, Japan, and South Korea), which could be rationalized into a single agreement; yet another approach could build on a China-India free trade agreement. Regardless of the strategy, however, progress has been slow because of rivalries, historical mistrust, and unwillingness to rationalize key industries such as autos.

Asia's variable geometry nonetheless serves a distinct purpose in the region: by providing channels for cooperation among ad hoc groups with common interests, it aids trust building and cooperation. Regional initiatives in trade and finance are building blocks, but construction can move ahead only at the speed of the slowest member. Leadership is modest and so are results. Where Europe has created a common house in which members have pooled their sovereignty, Asian rivalries and sovereignty concerns constrain them to living in separate but increasingly connected rooms. Variable geometry has its limits, however, for the simple reason that there is no acknowledged leader – no accepted champion to provide focus and set priorities. As a result, Asian governments have had to be content with incremental change. For some time, ASEAN has been regarded as the core, particularly by China, which assumes that any initiative it might take would be regarded as highly suspect by the smaller countries. Cooperative regional institutions serve China's objective of developing closer friendly relationships in the neighborhood and its desire to counterbalance U.S. influence, but others must provide the impetus. Good relationships with its neighbors also allow China to concentrate on its many distractions at home. Indeed, when government representatives talk about China's 'peaceful development,' they are at pains to elaborate that this means 'Three Nos:' no expansion, no hegemony, and no alliances. The message is clear but has an implicit subtext: if China gets its domestic development right, its influence will expand automatically along with its growing economic and political clout.

With some notable exceptions, such as anti-Japanese demonstrations in 2005 and strident rhetoric and actions around Tibet, China's nationalist sentiments and territorial claims have been replaced with friendly, even magnanimous, gestures. During the financial volatility of the 1997–98 crisis, China earned much goodwill in the region by choosing not to devalue its exchange rate, as its smaller neighbors were doing in order to enhance their competitiveness. Cooperative networks also help to address the ambivalence many feel about China, which is summed up by observations by Asian neighbors, some of whom say, 'Don't call China a threat,' while others admonish, 'Don't forget, China is a threat.'

What can be achieved within these constraints? Increasingly, members of these networks and outsiders alike are looking for evidence of tangible cooperation to prevent negative spillovers from the giants to their neighbors, to improve economic performance, head off future crises, and manage them when they occur. ASEAN + 3 is beginning to gain traction, with regular economic reviews and policy dialogues, but the structure lacks such institutional support as a permanent secretariat. The emergency financing available under the Chiang Mai Initiative was not drawn on during the 2008–09 crisis in part because most economies unilaterally took actions to self-insure against financial crises by running current account surpluses and managing their exchange rates to build foreign-exchange reserves.[35] At the end of 2008, the combined reserves of China, Japan, Singapore, India, and Hong Kong totaled almost US$4 trillion, which is far in excess of what most countries try to set aside to cover shortfalls between what they earn from their exports and what they need to pay for their imports.[36]

In this context, the 2008–09 crisis was a needed catalyst. The precipitous drop in export demand prompted east Asian countries to reduce future risks by stepping up their efforts to create regional financial markets and shifting away from exporting outside the region toward meeting demand within the region. But there was little talk about allowing the market to determine exchange rates or about reducing self-insurance. Instead, they looked to exploit the vast potential demand in China and India, arguing that more of the region's savings should be intermediated within the region and that intraregional production networks could be integrated better by investing in infrastructure to speed up shipments, promoting trade in green technologies, and relying more on trade in services.

At the same time, the inclusion of Australia, China, India, Indonesia, Japan, and South Korea in the G20 has created new possibilities. One is that the G20 displaces governments' interest in regional institutions. Another is that, by elevating the status of these economies to that of global players, the G20 encourages them to lead in the region. Much will depend on how China behaves. Its preference is to provide leadership without appearing to do so, given its neighbors' fears that it will become the regional hegemon, and to pursue its global interests in international forums such as the G20. But its behavior in regional institutions continues to reflect parochial concerns about India's membership and its mistrust of Japan. For their part, China's large and democratic neighbors exert peer pressure to align its values with theirs by promoting greater pluralism, transparency, the rule of law, and respect for human rights.

Regional leadership is further complicated by a preference on the part of many countries for greater participation by the United States. Although it is a member of APEC, the United States is absent from the ASEAN-plus institutions and was not invited to join the East Asian Summit. Moreover, US administrations have chosen not to sign the Treaty of Amity and Cooperation – a pledge to refrain from interference in each other's internal affairs – which is ASEAN's cornerstone and a condition of membership in the ASEAN-plus architecture, although the Obama administration has indicated its willingness to come aboard. U.S. engagement on trade would be particularly welcome as the regions' economies look for ways to rationalize proliferating subregional free trade agreements. For its part, the United States is looking for ways to promote comprehensive trans-Pacific trade despite domestic protectionist sentiment in Congress, and in 2008 committed to join the Trans-Pacific Strategic Economic Partnership Agreement, a comprehensive trade agreement among New Zealand, Chile, Brunei, and Singapore that is designed to let other countries join.[37]

The G20, New Players, and the Global Economic Architecture

The G20 has opened a new channel for both regional and global cooperation and might serve as a catalyst for leadership and strategic discussions within the region. This catalytic role is still playing out – there was no coordinated response to the global crisis in 2008–09 beyond public commitments to refrain from protectionism. China, India, and Japan each introduced substantial stimulus packages, with no discernible attempt to coordinate them. The G20 is a convenient and timely bandwagon, but it is still led by the Americans and Europeans.

Yet one must acknowledge that recent G20 leaders' summits have given equal voice to the leaders of the world's systemically significant economies.[38] Like other global organizations – particularly the WTO, the World Bank, and the IMF – the G20 is based on universal principles that promote openness and growth. They include transparency and nondiscrimination on which the WTO is based, as well as monetary cooperation, exchange-rate stability, and exchange-rate flexibility, which are the IMF's contribution. Asians accept these principles, but, with the exception of the Japanese and Indians, argue that these institutions were created without their input and now lack legitimacy because the institutions' governing structures fail to reflect Asia's growing economic importance. Thus, the G20 is a timely innovation because of the growing list of collective issues that require strategic direction and international cooperation to address.

The reality, however, is less straightforward. What will the new players do with their increased voice and clout? The principles on which Asia's regional institutions are based are carefully aligned with global principles, in part reflecting the dependence of Asian countries on an open world economy. What about China and India? Do they wish to use the institutions to serve their own objectives, or to second-guess the established powers, or do they have global views and value to add? Each has a different world view. That of the Chinese is currently expressed as 'peaceful development,' which implicitly assumes it eventually will reassert its historical preeminence and become a counterbalance to the United States. As a Chinese academic expressed in an interview in Beijing in 2005, 'Think of the world order as dragons in the sky. When there is only one dragon, it becomes arrogant and lazy. Two or three dragons are better because they counterbalance each other.' India's world view is more influenced by its regional hegemony in south Asia, where it sees itself as a pole of influence in a polycentric world. But its recent acceptance as a nuclear power by the United States has raised elite ambitions to assume Great Power status.

Will the two new dragons put forward alternative objectives that will increase the effectiveness of the global system and its governing institutions? So far they are working within the existing system. China carved out a high public profile around the April 2009 leaders' summit through its contributions to financing facilities and central bank publications on its perspectives and proposals. These may have played well to nationalist audiences at home, demonstrating China's return to the global stage, but the substance was less than met the eye. Neither China's nor India's leader played much of a role in the actual talks, but each advanced an interest in reforming the IMF to reflect their growing economic clout.[39]

Political scientist John Ikenberry makes a strong case that, although China has very different political and domestic institutions from those of the western democracies and India, the international system can accommodate it. True, the system was constructed by western governments, but in a way that welcomes newcomers. It works through cooperation and shared authority, and it is open to any country willing to observe its dense networks of rules and institutions. The system does not rely on any one country for leadership, but allows leadership to shift without bringing about its own demise.[40]

Both China and India have benefited from this rules-based international system – the WTO and IMF have served them well. Each has gained enormously from open markets, and it is in their long-term interests to maintain that openness and manage the vulnerabilities that go with it. India was a charter member of the General Agreement on Tariffs and Trade, the WTO's predecessor. China became a member in 2001 after fifteen years of arduous negotiations that played a major role in encouraging it to undertake domestic reforms – 'to join the WTO we must make these changes'; its economy is now the most open of any emerging market. The World Bank has been a valuable advisor to both countries on development and, in turn, they are now becoming donors to and investors in very poor countries in Africa and central Asia, sometimes in concert with the World Bank. Individuals from the two countries are also beginning to make their presence felt in international organizations: in 2001, an Indian was the founding director of the IMF's Independent Evaluation Office; in 2008, a Chinese became the World Bank's chief economist.

But the global trading system is under stress. Since late 2008, seventeen of the G20 have taken protectionist actions.[41] The Chinese and Indian governments are skeptical of the priority the United States has accorded labor and environmental issues. India was opposed even to starting the Doha Round of multilateral trade negotiations, and China stayed on the sidelines because of the many unilateral changes it made during the process of joining the WTO. Along with the United States and the European Union, however, China and India share responsibility for the collapse of the Doha Round in July 2008 for their unwillingness to compromise on agriculture and other issues. Global negotiations now languish; if they continue to do so, interest in a regional free trade area will grow among various groups of Asian countries. A pan-Asian free trade area would provoke fear that the world was dividing into competing trade blocs, but it could also be the catalyst for an initiative to rationalize all large regional trade agreements so that they accord with global rules.[42] China and India should expect to be thrust into leadership roles as architects of this new system, and much will depend on their reaction.

The international financial system is also under stress. The IMF as its centerpiece has declined in influence since the 1997–98 financial crisis, when Asians concluded that it had treated them differently than others and was too much under the influence of the U.S. and European governments. When the crisis broke, the G20 initially was the preferred forum for crisis management. In 2009, however, G20 leaders brought the IMF back to center stage, trebling its resources to US$750 billion using channels that included loans of US$100 billion each from Japan and the European Union and US$40 billion from China. Even so, the IMF's resources pale in comparison with the US$2 trillion managed by sovereign wealth funds in 2006 or the US$5 trillion in foreign-exchange reserves the world's central banks had in hand in 2007.[43]

Perhaps the most significant outcome of the 2008 and 2009 G20 meetings was the centrality of Chinese-U.S. cooperation in maintaining an open world economy during the recovery from the financial collapse. China presented a series of high-profile suggestions and initiatives that demonstrated its willingness to assume some global responsibility. It expanded bilateral currency swap arrangements with central banks beyond the members of the Chiang Mai Initiative and contributed to trade finance initiatives by the World Bank and regional development banks.

China also proposed a Big Idea. Zhou Xiaochuan, governor of the People's Bank of China, proposed that a new reserve currency replace the U.S. dollar, which Chinese leaders had worried publicly would soon depreciate, undercutting the value of their large holdings of U.S. government bonds. Governor Zhou suggested stepping up the role of the Special Drawing Right (SDR), a currency unit used by the International Monetary Fund that is denominated in the currencies of its major members. The idea was given added weight by the G20, which agreed to expand the use of the SDR by issuing US$250 billion to expand the IMF's resources. The proposed SDR-denominated fund could allow China to diversify its reserve assets of U.S. dollars by exchanging them for SDRs. U.S. economist Fred Bergsten points out that the SDR would be liquid, pay market rates of return, and allow for diversification into the other currencies in which it is denominated. This kind of diversification would head off volatility in the underlying currencies that would occur if it were done through currency markets.[44]

The creditor-debtor relationship between China and the United States has locked the two in an unintended and unwanted interdependence: China needs a safe investment for its foreign-exchange reserves, while the United States needs to borrow abroad to finance its current account deficit. This relationship was mutually convenient while trade was booming and both economies were growing. But the ready availability of foreign funds also fueled U.S. liquidity, which was one of the causes of the U.S. financial crisis. In future, both the willingness of the United States and China to cooperate and their disagreements will have global repercussions. One interest they have in common is to find ways to manage and eventually to unwind the bilateral imbalance, although they may disagree on how to go about it. The Obama administration recognizes, as Secretary of State Clinton made clear during her visit to Beijing in January 2009, that U.S. savings will not suffice to finance Washington's fiscal stimulus plans and the deficits that stretch to the horizon. The Chinese are in the same boat: they cannot reverse their U.S. dollar investments without endangering their value; they can only diversify their investments and reduce the future use of the dollar in their transactions. The SDR proposal serves a common interest because it provides China with a method of diversifying its investments while maintaining their value and it helps the United States to avoid a dollar crisis that any large market-based transactions by the Chinese would bring about.

The SDR proposal also raises the question of the future of the yuan. Just as political scientists predict a new world order, so financial market participants predict the yuan will become a world currency. Both predictions might prove correct, but are unlikely to come to pass in the next decade. For the latter to occur, China's leaders would have to free up both the exchange rate and the capital account. Freeing up the exchange rate would free up monetary policy conduct, allow interest rates to be determined by the market, and raise the artificially low cost of capital. Greater market discipline would pressure China's banks to modernize their ability to evaluate and manage risk – which has not been a priority of theirs while their profits are assured by income from riskless spreads. China has taken steps, however, to increase the crossborder use of the yuan in trade invoicing within southeast Asia, mainly through transactions in Hong Kong and contiguous regions.[45] In the longer term, it would be necessary for market participants to want to diversify out of the U.S. dollar, yet the evidence in the current crisis is the opposite: U.S. dollar assets are considered the world's safe haven, backed by the country's hard and soft power. Even the euro has not yet come close in usage.

One development that could accelerate China's exchange-rate and capital account liberalization would be serious inflation in the United States. An exchange rate determined by market forces would eliminate the need to build foreign-exchange reserves and the value of the dollar would plunge. Inflation is possible if the U.S. Federal Reserve continues to print large quantities of dollars to provide liquidity during the financial crisis and fails to withdraw liquidity quickly enough as the economy recovers. High U.S. inflation would damage the value of reserve assets denominated in U.S. dollars; it would also greatly damage the dollar's status as a global currency and accelerate the use of the yuan.

The responses of the two countries to such a scenario are fraught with peril. In getting into separate boats again, uncoordinated disembarkation would cause problems for both. China could allow the yuan to appreciate in value to slow the accumulation of reserves, but a stronger yuan would make Chinese exporters less competitive when they have already laid off millions of workers. In the United States, a stronger yuan would cause interest rates to rise, threatening the U.S. recovery. If Americans saved more and paid for their stimulus package, rather than borrowing, U.S. taxpayers would face higher taxes and spending cuts. Either way, both countries are in for changes, which the Chinese prefer would be gradual and controlled. The most likely way out would be for U.S. consumers to save more and spend less, causing China's exports to decline and reducing the number of dollars to be recycled. This assumes that China would accept the loss of exports and refrain from subsidies or measures to manage the exchange rate to make its exports artificially competitive. Rather, China would have to offset its export dependence by stimulating domestic demand – an inherent element of its rebalancing strategy. As the Chinese spent more at home, they would have less to lend to the United States. This eventually will happen anyway, but it will take time to rebalance China's pattern of growth, raise consumer incomes, and restore citizens' faith in publicly provided social services sufficient to increase consumption. In the meantime, China will stabilize the U.S. recovery by continuing to buy U.S. government bonds as long as it remained confident about the value of the dollar. Americans should expect to continue to hear from its largest creditor about this concern.

China and the United States have other areas of common interest. One is the environment. China faces rising international pressure to commit to global targets for pollution and emissions reductions. China is the world's largest emitter in absolute terms, although the United States will continue to be the largest emitter per capita even in 2030. As the world's two largest energy consumers and emitters of greenhouse gases, China and the United States have strong common interests in stepping up cooperative R&D efforts on conservation and emissions reduction.[46] Domestic pressure to clean up the air and water is pushing the Chinese government toward participating in the new global environmental architecture, and officials have signaled China's willingness to make commitments if the United States does. A Chinese academic put it this way in 2008: 'If the United States makes commitments on climate change, we will meet them, but less than half way.' In preparations for the UN conference on climate change to be held in Copenhagen in December 2009, Chinese delegates were willing only to commit to what is best for China's development rather than to any global reduction targets. As an aside, India's emissions are expected to increase fourfold by 2030, but its government has similarly resisted any target for emissions reduction, arguing that it must give greater weight to continued economic development.[47] In 2008, however, Prime Minister Manmohan Singh pledged that India's per capita CO_2 emissions would not exceed those of developed countries. Thus, both China and India in their own way are providing implicit incentives to developed countries to set the example for them to follow.

The U.S.-China relationship will also have its tensions, the most likely to be protectionism by a Democrat-controlled U.S. Congress if unemployment remains high over the next few years. U.S. protectionism would cause slower growth in Asia and augment the argument of those who call for more nationalist policies in the large economies and more inward-looking regionalism in Asia. China's exchange-rate policy also will continue to be a focus of the U.S. Congress, and the bilateral relationship would come under strain if China were to use labor-intensive manufactured exports to head off political instability as its unemployment rises. Although geopolitical analysis is beyond the scope of this book, tension could also be exacerbated by U.S. foreign policy that placed more emphasis on military power and moved to contain or otherwise challenge China's rising military expenditures.[48]

The longer-term economic issue is the popular perception in the United States that the net costs of globalization to U.S. workers are rising. This is not just a China-related issue but a question of whether the United States will continue to lead the open global trading system. Foreign competition and free trade are widely blamed in populist rhetoric for the electorate's deeply held anxiety about economic change. But charges that unfair competition, free trade, and cheap labor are taking Americans' jobs are based on faulty assumptions, not facts. While unemployment skyrocketed in the recession, most of the turmoil in U.S. labor markets is the result of technological change and the normal workings of market forces. Most important, the debate ignores the flaws in the United States' own incentives and institutions. Workers' concerns are about the burdens of economic change on individuals; providing universal access to health care and making pensions portable would help to reduce these concerns among workers and vitiate fears about globalization.

The United States, China, and India in 2030:
First among Equals

The conduct of the U.S.-China relationship is central to the global recovery and to long-term economic prospects. Uncertainty will continue about how the United States will pay for its recovery packages and whether China will rebalance its economy. Judging by its behavior to date, China has chosen to play a stabilizing role. Both countries find themselves in the same boat and, barring serious inflation in the United States, are likely to remain there for the next decade.

By 2030, however, the world economy should have been reshaped and the outlines of a new world order have become clear. China has begun to take on global responsibilities. India, not yet a player, is still learning to balance its domestic agenda and regional objectives. There will be tensions: protectionism emanating from the United States, and competition for influence in Asia among the United States, China, Japan, and India. The world of the next two decades will have two remarkable features: first, despite their rivalry, the key Asian players will be committed to globalization and the peaceful development of Asia and to projecting Asia's voice in the rest of the world; second, they will be seeking a common purpose and a shared strategy. Surprisingly, perhaps, the United States will help to set both purpose and strategy as its attention shifts back to Asia's growing geopolitical significance. The U.S. economy will be down but not out. It will be slower growing, as taxpayers foot the bill for rescuing the economy from financial collapse. But the U.S. dollar will still be the reserve currency. The United States will still be the global policeman. The United States will still provide global leadership, albeit in a cooperative manner that treats Asians as equals. It will also be the author of trans-Pacific initiatives, particularly in trade and security, which will counterbalance Chinese ambitions.

China is further along than India in having the economic strength to be another 'dragon in the sky,' and in 2009 raised its global profile astutely. Both countries will grow more rapidly than the United States, but both will be able to sustain growth only if they address their lopsided economies. China's is unbalanced because its monetary and financial system supports high investment at the expense of consumption and the environment. Its dependence on the United States as a place to invest its foreign assets has deepened their interdependence for the foreseeable future. India's economy is lopsided because of its rigid labor market institutions whose impacts are serious but felt entirely in the domestic economy. How each country reconciles industrial growth with these domestic weaknesses will also affect its soft power and international standing. China's economy in 2030 will be larger and richer than India's, but the gap could be narrower than projected if government continues to direct and own much of China's financial system and if India were to have greater-than-expected success in educating, connecting, and financing the integration of Second India into more productive activities.

Progress will be slow and things could go wrong. The Chinese government's commitment to rebuild the social safety net that was dismantled during reform and opening the economy might be sufficient to head off social unrest, but it will take many years to rebuild people's trust in the state sufficiently for them to save less and consume more. Neither is it clear how local officials, used to years of industrial growth projects from which they benefited directly, will respond to new marching orders to step up social services and redistribute incomes. There could be significant social discontent. India's indifference to opening the door to good jobs for Second India will cause similar inertia unless spreading discontent sparks protests and internal disruption – the worst nightmare for both governments. India's political nightmare is twofold: increasing communal violence and Islamic terrorism, and internal fragmentation caused by organized, disaffected, and marginalized groups in more remote areas.

The global financial crisis marks a turning point in reshaping the world economic order. It has accelerated the decline of U.S. economic influence and shocked Asian governments into reducing their export dependence on U.S. consumers and to explore ways to rely more on their own domestic and regional demand. The world order of 2030 likely will be a multi-polar one with no dominant power. The new order will need a common vision and a shared strategy that attracts Asian governments into global institutions. The United States will continue to lead, but it will have to learn to listen and cooperate as an equal, not only with China, its major creditor, but also with India. With the recognition of Asia's new economic powerhouses as equal voices at the G20 leaders' summits, the gravity shift is well under way.

Notes

1: Why Are They Growing So Fast?

1 The projections I use in this book are based on the work of Angus Maddison, *Contours of the World Economy, 1–2030 AD: Essays in Macro-economic History*, (Oxford: Oxford University Press, 2007); and idem, 'Asia in the World Economy 1500–2030 AD,' *Asian-Pacific Economic Literature* 20 (2, 2006): 1–37. Maddison's projections have some unique features: his historical series of population change and growth of gross domestic product for most major countries reach as far back as the beginning of the Common Era, and his statistical series draw on a wide range of authoritative sources that provide one of the few internally consistent measures across countries and over such a long period of time. The Asian Development Bank, using purchasing power parity measures (which eliminate differences in price levels across countries), projects that, by 2020, China and India together will account for 21 percent of world output.

2 Kalpana Kochhar, Utsav Kumar, Raghuram Rajan, Arvind Subramanian, and Ioannis Tokatlidis, 'India's Pattern of Development: What Happened, What Follows?' IMF Working Paper WP 06/22 (Washington, DC: International Monetary Fund, 2006), table 11. The lagging states include Assam, the large states of Bihar, Madhya Pradesh, Uttar Pradesh, and Orissa, and the smaller states of Chhattisgarh and Jarkhand, which were recently carved out of their larger neighbors.

3 India, Planning Commission, *Towards Faster and More Inclusive Growth: An Approach to the 11th Five Year Plan (2007–2012)* (New Delhi: Government of India Planning Commission, 2006), p. 5.

4 Dwight Perkins and Thomas G. Rawski, 'Forecasting China's Economic Growth to 2025,' in *China's Great Economic Transformation*, ed. Loren Brandt and Thomas G. Rawski (Cambridge: Cambridge University Press, 2008).

5 Dominic Wilson and Roopa Purushothaman, 'Dreaming with BRICs: The Path to 2050,' Global Economics Paper 99 (New York: Goldman Sachs, 2003).

6 See, for example, Richard Herd and Sean Dougherty, 'Growth Prospects in China and India Compared,' *European Journal of Comparative Economics* 4 (1, 2007): 65–89; and Barry Bosworth and Susan M. Collins, 'Accounting for Growth: Comparing China and India,' *Journal of Economic Perspectives* 22 (1, 2008): 45–66.

7 Douglass North and R.P. Thomas, *The Rise of the Western World: A New Economic History* (Cambridge: Cambridge University Press, 1973), p. 2.

8 These issues are developed and discussed in Daron Acemoglu, Simon Johnson, and James Robinson, 'Institutions as a Fundamental Cause of Long Run Growth,' in *Handbook of Economic Growth*, ed. Philippe Aghion and Stephen Durlauf (North Holland: Elsevier, 2005); and International Monetary Fund, *World Economic Outlook 2005* (Washington, DC: International Monetary Fund, 2005).

9 See International Monetary Fund, *World Economic Outlook 2005*, pp. 125–50.

10 These surveys of the quality of governance, carried out by Daniel Kaufmann, Aart Kraay, and others, are available at the World Bank's website at: www.worldbank.org.

11 Maddison, *Contours of the World Economy, 1–2030 AD*.

12 Maddison, 'Asia in the World Economy 1500–2030 AD,' p. 29.

13 Quoted in Ann Kent, *Beyond Compliance: China, International Organizations and Global Security* (Stanford, CA: Stanford University Press, 2007), pp. 105–7.

14 This experiment is described by Barry Naughton, *The Chinese Economy* (Cambridge, MA: MIT Press, 2007), pp. 239–40.

15 The timing could not have been better for the diaspora, since labor costs were rising and profitability was falling in both Taiwan and Hong Kong. A fuller account of this approach can be found in Thomas G. Rawski, 'Chinese Industrial Reform: Accomplishments, Prospects, and Implications,' *American Economic Review* 84 (2, 1994): 271–5.

16 Indeed, this saying was first attributed to Premier Zhao Ziyang, who led the reform drive in its early years; see Susan Shirk, *The Political Logic of Economic Reform in China* (Berkeley: University of California Press, 1993), pp. 130–1.

17 Similarly, the incentives to individual agricultural households were also partial and built on ancient incentives to increase agricultural production. The government retained control over agricultural procurement and, therefore, prices for products and fertilizer for many more years. But the basis for markets had been created, and with them the financial and competitive incentives to change.

18 John Fairbanks, *The Great Chinese Revolution: 1800–1995* (New York: Harper and Row, 1986), p. 7.

19 The equity of the Industrial and Commercial Bank of China (ICBC), for example, is distributed among state-owned shares (70.7 percent), domestic entities (5.1 percent), foreign strategic investors (7.2 percent), and public investors (17 percent); see Industrial and Commercial Bank of China, *ICBC Interim Report 2008* (Beijing: ICBC, 21 August 2008), p. 12.

20 Ian Johnson, *Wild Grass: Three Stories of Change in Modern China* (New York: Vintage, 2005); and Chen Guidi and Wu Chuntao, *Will the Boat Sink the Water? The Life of China's Peasants* (New York: Public Affairs, 2006).

21 Yang Binbin et al., 'Why Did So Many Sichuan Schools Collapse?' *Caijing*, June 2008, pp. 14–21.

22 See Tony Saich, 'Negotiating the State: The Development of Social Organizations in China,' *China Quarterly* 161 (March 2000): 124–41.

23 The measures include public housing projects, rural and transportation infrastructure investment, health and education, the environment, and support for the development of high-tech and services industries; see World Bank, 'Quarterly Update, December 2008' (Beijing: World Bank Office, 2008).

24 Sunil Khilnani, *The Idea of India* (New Delhi: Penguin Books, 1997).

25 Francine Frankel, 'Introduction,' in *The India-China Relationship: What the United States Needs to Know*, ed. Francine R. Frankel and Harry Harding (Washington, DC; New York: Woodrow Wilson Center Press and Columbia University Press, 2004).

26 Deepak Lal, *The Hindu Equilibrium*, vol. 1, *Cultural Stability and Economic Stagnation* (Oxford: Clarendon Press, 1988).

27 As Figure 2 shows, India's share of world output increased during this period as China turned inward.

28 James Clad, 'Convergent Chinese and India Perspectives on the Global Order,' in *The India-China Relationship*.

29 The independent country of Bangladesh was created when rising ethnic tension and the violent suppression of East Pakistan by West Pakistan resulted in a war with India in 1971.

30 Ramachandra Guha, *India after Gandhi: The History of the World's Largest Democracy* (Basingstoke; Oxford: Macmillan, 2007).

31 Ibid., p. 771.

32 Arvind Panagariya, *India: The Emerging Giant* (Oxford: Oxford University Press, 2008), p. 8 .

33 For a full account of this interesting case, see ibid., pp. 375–95.

34 Nandan Nilekani, *Imagining India: The Idea of a Renewed Nation* (New Delhi: Penguin, 2008), p. 28.

2: Developing Human Capital

1 This is not his real name; he reveals his remarkable story in a personal interview with the author.
2 This profile is drawn from Jo Johnson, 'Midnight's grandchildren,' *Financial Times,* June 7, 2008.
3 United Nations Development Programme, *Human Development Report 2006* (New York: UNDP, 2006), table 1.
4 Zhang Yongsheng, 'To Achieve the Goals of China's 11th Five-Year Plan through Reforms' (presentation to the Tokyo Club Foundation for Global Studies, 6–7 December 2006). These commitments were reiterated in government work reports to the March 2009 National People's Congress.
5 Naughton, *The Chinese Economy,* p. 196; Naughton also notes that, by 2004, nearly 7 percent of those over age 15 had some college or university education.
6 Loren Brandt, Hsieh Chang-tai, and Zhu Xiaodong, 'Growth and Structural Transformation in China,' in *China's Great Economic Transformation,* ed. Loren Brandt and Thomas G. Rawski (Cambridge: Cambridge University Press, 2008).
7 Ross Garnaut, Song Ligang, Stoyan Teneve, and Yao Yang, *China's Ownership Transformation: Process, Outcomes, and Prospects,* (Washington, DC: International Finance Corporation and the World Bank, 2005).
8 This estimate is based on a detailed statistical study by Judith Banister, 'Manufacturing Employment and Compensation in China' (Washington, DC: Department of Labor, Bureau of Labor Statistics, November 2005); available online at http://www.bls.gov/fls/chinareport.pdf. Banister's estimate reported in Table 2 relies on census data.
9 Naughton, *The Chinese Economy,* p. 191.
10 China's migrant labor policy originated in 1950s' state planning, when movement of rural labor was restricted to prevent food shortages developing in the cities. The policy has been eased since liberalization, but movement of agricultural labor continues to face restrictions except where the state explicitly or implicitly permits it. For example, migrant labor is encouraged in construction, infrastructure, and labor-intensive manufacturing, and is tolerated in labor-intensive services.
11 Naughton, *The Chinese Economy,* p. 190.
12 See, for example, Gillian Wong, 'China's Communist Party approves rural land reform,' Associated Press, 24 October 2008; and 'Land reform in China: Still not to the tiller,' *The Economist,* 23 October 2008.
13 With the global recession that began in 2008, however, China's exporters faced increasing cost pressures at the same time that export demand was

drying up. The way the government responds to the slowdown – whether by protecting manufacturing jobs or by promoting adjustment – will affect China's future growth prospects. As the global recession deepened in early 2009, Chinese officials publicly acknowledged that an estimated twenty million migrant workers had been sent home as low-margin suppliers in global supply chains closed their doors and construction projects were delayed or canceled.

14 Herd and Dougherty, 'Growth Prospects in China and India Compared,' 69–70.

15 Quoted in Johnson, 'Midnight's grandchildren.'

16 India, Planning Commission, *Towards Faster and More Inclusive Growth*, p. 12.

17 Asian Development Bank, *Asian Development Bank Outlook 2007* (Manila: Asian Development Bank, 2007), pp. 177–9.

18 The 'other and residual' category in the Chinese statistics reflects statistical difficulties associated with reporting and categorizing large numbers of workers who changed employment status during the massive restructuring of state-owned enterprises between 1998 and 2004.

19 Panagariya, *India*, p. 288.

20 Nandan Nilekani (*Imagining India*, p. 21) tells the story of how Mrs. Gandhi had to cancel a flight to meet U.S. president Lyndon Johnson because Air India's navigators were striking for higher pay.

21 Timothy Besley and Robin Burgess, 'Can Labor Market Regulation Hinder Economic Performance? Evidence from India,' *Quarterly Journal of Economics* 119 (1, 2004): 124.

22 See Panagariya, *India*, pp. 282–9.

23 World Bank, *India – Inclusive Growth and Service Delivery: Building on India's Success*, Development Policy Review (Washington, DC: World Bank, 2006), p. 123.

24 On an index of infrastructure penetration by state, the leading states scored 3 (out of a possible 4 awarded to New Delhi), while the lagging states scored less than 1; Bihar scored zero. See Kochhar et al., 'India's Pattern of Development,' table 11.

25 Institute of International Finance, 'Special Briefing: India' (Washington, DC: IIF, 2007).

26 World Bank, *India*, p. 141.

27 Labor force participation is determined by the size of the labor force and the entry of people into economic activity, as well as by definitions and measures of employment and unemployment. Unemployment in India is a relatively meaningless term because of the large number of casual workers in both agriculture and the informal nonagricultural sectors.

28 Kirsty McNay, Jeemol Unni, and Robert Cassen, 'Employment,' in *Twenty-*

first Century India: Population, Economy, Human Development, and the Environ-ment, ed. Tim Dyson, Robert Cassen, and Leela Visaria (New Delhi: Oxford India Paperbacks, 2005), p. 170.

29 United Nations Development Programme, *Human Development Report 2006*, table 1. In 2000, nearly 40 percent of Indians over age 15 – more than 250 million people – were illiterate; the comparable number in China was 86 million.

30 For a fuller account, see Johnson, 'Midnight's grandchildren.'

31 See 'How to get 100 million children in India reading in three years,' 1 August 2008; available at website: http://cbpm.blogspot.com/2008/08/how-to-get-100-million-children-in.html.

32 China's state-owned enterprises include huge, capital-intensive conglomerates that often span several industries, foreign-invested or -owned enterprises, and public sector jobs in education and social services. Nonstate enterprises, which include private ones, are subject to labor laws that increasingly are being enforced, but they are free to hire and fire within the confines of the law.

33 Arvinder Singh, 'Labor Mobility in China and India: The Role of Hukou, Caste, and Community," in *China and India: Learning from Each Other – Reforms and Policies for Sustained Growth*, ed. Aziz Jahangir, Steven Dunaway, and Eswar Prasad (Washington, DC: International Monetary Fund, 2005).

34 See Richard N. Cooper, 'How Integrated Are Chinese and Indian Labor into the World Economy?' Working Paper 2008-0017 (Cambridge, MA: Harvard University, Weatherhead Center for International Affairs, February 2006).

35 World Bank, *India*, p. 123.

36 Between 1991 and 2001, overall literacy rates increased by as little as 11 percentage points (to a mere 49 percent) in Bihar and as much as 22 percentage points (to 61 percent) in Rajasthan; see Geeta Ghandi Kingdon et al., 'Education and Literacy,' in *Twenty-first Century India*, p. 133.

37 It is not clear whether the intent of the report's recommendations was to make the unorganized sector more like the organized sector, but by stealth; see India, National Commission for Enterprises in the Unorganised Sector, *Report on Conditions of Work and Promotion of Livelihoods in the Unorganised Sector* (New Delhi: NCEUS, August 2007).

38 Tim Dyson and Pravin Visaria, 'Migration and Urbanization: Retrospect and Prospects,' in *Twenty-first Century India*, p. 123.

39 Ibid.

40 Kochhar et al., 'India's Pattern of Development,' pp. 25–26.

41 The problems with the system's structure are laid out in Panagariya, *India*,

chap. 20. Press reports on the struggle to increase the skills and employability of recent graduates are plentiful; see, for example, Amy Yee, Andrew Hill,
and Paul Betts, 'India struggles to plug gaps in burgeoning IT industry,'
Financial Times, 10 July 2008.

42 For a good analysis, see Panagariya, *India,* pp. 441–54.

43 Ibid., p. 437.

44 Herd and Dougherty, 'Growth Prospects in China and India Compared.'

45 Asian Development Bank, *Asian Development Bank Outlook 2007.*

46 India also faces the risk of growing external competition in labor-intensive
manufacturing where other emerging market economies such as Vietnam
are more agile and their policies more pragmatic than India's.

3: Finance: Sharper Scissors Required

1 This observation is informed by the lessons of the global financial crisis,
which have demonstrated the value of conservatively regulated banks and
equity and bond markets to ensure their soundness to carry out basic and
essential services in the modern economy.

2 McKinsey Global Institute, 'Mapping Global Capital Markets, Fifth Annual
Report' (San Francisco: MGI, October 2008). Part of the growth is attributed to depreciation of the U.S. dollar over that period.

3 McKinsey Global Institute, 'Mapping Global Capital Markets, Fourth Annual
Report' (San Francisco: MGI, January 2008), p. 9.

4 See Rafael LaPorta, Florencio López-de-Silanes, and Andrei Shleifer, 'Government Ownership of Commercial Banks,' *Journal of Finance* 57 (1, 2002):
265–301.

5 See Wendy Dobson and Paul Masson, 'Will the Renminbi Become a World
Currency?' *China Economic Review* 20 (1, 2009): 124–35. The six agencies are
the People's Bank of China, the Ministry of Finance, the State Council, and
separate regulators for securities, banking, and insurance.

6 In the 1960s, Japan's incremental ratio of capital to output was 3.5, while
in China and India the ratio currently averages 5; see McKinsey Global
Institute, 'Putting China's Capital to Work: The Value of Financial System
Reform' (San Francisco: MGI, May 2006), p. 78.

7 From a profile developed by Johnson, 'Midnight's grandchildren.'

8 Interview with the author, Beijing, 2008; Xiaodong is not his real name.

9 The Chinese Securities Regulatory Commission oversees investment banks.
The formation of a single regulator has been under discussion since the
17th People's Congress in October 2007.

10 Trading is subject to restrictions on the size of the foreign investor's equity

stake and its ability to repatriate its investment; in 2007, such investments accounted for 3 percent of China's market capitalization.

11 Oversight is exercised by the central bank, the National Development Reform Commission, the China Securities Regulatory Commission (which also supervises listed company bonds and the issuance of convertible bonds), and the National Association of Financial Market Institutional Investors, a self-regulatory organization of institutional investors.

12 Competitive pressures are growing as city commercial banks are allowed to diversify geographically. Moreover, the rural financial system has been strengthened by carving out a new Postal Savings Bank from the national post office and allowing villages and townships to set up banks following an initial six-province pilot project. A new national joint stock bank was also founded in February 2006 when the Bohai Bank in Tianjin began operations with a new ownership structure that allows nearly equal shares between Tianjin's municipal government's 25 percent stake and Standard Chartered Bank's 20 percent.

13 See Ma Guonan, 'Sharing China's Bank Restructuring Bill,' *China & World Economy* 14 (3, 2006): 19–37.

14 See Jonathan Anderson, *How to Think about China* (Hong Kong: UBS Investment Research, 2008). In the depths of the global financial crisis in 2009 several of these strategic investors either reduced or sold off their stakes in China Construction Bank, Bank of China and ICBC.

15 In September 2007, central bank governor Zhou Xiaochuan outlined the government's supportive policy framework, which includes fostering foreign-exchange market development to assist enterprises to manage interest-rate and exchange-rate risk, reduced controls on foreign-exchange transactions, assistance to qualifying financial enterprises to establish overseas operations, and development of 'regional financial platforms' through cooperation with regional development banks.

16 Both the Industrial and Commercial Bank of China and the China Merchants Bank applied to the U.S. Federal Reserve for banking licenses, but initially were met with caution because of governance issues and a lack of transparency. Subsequently, the China Banking Regulatory Commission indicated it would link its stance toward foreign investors in China's banking system to other governments' willingness to grant banking licenses to Chinese applicants. Eventually, both Chinese institutions received their banking licenses.

17 China Banking Regulatory Commission, 'NPLs of Commercial Banks as of end-2007' (Beijing: CBRC, 2007).

18 Wendy Dobson and Anil Kashyap, 'The Contradictions in China's Gradualist Banking Reforms,' *Brookings Papers on Economic Activity* (2, 2006).

19 Barry Naughton, 'The State Asset Commission: A Powerful New Government Body,' *China Leadership Monitor*, Fall 2003.

20 My interviews with foreign managers installed by strategic investors suggest outsiders are hampered by their exclusion from these parallel political structures. One senior manager recruited from abroad recalled how he arrived at work one day to find most of his employees absent; only then was he informed that they had been assigned to classes at the Party School for the day.

21 These interconnections are traced in detail in Eswar Prasad, 'Is the Chinese Growth Miracle Built to Last?' *China Economic Review* 20 (1, 2009): 103–23.

22 The renminbi (RMB), or 'people's currency' in literal translation, is China's official unit of account (like the pound Sterling in the United Kingdom), while the principal unit of denomination in everyday use is the yuan.

23 For an illustration of the size of the spread and a discussion of its impact on bank business plans, see Dobson and Kashyap, 'The Contradictions in China's Gradualist Banking Reforms.'

24 As the effects of the U.S. recession began to bite in 2008, the central bank reversed course and encouraged new lending; see UBS Investment Research, 'China's Stimulus Package Focuses on Investment and Consumption,' 10 November 2008.

25 In gross terms, consolidated government deficits reached 10 percent of GDP in fiscal year 2000/01, then declined to 6.5 percent in 2007 before rising again during the financial crisis of 2009.

26 Banks must invest at least 25 percent of their deposits in these bonds, while insurers must invest 50 percent, noninsurers 30 percent, and private provident funds 40 percent of their assets.

27 Percy S. Mistry, 'The Mumbai-IFC Report: Of Discourse, Garlands and Brickbats!' 10 June 2007; available at http://ajayshahblog.blogspot.com/2007/04/mumbai-as-international-financial.html. For most of its life, Mistry was the chairman of the committee that issued the report.

28 See Nicholas Lardy, 'State-owned Banks in China,' in *The Future of State-Owned Financial Institutions*, ed. Gerard Caprio (Washington, DC: Brookings Institution, 2004); and Dobson and Kashyap, 'The Contradictions in China's Gradualist Banking Reforms.'

29 McKinsey Global Institute, 'Putting China's Capital to Work.'

30 McKinsey Global Institute, 2006, 'Accelerating India's Growth through Financial System Reform' (San Francisco: MGI, 2006), pp. 82–86.

31 Other reforms have also been suggested, such as creating stronger and more independent bank boards, with private investors (not necessarily foreigners) taking strategic stakes, and allowing bank mergers so that smaller and less efficient banks can be taken over by those with more profitable

business models; see Eswar Prasad and Raghuram G. Rajan, 'Next Generation Financial Reforms for India,' *Finance and Development* 45 (3, 2008):
23–27.

32 Zhou Xiaochuan, 'China's Corporate Bond Market Development: Lessons
Learned,' BIS Papers 26 (Basle: Bank for International Settlements, 2005).

33 India, High Powered Expert Committee on Making Mumbai an Internation-
al Financial Centre, *Report* (New Delhi: Ministry of Finance, 2007); idem,
Committee on Financial Sector Reforms, *A Hundred Small Steps* (New Delhi:
Planning Commission, 2008).

34 Philip R. Lane and Sergio L. Schmukler, 'International Financial Integration of China and India,' in *Dancing with Giants: China, India and the Global
Economy*, ed. L. Alan Winters and Shahid Yusuf (Washington, DC, and Singapore: World Bank and the Institute of Policy Studies, 2007).

35 FDI data are from United Nations Conference on Trade and Development,
*World Investment Report 2008: Transnational Corporations and the Infrastructure
Challenge* (Geneva: UNCTAD, 2008).

36 'Beijing fund chief seeks to calm fears,' *Financial Times*, 16 October 2007.

37 Ma Guonan and Robert N. McCauley, 'Do China's Capital Controls Still
Bind?' in *China, Asia, and the New World Economy*, ed. Barry Eichengreen,
Yung Chul Park, and Charles Wyplosz (Oxford: Oxford University Press,
2008).

38 Interview with the author, July 2008.

39 Dobson and Kashyap, 'The Contradictions in China's Gradualist Banking
Reforms,' 121.

40 These patterns are discussed in Richard Podpiera, 'Progress in China's
Banking Sector Reform: Has Bank Behavior Changed?' Working Paper
WP/06/71 (Washington, DC: International Monetary Fund, 2006); and
Dobson and Kashyap, 'The Contradictions in China's Gradualist Banking
Reforms.'

41 See Franklin Allen, Jun Qian, and Meijun Qian, 'China's Financial System:
Past Present and Future,' in *China's Great Economic Transformation*.

42 Li Hongbin et al. 'Political Connections and Firm Performance: Evidence
from Chinese Private Firms,' Working Paper 2005-E-11-CIG (Hong Kong:
Center for Institutions and Governance, Chinese University of Hong Kong,
2005).

43 See India, National Commission for Enterprises in the Unorganised Sector,
Financing of Enterprises in the Unorganised Sector (New Delhi: NCEUS, 2007).
NGOs and microfinance institutions have organized groups of small savers,
mainly women, to pool their savings and make small loans to their members. Both public sector banks and private banks are also experimenting

with ways to turn microlending into a profitmaking business. These institutions use group guarantees of repayment as collateral and rely on pressure from group members to ensure loan repayment. These efforts are in their early stages, and their sustainability will be tested in the next economic downturn by whether or not their credit quality is maintained.

44 See Franklin Allen et al., 'Financing Firms in India' (paper presented to the 33rd Annual Meeting of the European Finance Association, Zurich, 23–6 August 2006).

45 Ibid.

46 Reported in Organisation for Economic Co-operation and Development, *Economic Survey of India 2007* (Paris: OECD, 2007).

47 Mistry, 'The Mumbai-IFC Report,' p. 6.

4: From Latercomers to Technology Titans?

1 'High-tech hopefuls: A special report on technology in India and China,' *The Economist*, 10 November 2007.

2 It is useful to note, however, that some countries have grown rapidly even though they have lagged in terms of innovation, but that has been due to strong demand for their natural resources.

3 Richard Nelson, *National Innovation Systems: A Comparative Analysis* (Oxford: Oxford University Press, 1993).

4 Organisation for Economic Co-operation and Development, *Science, Technology and Industry Outlook* (Paris: OECD, 2006), p. 22.

5 Measures of spending on R&D are influenced by a number of factors. For example, salary payments may push them up in some countries while lower costs may reduce them in lower-income countries.

6 See Rebecca Catching and Anurag Viswanath, 'Can China and India Move Up the Value Chain?' *Far Eastern Economic Review*, July 2007.

7 Before its split with the Soviet Union in the 1960s, however, China spent as much as 2 percent of its GDP on science and technology; after the split, such spending declined by half; see Naughton, *The Chinese Economy*, p. 355.

8 A similar incident occurred in China in 2007 when a Shanghai university researcher accepted national research funds for semiconductor research that produced a copy of an already-patented chip.

9 See Thomas Hout, 'The Ecology of Innovation,' *China Economic Quarterly* (3rd quarter, 2006): 34–8.

10 Wendy Dobson and A.E. Safarian, 'The Transition from Imitation to Innovation: An Enquiry into China's Evolving Institutions and Firm Capabilities,' *Journal of Asian Economics* 19 (4, 2008): 301–11.

11 Signs are appearing, however, that the playing field for small private firms and large state-owned enterprises is gradually being leveled, as an increasing number of Chinese firms are filing patents they want to defend. Between 2003 and 2008, trademark applications grew by 60 percent, and nearly a million patents have been filed. To deal with the rising volume of disputes, more than fifty courts now deal with intellectual property cases; see '850,000 lawsuits in the making,' *The Economist,* 10 April 2008.

12 Gu Shulin and Bengt-Åke Lundvall, 'China's Innovation System and the Move Toward Harmonious Growth and Endogenous Innovation,' *Innovation: Management, Policy and Practice* 8 (1-2, 2006): 1–26.

13 See Toshiki Kanamori and Zhao Zhijun Zhao, 'Private Sector Development in the People's Republic of China,' ADBI Policy Papers 5 (Tokyo: Asian Development Bank Institute, 2004).

14 See India, Planning Commission, *Towards Faster and More Inclusive Growth.*

15 Between 1998 and 2003, India attracted US$1.3 billion in such investments; see World Bank, *Unleashing India's Innovation: Towards Sustainable and Inclusive Growth* (Washington, DC: World Bank, 2007), p. 52.

16 'High-tech hopefuls,' *The Economist,* p. 20. Since 2005, however, the deregulation of the telecommunications sector has unleashed explosive growth in the number of Indians with access to mobile and fixed-line telephones.

17 See 'A global love affair:.A special report on cars in emerging markets,' *The Economist,* 15 November 2008.

18 Ibid.

19 PricewaterhouseCoopers, 'Gearing Up for a Global Gravity Shift: Growth, Risk and Learning in the Asia Pharmaceutical Market' (London: PricewaterhouseCoopers, 2007).

20 'High-tech hopefuls,' *The Economist,* p. 21.

21 Quoted in World Bank, *Unleashing India's Innovation,* p. 140.

22 Author's interview with China expert Loren Brandt of the University of Toronto, January 2009.

23 Chris Hall, 'When the Dragon Awakes: Internationalisation of SMEs in China and Implications for Europe,' *CESifo Forum* (2, 2007): 29–34.

24 See, for example, Geoff Dyer, 'Unmade in China,' *Financial Times,* 17 December 2008.

25 World Bank, *Unleashing India's Innovation,* pp. 83–5.

26 See George Gilboy, 'The Myth behind China's Miracle,' *Foreign Affairs* 83 (4, 2004): 33–49.

27 This view is advanced by Albert Z. Hu and Gary H. Jefferson, 'Science and Technology in China,' in *China's Great Economic Transformation.*

28 Zhou Yu, 'The Making of an Innovative Region from a Centrally Planned

Economy: Institutional Evolution in Zhongguancun Science Park in Beijing,' *Environment and Planning* 37 (6, 2005): 1128.

29 Sean Dougherty, Richard Herd, and Ping He, 'Has a Private Sector Emerged in China's Industry? Evidence from a Quarter of a Million Chinese Firms,' *China Economic Review* 18 (2007): 309–34.

30 Gary Jefferson, Bai Huamao, Guan Xiaojing, and Yu Xiaoyun, 'R&D Performance in Chinese Industry,' *Economics of Innovation and New Technology* 15 (4-5, 2006): 345–66.

31 Dobson and Safarian, 'The Transition from Imitation to Innovation.'

32 John Sutton, 'The Globalization Process: Auto-Component Supply Chains in China and India,' in *Are We on Track to Achieve the Millennium Development Goals?* ed. François Bourgvignon, Boris Pleskovic, and André Sapir (Washington, DC: World Bank; New York: Oxford University Press, 2005). For a detailed study of how Chinese industries have developed their capabilities, measured by their ability to sell abroad, in a growing array of products and sectors, see Loren Brandt, Hsieh Chiangtai, and Zhu Xiaodong, 'Growth and Structural Transformation in China,' in *China's Great Economic Transformation.*

33 Zhang Haizhou, 'As old industry bites the dust, new sectors begin to bloom,' *China Daily*, 4 November 2008.

34 World Bank, *World Development Indicators* (Washington, DC: World Bank, 2008).

35 See Lee Branstetter and Nicholas R. Lardy, 'China's Embrace of Globalization,' in *China's Great Economic Transformation.*

36 See Robert Feenstra and G.H. Hanson, 'Ownership and Control in Outsourcing to China,' *Quarterly Journal of Economics* 120 (2, 2005): 729–61; and John Whalley and Xin Xian, 'China's FDI and Non-FDI Economies and the Sustainability of Future High Chinese Growth,' NBER Working Paper 12249 (Cambridge, MA: National Bureau of Economic Research, 2006).

37 Gilboy, 'The Myth behind China's Miracle.'

38 Branstetter and Lardy, 'China's Embrace of Globalization,' p. 662.

39 See Liu Xielin, 'China's Development Model: An Alternate Strategy for Technological Catchup,' Working paper (Tokyo: Hitotsubashi University, Institute of Innovation Research, 2005). More recent reports indicate that the number of invention patents began to rise in 2008.

40 'High-tech hopefuls,' *The Economist*, pp. 16–17.

41 World Bank, *Unleashing India's Innovation*, chap. 3.

42 Author's interview with Dr A.L. Rao, Wipro's president-technology and chief operating officer, Bangalore, December 2004.

43 Author's interviews in 2006 and 2007.

44 Ibid.

45 Ashish Arora, V.S. Arunachalam, Jai Asund, and Ronald Fernandes, 'The Indian Software Services Industry,' *Research Policy* 30 (8, 2001): 1267–87.

46 Economist Amar Bhidé of the Columbia Business School similarly argues that one should not overemphasize the role of production in innovation – that consumers, whether individuals or firms, who are prepared to try new goods and services and managers who are able to adapt their organizations to innovations can be significant drivers of innovation. See Amar Bhidé, 'Venturesome Consumption, Innovation and Globalization' (paper prepared for the joint conference of CESifo and the Center on Capitalism and Society, 'Perspectives on the Performance of the Continent's Economies,' Venice, 21–22 July 2006).

47 Author's interviews, Mumbai, 2006 and 2007.

48 These and other innovations are summarized in World Bank, *Unleashing India's Innovation*, pp. 110–11.

49 These innovations are described in 'High-tech hopefuls,' *The Economist*, pp. 15–16.

5: Sprints, Spurts, and Stumbling Blocks

1 United Nations Development Programme, *Human Development Report 2006*, pp. 292–3.

2 UNICEF, *Progress for Children: A World Fit for Children Statistical Review* 6 (New York: UNICEF, December 2007).

3 Economists often measure income inequality using what is known as the Gini coefficient, an estimate of the shares of total income earned by segments of the population, whereby the higher the coefficient, which ranges from 0 to 1, the more unequal the distribution of income. World Bank comparisons of Gini coefficients over time and across countries show that India's rose from 0.315 in 1993–4 to nearly 0.370 in 2004–05, while China's rose from 0.335 in 1990 to nearly 0.470 in 2004. By way of comparison, Brazil's was 0.610 in 1990 but declined by 2004 to 0.570; in other words, income inequality is very high in Brazil but declined somewhat over that period. See World Bank, Commission on Growth and Development, *The Growth Report: Strategies for Sustained Growth and Inclusive Development* (Washington, DC: World Bank, 2008), statistical appendix table 3.2.

4 Dwayne Benjamin, Loren Brandt, John Giles, and Wang Sangui, 'Income Inequality during China's Economic Transition,' in *China's Great Economic Transformation*.

5 Panagariya, *India*, p. 166.

6 Compared with 58 percent in India and 70 percent in the United States; see

'Economics focus: A worker's manifesto for China,' *The Economist*, 13 October 2007.

7 Justin Yifu Lin, 'Rebalancing Equity and Efficiency for Sustained Growth,' in *China's Dilemma: Economic Growth, the Environment, and Climate Change*, ed. Song Ligang and Woo Wing Thye (Washington, DC: Brookings Institution Press, 2008).

8 The decline in household saving is not apparent in the overall savings rate because rising corporate and government saving have more than compensated for it.

9 He Jianwu and Louis Kuijs, 'Rebalancing China's Economy: Modeling a Policy Package,' World Bank China Research Paper 7 (Washington, DC: World Bank, 2007).

10 Benjamin, Brandt, Giles, and Wang, 'Income Inequality during China's Economic Transition,' pp. 730–1.

11 He and Kuijs, 'Rebalancing China's Economy.'

12 See Panagariya, *India*, especially chaps 7 and 8.

13 World Bank, *India – Inclusive Growth and Service Delivery*.

14 India, Prime Minister's Office, 'Prime Minister addresses 40th Indian Labour Conference,' New Delhi, 9 December 2005.

15 See Paul Rogers, 'China and India: Heartlands of Global Protest,' *Open Democracy*, 8 July 2008.

16 The one-child policy has also contributed to the phenomenon of 'missing girls,' with the sex ratio at birth having risen from 108.5 males per female in 1982 to 117 in the 2000 census. The burden of this imbalance is borne mainly by rural males, who are lacking in skills and education. For an analysis of these issues, see Wang Feng and Andrew Mason, 'The Demographic Factor in China's Transition,' in *China's Great Economic Transformation*.

17 See Andrew Taylor, 'Asian economies near "demographic cliff",' *Financial Times*, 13 August 2007.

18 Jonathan Anderson, 'The Aging of China,' UBS *Asian Economic Perspectives*, 21 January 2008.

19 World Bank, 'Quarterly Update, June 2008' (Beijing: World Bank Office, 2008).

20 Anderson estimates that China's potential growth rate could slow by as much as two percentage points for this reason; see 'The Aging of China.'

21 China's consumption of commodities also affects world markets. In 2005, its share of world consumption exceeded the U.S. share in aluminum, copper, lead, zinc, and iron ore, and its steel production exceeded that of the United States nearly fourfold. The same is true for a range of agricultural commodities, such as soybean, soy, and palm oil (India's shares were be-

tween one-seventh and one-tenth of China's). See Shahid Yusuf and L. Alan
Winters, eds., *Dancing with Giants: China, India and the Global Economy* (Washington, DC, and Singapore: World Bank and the Institute of Policy Studies,
2007).

22 'Melting Asia,' *The Economist*, 5 June 2008.

23 A growing literature explores the growing investments of China and, to a
lesser extent, India in Africa and central Asia in the search of dedicated energy supplies and other natural resources, and articles in the popular press
speculate about whether China is becoming a new 'imperialist.' I have chosen not to enter into this debate.

24 See Shalizi Zmarak, 'Energy and Emissions,' in *Dancing with Giants*.

25 Ibid., p. 138.

26 Edward Steinfeld, Richard Lester, and Edward Cunningham, 'Lessons from
Sulfur,' *China Economic Quarterly* (September 2008): 28–32.

27 Andy Rothman, 'Thirsty China,' *Asia Pacific Markets*, Summer 2006.

28 World Bank, *India's Water Economy: Bracing for a Turbulent Future* (Washington, DC: World Bank, 2005).

29 Ibid.

30 Marcos Chamon, Paolo Mauro, and Yohei Okawa, 'Mass Car Ownership in
the Emerging Market Giants,' *Economic Policy* 23 (54, 2008): 243–96.

31 'Don't drink the water and don't breathe the air,' *The Economist*, 26 January
2008; 'A ravenous dragon,' *The Economist*, 15 March 2008.

32 Cited in Rothman, 'Thirsty China,' p. 17.

33 Deborah Seligsohn, 'Doing More than You Think,' *China Economic Quarterly*,
21 September 2008.

34 See 'Don't drink the water and don't breathe the air,' *The Economist*, 26 January 2008.

35 In contrast, nuclear power accounts for 15 percent of total power generation in Canada and 19 percent in the United States, according to the International Atomic Energy Agency.

36 The commission looked at thirteen highly diverse success stories – countries
of varying size, location, and resources – and found that all shared five characteristics: open economies; committed, credible, and capable governments;
resources allocated by market forces; high savings and investment rates; and
macroeconomic stability. See World Bank, Commission on Growth and Development, *The Growth Report*.

37 Beijing would like to consolidate China's 7,000 steel plants and 381 aluminum plants into fewer, but larger, more efficient national champions.

38 Web commentators, trained and financed by Party organizations, monitor
discussions in chat rooms and forums and engage in posting techniques
aimed at influencing public opinion by advocating pro-Party views; see, for

example, David Bandurski, 'China's guerrilla war for the Web,' *Far Eastern Economic Review*, July/August 2008, pp. 41–44.

39 See Rogers, 'China and India.'

40 For an excellent account, see Fred C. Bergsten et al., 'Corruption in China: Crisis or Constant?' in *China's Rise: Challenges and Opportunities* (Washington, DC: Peterson Institute for International Economics and Center for Strategic and International Studies, 2008).

41 See 'Land reform in China: Still not to the tiller,' *The Economist*, 23 October 2008.

42 John L. Thornton, 'Long Time Coming,' *Foreign Affairs* 87 (1, 2008): 2–22. The section that follows incorporates some of Thornton's observations.

43 These questions are examined in Joseph Fewsmith, 'Staying in Power,' in *China's Changing Political Landscape*, ed. Cheng Li (Washington, DC: Brookings Institution Press, 2008); and in Bergsten et al., 'Democracy with Chinese Characteristics? Political Reform and the Future of the Chinese Communist Party,' in *China's Rise*.

44 Kathleen Hartford, 'Dear Mayor,' *China Information* 19 (2, 2005): 217–20.

45 'The people speak and Maglev is put on hold,' *Shanghai Daily*, 28 May 2007. Construction has since restarted but the issue now receives much less attention.

46 Zhan Jiang, 'News Media, Cautious Change,' *Caijing Annual Edition 2008* (Beijing, 2008): 128–9.

47 Author's interview with a senior foreign diplomat with knowledge of the case, Beijing, 2005.

48 Matthew Forney, 'Behind the wheel in China,' *Washington Post*, 21 February 2009.

49 This interpretation relies on a translation of the original by Sophie Liang; and on Richard McGregor, 'Party think tank calls for checks on China's rulers,' *Financial Times*, 20 February 2008.

50 'Smoke clears, doubts linger at CCTV fire,' *Caijing*, 3 March 2009.

51 Despite the ban, the document became widely available on the Internet; see, for example, Perry Link, trans., 'China's Charter 08,' *New York Review of Books*, 15 January 2009.

52 See Fred C. Bergsten et al., *China's Rise*, p. 69.

53 In 2006, after I had delivered a public lecture on China, an older member of the audience recounted his recent visit to his home village, and emphasized the material improvements that had provided more freedom. Over the years, my Chinese students (who average 30 years of age) have been divided on this point; a few who are critical of the Party's insistence on absolute political control have chosen to remain in the West.

54 Surveys of urban attitudes along these lines are cited in Teresa Wright, 'Dis-

incentives for Democratic Change in China,' *Asia Pacific Issues* 82 (February 2007). My own interviews corroborate these findings.

55 'Battling the babu raj,' *The Economist,* 8 March 2008.

56 Jo Johnson, 'Engaging India: Creative destruction,' *Financial Times,* 4 October 2007.

57 Jean Drèze and Christian Oldiges, 'How is NREGA doing?' (PowerPoint presentation, A.N. Sinha Institute of Social Studies, Patna, Bihar, India, 2008); available at website: http://www.ansiss.org/doc/seminar2007July20-22/jean_dreze.doc.

58 Amar Bhidé, 'What Holds Back Bangalore Business?' (New York: Columbia Business School, 2006)', manuscript.

59 Reported in Panagariya, *India.*

60 'Gujarat has shown how to tackle the power problem,' *Times of India,* 3 November 2007.

61 Dividends paid to the government will vary by industry: chemicals, coal, oil, power, telecommunications, and tobacco will pay 10 percent; all others will pay 5 percent. See World Bank, 'Quarterly Update, June 2008.'

62 Robert Feenstra and Hong Chang, 'China's Exports and Employment," NBER Working Paper 13552 (Cambridge, MA: National Bureau of Economic Research, October 2007). The impact of exports on employment should not be overestimated. Analysis of employment growth during the 1997–2002 period shows that, while export growth contributed 2.5 million jobs a year, most of the employment gains came from nontraded goods, such as construction. Between 2000 and 2005, domestic demand contributed three times the employment growth that exports did.

63 For a sober assessment, see 'Melting Asia,' *The Economist,* 5 June 2008.

6: As Gravity Shifts

1 See Anil K. Gupta and Wang Haiyan, *Getting China and India Right: Strategies for Leveraging the World's Fastest Growing Economies for Global Advantage* (New York: Jossey-Bass/Wiley, 2009).

2 Ibid.

3 'A global love affair: A special report on cars in emerging markets,' *The Economist,* 15 November 2008.

4 For a survey of the attitudes of multinational pharmaceutical companies, see PricewaterhouseCoopers, 'Gearing Up for a Global Gravity Shift.'

5 For the case study on which this example is based, see Tarun Khanna, *Billions of Entrepreneurs: How China and India Are Reshaping Their Futures and Yours* (Cambridge, MA: Harvard Business School Press, 2007).

6 Gupta and Wang, *Getting China and India Right.*

7 Daniel Pimlott, 'Bangladesh bank offers loans to US poor,' *Financial Times*, 16 February 2008. As many as 28 million Americans do not have bank accounts and an estimated 45 million have only limited access to financial institutions.

8 Tata, it was later learned, borrowed US$3 billion for the Ford transaction and US$11 billion for the Corus acquisition; see Joe Leahy, 'Family stakes back Indian debt,' *Financial Times*, 20 February 2009.

9 Mary Amiti and Caroline Freund, 'An Anatomy of China's Export Growth' (paper prepared for the Global Implications of China's Trade, Investment and Growth Conference, sponsored by the National Bureau of Economic Research, Washington, DC, 6 April 2007).

10 Li Cui and Syed Murtaza, 'The Shifting Structure of China's Trade and Production,' Working Paper WP/07/214 (Washington, DC: International Monetary Fund, 2007).

11 World Trade Organization, *International Trade Statistics, 2007* (Geneva: WTO, 2007).

12 McKinsey Global Institute, 'The Emerging Global Labor Market' (San Francisco: MGI, 2007). Although the numbers of Chinese and Indians working abroad are difficult to estimate, it is thought that each diaspora is around 20 million people. Students studying abroad tend to pursue postsecondary and graduate education – China is thought to have had about 3.6 percent of its total student population at these levels studying abroad since 2000, a share that is stationary in the face of a doubling of enrollment at these levels. India's share is approximately 1 percent but growing quickly.

13 Winters and Yusuf, *Dancing with Giants*.

14 Rothman, 'Thirsty China.'

15 Daniel Rosen, 'What China Can't Do,' *China Economic Quarterly* (3rd quarter, 2006): 45–51.

16 Alan Blinder, 'Offshoring: The Next Industrial Revolution?' *Foreign Affairs*, March/April 2006, pp. 113–28.

17 J. Bradford Jensen and Lori G. Kletzer, '"Fear" and Offshoring: The Scope and Potential Impact of Imports *and* Exports of Services,' Policy Brief PB08-1 (Washington, DC: Peterson Institute for International Economics, 2008).

18 Amar Bhidé, *The Venturesome Economy: How Innovation Sustains Prosperity in a More Connected World* (Princeton, NJ: Princeton University Press, 2008); he uses total factor productivity as the indicator of catch-up.

19 Suzanne Berger, *How We Compete: What Companies Around the World Are Doing to Make It in Today's Global Economy* (New York: Random House, 2005).

20 McKinsey Global Institute, 'The Emerging Global Labor Market.'

21 Lori G. Kletzer, *Job Loss from Imports: Measuring the Costs* (Washington, DC: Peterson Institute for International Economics, 2001).

7: The New Asian Powerhouses and the World Economy in 2030

1 See Maddison, 'Asia in the World Economy 1500–2030'; Goldman Sachs,
'India's Rising Growth Potential,' Global Economic Paper 152 (New York:
Goldman Sachs, 27 January 2008); and Asian Development Bank, *Emerging
Asian Regionalism* (Manila: Asian Development Bank, 2008). Projections depend, of course, on measures and assumptions about sources of economic
growth. Maddison uses constant 1990 U.S. dollars estimated using purchasing power parity (PPP) weights; the Asian Development Bank also presents
PPP estimates, while Goldman Sachs uses 2003 U.S. dollar measures adjusted for inflation. Most economists agree that the U.S. economy will grow
at a rate of 3 percent or less during this period. In contrast, Goldman Sachs
assumes that India sustains 8 percent and China 10 percent growth, while
Maddison and the Asian Development Bank assume more conservative
growth of around 7 percent for China and 6 percent for India.
2 The January update of global economic prospects for 2009 by the International Monetary Fund predicted a global average of no growth, a 2 percent
contraction in the advanced countries, and growth of as much as 6.7 percent in China and 5.1 percent in India. In absolute terms, however, China's
slowdown from 13 percent growth in 2007 was the world's largest, because
of the drop in exports and a property market correction. India's slowdown
from 9 percent was less pronounced because its economy is less open and
good weather buoyed agriculture, which still accounts for nearly one-fifth of
GDP and provides a livelihood for two-thirds of the population.
3 Wang Tao, 'How Will China Grow? Export Slowdown, Reverse Migration,
and Urbanization,' UBS *Asian Economic Perspectives,* 7 January 2009.
4 These reforms are reported to include the introduction of pension portabil-
ity, basic medical insurance coverage for 90 percent of the population by
2010, the beginnings of a national drug insurance system, a comprehensive
medical services system in rural areas, and a unified resident health record;
see Yu Song and Helen Qiao, 'A preview of the upcoming National People's
Congress meeting: Don't expect too many new policies,' *China Views*, 27
February 2009.
5 Perkins and Rawski, 'Forecasting China's Economic Growth to 2025,' table
20.6.
6 These projections are found in Maddison, 'Asia in the World Economy
1500–2030 AD' (he discusses his assumptions in *Contours of the World
Economy, 1–2030 AD*). They are relatively conservative: that China's growth
will slow because of its aging population and rising wages, and that more
resources will be channeled toward the costly environmental fallout from
its dash for growth and toward more growth and social development in the

rural areas. He predicts India will continue to grow as it abandons its historical emphasis on heavy industry and self sufficiency, drops its controls on the
private sector, and opens the economy.

7 Herd and Dougherty, 'Growth Prospects in China and India Compared.'

8 Perkins and Rawski, 'Forecasting China's Economic Growth to 2025.'

9 See Cheng Li, 'China's Team of Rivals,' *Foreign Policy*, March/April 2009.

10 Pei Minxin, 'How Beijing can boost its human capital,' *Financial Times*, 9
January 2009.

11 Wang Tao and Harrison Hu, 'How Will China Grow? The Re-leveraging of
China,' *Asian Economic Perspectives*, 9 December 2008.

12 In 2009, the State Council encouraged consolidation of the auto and steel
industries in return for government support during the downturn. It intends to create two or three large automotive groups with capacity to produce two million vehicles a year, and four or five smaller groups making one
million vehicles a year. It also proposed to consolidate the steel industry,
allocating nearly half the market to five top producers and closing outdated
production facilities. See Kathrin Hille, 'Beijing drives car and steel mergers
message,' *Financial Times*, 23 March 2009.

13 Cited in Perkins and Rawski, 'Forecasting China's Economic Growth to
2025,' p. 863.

14 Ibid., pp. 863–5.

15 See North and Thomas, *The Rise of the Western World*, pp. 1–8.

16 A point made by Perkins and Rawski, 'Forecasting China's Economic
Growth to 2025.'

17 Keith Bradsher, 'As trade slows China rethinks growth strategy,' *New York
Times*, 31 December 2008.

18 See World Bank, 'Orissa in Transition: From Fiscal Turnaround to Rapid
and Inclusive Growth' (Washington, DC: World Bank, 2008).

19 The Indian statistics are from Panagariya, *India*, p. 299; the Chinese figure is
from Perkins and Rawski, 'Forecasting China's Economic Growth to 2025,'
p. 862.

20 Panagariya, *India*, pp. 300–1.

21 These restrictions are analyzed in ibid., chap 13.

22 See Ashley Tellis, 'China and India in Asia,' in *The India-China Relationship*.

23 Ibid.

24 James Clad makes this point in 'Convergent Chinese and Indian Perspectives on the Global Order.'

25 Harry Harding argues, however, that competition will be the main characteristic; see 'The Evolution of the Strategic Triangle: China, India, and the
United States,' in *The India-China Relationship*, p. 346.

26 Following a bilateral meeting in March 2009, India's commerce secretary

called on China to increase market access for Indian agricultural and pharmaceutical products. He also called for stepped-up bilateral FDI in a number of sectors, including energy, steel, health care, IT, and autos. See India, Department of Commerce, 'Need to Strengthen Trade between India and China: Commerce Secretary' (New Delhi: Department of Commerce, 19 March 2009); available at website: http://www.commerce.gov.in/pressrelease/pressrelease_detail.asp?id=2399.

27 India-China Joint Study Group on Comprehensive Trade and Economic Cooperation, *Report* (New Delhi, 2005).

28 Arvind Panagariya, 'India and China: Past Trade Liberalization and Future Challenges' (paper prepared for a Tokyo Club Foundation for Global Studies conference, Tokyo, 6–7 December 2006, updated 4 February 2007); available at website: http://www.tcf.or.jp/data/2006120607_Arvind_Panagariya.pdf.

29 See Kishore Mahbubani, *The New Asian Hemisphere: The Irresistible Shift of Global Power to the East* (New York: Public Affairs, 2008).

30 The ten-member ASEAN will also be a player, accounting collectively for 14 percent of the regional total. These estimates are based on purchasing power parity measures presented in Asian Development Bank, *Emerging Asian Regionalism*, p. 38.

31 These views are expressed in Jusuf Wanandi and Tadashi Yamamoto, *East Asia at a Crossroads* (Tokyo: Japan Center for International Exchange, 2008).

32 Significantly, the latter three leaders, who have met each other repeatedly on the fringes of other meetings, finally held their own summit in December 2008 in Japan.

33 A joint statement issued at a summit meeting of Japanese, Chinese, and South Korean leaders acknowledged recent increases in the size of bilateral swap arrangements and committed to work with ASEAN members to multilateralize the swaps and strengthen 'monitoring on the regional economy and financial markets'; see Japan-China-Republic of Korea Trilateral Summit, 'Joint Statement on the International Finance and Economy,' Fukuoka, Japan, 13 December 2008; available at website: http://www.mofa.go.jp/region/asia-paci/jck/summit0812/economy.html.

34 Asian Development Bank, *Emerging Asian Regionalism*, table A3.3.

35 Current account surpluses and rising foreign-exchange reserves can be tracked in ibid., pp. 173–5.

36 Wendy Dobson, 'A Window of Opportunity Opens? Asian and US Views of the International Financial Architecture,' *Asian Economic Policy Review* 4 (2, 2009).

37 Australia and Peru have applied to join and Vietnam is showing interest.

38 The twenty economies are Argentina, Australia, Brazil, Canada, China, France, Germany, India, Indonesia, Italy, Japan, Mexico, Russia, Saudi Arabia, South Africa, South Korea, Turkey, the United Kingdom, the United States, and the European Union.

39 Author's interviews with other participants, April 2009. In the preparatory meetings involving officials, the Chinese participants lacked any apparent authority to stray beyond their briefing books, which limited their ability to contribute. India put forward no new ideas.

40 See John Ikenberry, 'The Rise of China and the Future of the West,' *Foreign Affairs* 87 (1, 2008): 23–37.

41 For example, the United States included 'buy America' provisions in its financial stimulus package, and India raised tariffs on certain steel products and restricted imports of Chinese toys. Many governments, including China's, have subsidized the auto industry, and antidumping complaints are on the rise.

42 Such a possibility is explored in Bergsten et al., *China's Rise.*

43 Estimates in Edwin M. Truman, 'Sovereign Wealth Funds: The Need for Greater Transparency and Accountability,' Policy Brief PB07-06 (Washington, DC: Peterson Institute for International Economics, 2007).

44 C. Fred Bergsten, 'We should listen to Beijing's currency idea,' *Financial Times*, 9 April 2009.

45 For an explanation of why, under current policies, the yuan is unlikely to be used more widely outside east Asia, see Dobson and Masson, 'Will the Renminbi Become a World Currency?'

46 See Council on Foreign Relations, *US-China Relations: An Affirmative Agenda, A Responsible Course* (New York: Council on Foreign Relations, 2007).

47 'Melting Asia,' *The Economist*, 5 June 2008.

48 Such analysis can be found in Robert Kagan, *The Return of History and the End of Dreams* (New York: Knopf, 2008).

Bibliography

Acemoglu, Daron, Simon Johnson, and James Robinson. 'Institutions as a Fundamental Cause of Long Run Growth.' In *Handbook of Economic Growth,* ed. Philippe Aghion and Stephen Durlauf. North Holland: Elsevier, 2005.

Allen, Franklin, et al. 'Financing Firms in India.' Paper presented to the 33rd Annual Meeting of the European Finance Association, Zurich, 23–26 August 2006.

Allen, Franklin, Jun Qian, and Meijun Qian. 'China's Financial System: Past Present and Future.' In *China's Great Economic Transformation,* ed. Loren Brandt and Thomas G. Rawski. Cambridge: Cambridge University Press, 2008.

Amiti, Mary, and Caroline Freund. 'An Anatomy of China's Export Growth.' Paper prepared for the Global Implications of China's Trade, Investment and Growth Conference, Washington, DC, 6 April 2007.

Anderson, Jonathan. 'The Aging of China.' UBS *Asian Economic Perspectives,* 21 January 2008.

– *How to Think about China.* Hong Kong: UBS Investment Research, 2008.

Arora, Ashish, V.S. Arunachalam, Jai Asund, and Ronald Fernandes. 'The Indian Software Services Industry.' *Research Policy* 30 (8, 2001): 1267–87.

Asian Development Bank. *Asian Development Bank Outlook 2007.* Manila: Asian Development Bank, 2007.

– *Emerging Asian Regionalism.* Manila: Asian Development Bank, 2008.

Bandurski, David. 'China's guerrilla war for the Web.' *Far Eastern Economic Review,* July/August 2008, pp. 41–44.

Banister, Judith. 'Manufacturing Employment and Compensation in China.' Washington, DC: Department of Labor, Bureau of Labor Statistics, November 2005.

'Battling the babu raj.' *The Economist,* 8 March 2008.

'Beijing fund chief seeks to calm fears.' *Financial Times*, 16 October 2007.

Benjamin, Dwayne, Loren Brandt, John Giles, and Wang Sangui. 'Income Inequality during China's Economic Transition.' In *China's Great Economic Transformation*, ed. Loren Brandt and Thomas G. Rawski. Cambridge: Cambridge University Press, 2008.

Berger, Suzanne. *How We Compete: What Companies Around the World Are Doing to Make It in Today's Global Economy*. New York: Random House, 2005.

Bergsten, C. Fred. 'We should listen to Beijing's currency idea.' *Financial Times*, 9 April 2009.

Bergsten, Fred C., et al. *China's Rise: Challenges and Opportunities*. Washington, DC: Peterson Institute for International Economics and Center for Strategic and International Studies, 2008.

Besley, Timothy, and Robin Burgess. 'Can Labor Market Regulation Hinder Economic Performance? Evidence from India.' *Quarterly Journal of Economics* 119 (1, 2004): 91–134.

Bhidé, Amar. *The Venturesome Economy: How Innovation Sustains Prosperity in a More Connected World*. Princeton, NJ: Princeton University Press, 2008.

– 'Venturesome Consumption, Innovation and Globalization.' Paper prepared for the joint conference of CESifo and the Center on Capitalism and Society, 'Perspectives on the Performance of the Continent's Economies,' Venice, 21–22 July 2006.

– 'What Holds Back Bangalore Business?' New York: Columbia Business School, 2006. Manuscript.

Blinder, Alan. 'Offshoring: The Next Industrial Revolution?' *Foreign Affairs*, March/April 2006, pp. 113–28.

Bosworth, Barry, and Susan M. Collins. 'Accounting for Growth: Comparing China and India.' *Journal of Economic Perspectives* 22 (1, 2008): 45–66.

Bradsher, Keith. 'As trade slows China rethinks growth strategy.' *New York Times*, 31 December 2008.

Brandt, Loren, Hsieh Changtai, and Zhu Xiaodong. 'Growth and Structural Transformation in China.' In *China's Great Economic Transformation*, ed. Loren Brandt and Thomas G. Rawski. Cambridge: Cambridge University Press, 2008.

Branstetter, Lee, and Nicholas R. Lardy. 'China's Embrace of Globalization.' In *China's Great Economic Transformation*, ed. Loren Brandt and Thomas G. Rawski. Cambridge: Cambridge University Press, 2008.

Brooks, Ray, and Ran Tao. 'China's Labor Market Performance and Challenges.' IMF Working Paper WP/03/210. Washington, DC: International Monetary Fund, 2003.

Catching, Rebecca, and Anurag Viswanath. 'Can China and India Move Up the Value Chain?" *Far Eastern Economic Review,* July 2007.

Chamon, Marcos, Paolo Mauro, and Yohei Okawa. 'Mass Car Ownership in the Emerging Market Giants.' *Economic Policy* 23 (54, 2008): 243–96.

Chen Guidi and Wu Chuntao. *Will the Boat Sink the Water? The Life of China's Peasants.* New York: Public Affairs, 2006.

Cheng Li. 'China's Team of Rivals.' *Foreign Policy,* March/April 2009.

China Banking Regulatory Commission. 'NPLs of Commercial Banks as of end-2007.' Beijing: CBRC, 2007.

Clad, James. 'Convergent Chinese and India Perspectives on the Global Order.' In *The India-China Relationship: What the United States Needs to Know,* ed. Francine R. Frankel and Harry Harding. Washington, DC; New York: Woodrow Wilson Center Press and Columbia University Press, 2004.

Cooper, Richard N. 'How Integrated Are Chinese and Indian Labor into the World Economy?' Working Paper 2008-0017. Cambridge, MA: Harvard University, Weatherhead Center for International Affairs, February 2006.

Council on Foreign Relations. *US-China Relations: An Affirmative Agenda, A Responsible Course.* New York: Council on Foreign Relations, 2007.

Dobson, Wendy. 'A Window of Opportunity Opens? Asian and US Views of the International Financial Architecture.' *Asian Economic Policy Review* 4 (2, 2009).

Dobson, Wendy, and Anil Kashyap. 'The Contradictions in China's Gradualist Banking Reforms.' *Brookings Papers on Economic Activity* (2, 2006).

Dobson, Wendy, and Paul Masson. 'Will the Renminbi Become a World Currency?' *China Economic Review* 20 (1, 2009): 124–35.

Dobson, Wendy, and A.E. Safarian. 'The Transition from Imitation to Innovation: An Enquiry into China's Evolving Institutions and Firm Capabilities.' *Journal of Asian Economics* 19 (4, 2008): 301–11.

'Don't drink the water and don't breathe the air.' *The Economist,* 26 January 2008.

Dougherty, Sean, Richard Herd, and Ping He. 'Has a Private Sector Emerged in China's Industry? Evidence from a Quarter of a Million Chinese Firms.' *China Economic Review* 18 (2007): 309–34.

Drèze, Jean, and Christian Oldiges. 'How is NREGA doing?' PowerPoint presentation, A.N. Sinha Institute of Social Studies, Patna, Bihar, India, 2008. Available at website: http://www.ansiss.org/doc/seminar2007July20-22/jean_dreze.doc.

Dyer, Geoff. 'Unmade in China,' *Financial Times,* 17 December 2008.

Dyson, Tim, and Pravin Visaria. 'Migration and Urbanization: Retrospect and

Prospects.' In *Twenty-first Century India: Population, Economy, Human Development, and the Environment*, ed. Tim Dyson, Robert Cassen, and Leela Visaria. New Delhi: Oxford India Paperbacks, 2005.

'Economics focus: A worker's manifesto for China.' *The Economist*, 13 October 2007.

'850,000 lawsuits in the making.' *The Economist*, 10 April 2008.

Fairbanks, John. *The Great Chinese Revolution: 1800–1995*. New York: Harper and Row, 1986.

Feenstra, Robert, and G.H. Hanson. 'Ownership and Control in Outsourcing to China.' *Quarterly Journal of Economics* 120 (2, 2005): 729–61.

Feenstra, Robert, and Hong Chang. 'China's Exports and Employment.' NBER Working Paper 13552. Cambridge, MA: National Bureau of Economic Research, October 2007.

Fewsmith, Joseph. 'Staying in Power.' In *China's Changing Political Landscape*, ed. Cheng Li. Washington, DC: Brookings Institution Press, 2008.

Forney, Matthew. 'Behind the wheel in China.' *Washington Post*, 21 February 2009.

Frankel, Francine. 'Introduction.' In *The India-China Relationship: What the United States Needs to Know*, ed. Francine R. Frankel and Harry Harding. Washington, DC; New York: Woodrow Wilson Center Press and Columbia University Press, 2004.

Garnaut, Ross, Song Ligang, Stoyan Teneve, and Yao Yang. *China's Ownership Transformation: Process, Outcomes, and Prospects*. Washington, DC: International Finance Corporation and the World Bank, 2005.

Gilboy, George. 'The Myth behind China's Miracle.' *Foreign Affairs* 83 (4, 2004): 33–49.

'A global love affair: A special report on cars in emerging markets.' *The Economist*, 15 November 2008.

'The Global 2000.' *Forbes Magazine*, special report, 8 April 2009.

Goldman Sachs. 'India's Rising Growth Potential.' Global Economic Paper 152. New York: Goldman Sachs, 27 January 2008.

Gu Shulin and Bengt-Åke Lundvall. 'China's Innovation System and the Move Toward Harmonious Growth and Endogenous Innovation.' *Innovation: Management, Policy and Practice* 8 (1-2, 2006): 1–26.

Guha, Ramachandra. *India after Gandhi: The History of the World's Largest Democracy*. Basingstoke; Oxford: Macmillan, 2007.

'Gujarat has shown how to tackle the power problem.' *Times of India*, 3 November 2007.

Gupta, Anil K., and Wang Haiyan. *Getting China and India Right: Strategies for*

Leveraging the World's Fastest Growing Economies for Global Advantage. New York: Jossey-Bass/Wiley, 2009.

Hall, Chris. 'When the Dragon Awakes: Internationalisation of SMEs in China and Implications for Europe.' *CESifo Forum* (2, 2007): 29–34.

Harding, Harry. 'The Evolution of the Strategic Triangle: China, India, and the United States.' In *The India-China Relationship: What the United States Needs to Know,* ed. Francine R. Frankel and Harry Harding. Washington, DC; New York: Woodrow Wilson Center Press and Columbia University Press, 2004.

Hartford, Kathleen. 'Dear Mayor.' *China Information* 19 (2, 2005): 217-20.

He Jianwu and Louis Kuijs. 'Rebalancing China's Economy: Modeling a Policy Package.' World Bank China Research Paper 7. Beijing: World Bank, 2007.

Herd, Richard, and Sean Dougherty. 'Growth Prospects in China and India Compared.' *European Journal of Comparative Economics* 4 (1, 2007): 65–89.

'High-tech hopefuls: A special report on technology in India and China.' *The Economist,* 10 November 2007.

Hille, Kathrin. 'Beijing drives car and steel mergers message.' *Financial Times,* 23 March 2009.

Hout, Thomas. 'The Ecology of Innovation.' *China Economic Quarterly* (3rd quarter, 2006): 34–38.

Hu, Albert Z., and Gary H. Jefferson. 'Science and Technology in China.' In *China's Great Economic Transformation,* ed. Loren Brandt and Thomas G. Rawski. Cambridge: Cambridge University Press, 2008.

Ikenberry, John. 'The Rise of China and the Future of the West.' *Foreign Affairs* 87 (1, 2008): 23–37.

India. Committee on Financial Sector Reforms. *A Hundred Small Steps.* New Delhi: Planning Commission, 2008.

– Department of Commerce. 'Need to Strengthen Trade between India and China: Commerce Secretary.' New Delhi: Department of Commerce, 19 March 2009. Available at website: http://www.commerce.gov.in/pressrelease/pressrelease_detail.asp?id=2399.

– High Powered Expert Committee on Making Mumbai an International Financial Centre. *Report.* New Delhi: Ministry of Finance, 2007.

– National Commission for Enterprises in the Unorganised Sector. *Financing of Enterprises in the Unorganised Sector.* New Delhi: NCEUS, 2007.

– National Commission for Enterprises in the Unorganised Sector. *Report on Conditions of Work and Promotion of Livelihoods in the Unorganised Sector.* New Delhi: NCEUS, August 2007.

- Planning Commission. *Planning Commission Reports on Labour and Employment.* New Delhi: Economica, 2002.
- Planning Commission. *Towards Faster and More Inclusive Growth: An Approach to the 11th Five Year Plan (2007–2012).* New Delhi: Government of India Planning Commission, 2006.
- Prime Minister's Office. 'Prime Minister addresses 40th Indian Labour Conference.' New Delhi, 9 December 2005.
India-China Joint Study Group on Comprehensive Trade and Economic Cooperation. *Report.* New Delhi, 2005.
Industrial and Commercial Bank of China. *ICBC Interim Report 2008.* Beijing: ICBC, 21 August 2008.
Institute of International Finance. 'Special Briefing: India.' Washington, DC: IIF, 2007.
International Monetary Fund. *World Economic Outlook 2005.* Washington, DC: IMF, 2005.
Japan-China-Republic of Korea Trilateral Summit. 'Joint Statement on the International Finance and Economy.' Fukuoka, Japan, 13 December 2008. Available at website: http://www.mofa.go.jp/region/asia-paci/jck/summit0812/economy.html.
Jefferson, Gary, Bai Huamao, Guan Xiaojing, and Yu Xiaoyun. 'R&D Performance in Chinese Industry.' *Economics of Innovation and New Technology* 15 (4-5, 2006): 345–66.
Jensen, J. Bradford, and Lori G. Kletzer. '"Fear" and Offshoring: The Scope and Potential Impact of Imports and Exports of Services.' Policy Brief PB08-1. Washington, DC: Peterson Institute for International Economics, 2008.
Johnson, Ian. *Wild Grass: Three Stories of Change in Modern China.* New York: Vintage, 2005.
Johnson, Jo. 'Engaging India: Creative destruction.' *Financial Times,* 4 October 2007.
- 'Midnight's grandchildren,' *Financial Times,* 7 June 2008.
Kagan, Robert. *The Return of History and the End of Dreams.* New York: Knopf, 2008.
Kanamori, Toshiki, and Zhao Zhijun. 'Private Sector Development in the People's Republic of China.' ADBI Policy Papers 5. Tokyo: Asian Development Bank Institute, 2004.
Kent, Ann. *Beyond Compliance: China, International Organizations and Global Security.* Stanford, CA: Stanford University Press, 2007.
Khanna, Tarun. *Billions of Entrepreneurs: How China and India Are Reshaping Their Futures and Yours.* Cambridge, MA: Harvard Business School Press, 2007.
Khilnani, Sunil. *The Idea of India.* New Delhi: Penguin Books, 1997.

Kingdon, Geeta Ghandi, et al. 'Education and Literacy.' In *Twenty-first Century India: Population, Economy, Human Development, and the Environment,* ed. Tim Dyson, Robert Cassen, and Leela Visaria. New Delhi: Oxford India Paperbacks, 2005.

Kletzer, Lori G. *Job Loss from Imports: Measuring the Costs.* Washington, DC: Peterson Institute for International Economics, 2001.

Kochhar, Kalpana, et al. 'India's Pattern of Development: What Happened, What Follows?' IMF Working Paper WP 06/22. Washington, DC: International Monetary Fund, 2006.

Lal, Deepak. *The Hindu Equilibrium,* vol. 1, *Cultural Stability and Economic Stagnation.* Oxford: Clarendon Press, 1988.

'Land reform in China: Still not to the tiller.' *The Economist,* 23 October 2008.

Lane, Philip R., and Sergio L. Schmukler. 'International Financial Integration of China and India.' In *Dancing with Giants: China, India and the Global Economy,* ed. L. Alan Winters and Shahid Yusuf. Washington, DC, and Singapore: World Bank and the Institute of Policy Studies, 2007.

LaPorta, Rafael, Florencio López-de-Silanes, and Andrei Shleifer. 'Government Ownership of Commercial Banks.' *Journal of Finance* 57 (1, 2002): 265–301.

Lardy, Nicholas. 'State-owned Banks in China.' In *The Future of State-Owned Financial Institutions,* ed. Gerard Caprio. Washington, DC: Brookings Institution, 2004.

Leahy, Joe. 'Family stakes back Indian debt.' *Financial Times,* 20 February 2009.

Li Cui and Syed Murtaza. 'The Shifting Structure of China's Trade and Production.' Working Paper WP/07/214. Washington, DC: International Monetary Fund, 2007.

Li Hongbin et al. 'Political Connections and Firm Performance: Evidence from Chinese Private Firms.' Working Paper 2005-E-11-CIG. Hong Kong: Center for Institutions and Governance, Chinese University of Hong Kong, 2005.

Lin, Justin Yifu. 'Rebalancing Equity and Efficiency for Sustained Growth.' In *China's Dilemma: Economic Growth, the Environment, and Climate Change,* ed. Song Ligang and Woo Wing Thye. Washington, DC: Brookings Institution Press, 2008.

Link, Perry. Trans. 'China's Charter 08.' *New York Review of Books,* 15 January 2009.

Liu Xielin. 'China's Development Model: An Alternate Strategy for Technological Catchup.' Working paper. Tokyo: Hitotsubashi University, Institute of Innovation Research, 2005.

Ma Guonan. 'Sharing China's Bank Restructuring Bill.' *China & World Economy* 14 (3, 2006): 19–37.

Ma Guonan and Robert N. McCauley. 'Do China's Capital Controls Still Bind?'

In *China, Asia, and the New World Economy*, ed. Barry Eichengreen, Yung Chul Park, and Charles Wyplosz. Oxford: Oxford University Press, 2008.

Maddison, Angus. 'Asia in the World Economy 1500–2030 AD.' *Asian-Pacific Economic Literature* 20 (2, 2006): 1–37.

– *Contours of the World Economy, 1–2030 AD: Essays in Macro-economic History*. Oxford: Oxford University Press, 2007.

Mahbubani, Kishore. *The New Asian Hemisphere: The Irresistible Shift of Global Power to the East*. New York: Public Affairs, 2008.

McGregor, Richard. 'Party think tank calls for checks on China's rulers.' *Financial Times*, 20 February 2008.

McKinsey Global Institute. 'Accelerating India's Growth through Financial System Reform.' San Francisco: MGI, 2006.

– 'The Emerging Global Labor Market.' San Francisco: MGI, 2007.

– 'Mapping Global Capital Markets.' San Francisco: MGI, 2006.

– 'Mapping Global Capital Markets, Fifth Annual Report.' San Francisco: MGI, October 2008.

– 'Mapping Global Capital Markets, Fourth Annual Report.' San Francisco: MGI, January 2008.

– 'Putting China's Capital to Work: The Value of Financial System Reform.' San Francisco: MGI, May 2006.

McNay, Kirsty, Jeemol Unni, and Robert Cassen. 'Employment.' In *Twenty-first Century India: Population, Economy, Human Development, and the Environment*, ed. Tim Dyson, Robert Cassen, and Leela Visaria. New Delhi: Oxford India Paperbacks, 2005.

'Melting Asia.' *The Economist*, 5 June 2008.

Mistry, Percy S. 'The Mumbai-IFC Report: Of Discourse, Garlands and Brickbats!' 10 June 2007. Available at website http://www.mayin.org/ajayshah/A/mifc/Mistry2007_mifc_response.pdf.

Naughton, Barry. 2007. *The Chinese Economy*. Cambridge, MA: MIT Press, 2007.

– 'The State Asset Commission: A Powerful New Government Body.' *China Leadership Monitor*, Fall 2003.

Nelson, Richard. *National Innovation Systems: A Comparative Analysis*. Oxford: Oxford University Press, 1993.

Nilekani, Nandan. *Imagining India: The Idea of a Renewed Nation*. New Delhi: Penguin, 2008.

North, Douglass, and R.P. Thomas. *The Rise of the Western World: A New Economic History*. Cambridge: Cambridge University Press, 1973.

Organisation for Economic Co-operation and Development. *Economic Survey of India 2007*. Paris: OECD, 2007.

– *Science, Technology and Industry Outlook*. Paris: OECD, 2006.

Panagariya, Arvind. *India: The Emerging Giant.* Oxford: Oxford University Press, 2008.

– 'India and China: Past Trade Liberalization and Future Challenges.' Paper prepared for a Tokyo Club Foundation for Global Studies conference, Tokyo, 6–7 December 2006, updated 4 February 2007. Available at website: http://www.tcf.or.jp/data/2006120607_Arvind_Panagariya.pdf.

Pei, Minxin. 'How Beijing can boost its human capital.' *Financial Times*, 9 January 2009.

'The people speak and Maglev is put on hold.' *Shanghai Daily*, 28 May 2007.

Perkins, Dwight, and Thomas G. Rawski. 'Forecasting China's Economic Growth to 2025.' In *China's Great Economic Transformation*, ed. Loren Brandt and Thomas G. Rawski. Cambridge: Cambridge University Press, 2008.

Pimlott, Daniel. 'Bangladesh bank offers loans to US poor.' *Financial Times*, 16 February 2008.

Podpiera, Richard. 'Progress in China's Banking Sector Reform: Has Bank Behavior Changed?' Working Paper WP/06/71. Washington, DC: International Monetary Fund, 2006.

Prasad, Eswar. 'Is the Chinese Growth Miracle Built to Last?' *China Economic Review* 20 (1, 2009): 103–23.

Prasad, Eswar, and Raghuram G. Rajan. 'Next Generation Financial Reforms for India.' *Finance and Development* 45 (3, 2008): 23–27.

PricewaterhouseCoopers. 'Gearing Up for a Global Gravity Shift: Growth, Risk and Learning in the Asia Pharmaceutical Market.' London: Pricewaterhouse-Coopers, 2007.

'A ravenous dragon.' *The Economist*, 15 March 2008.

Rawski, Thomas G. 'Chinese Industrial Reform: Accomplishments, Prospects, and Implications.' *American Economic Review* 84 (2, 1994): 271–5.

Rogers, Paul. 'China and India: Heartlands of Global Protest.' *Open Democracy*, 8 July 2008.

Rosen, Daniel. 'What China Can't Do.' *China Economic Quarterly* (3rd quarter, 2006): 45–51.

Rothman, Andy. 'Thirsty China.' CLSA *Asia Pacific Markets*, Summer 2006.

Saich, Tony. 'Negotiating the State: The Development of Social Organizations in China.' *China Quarterly* 161 (March, 2000): 124–41.

Seligsohn, Deborah. 'Doing More than You Think.' *China Economic Quarterly*, 21 September 2008.

Shirk, Susan. *The Political Logic of Economic Reform in China.* Berkeley: University of California Press, 1993.

Singh, Arvinder. 'Labor Mobility in China and India: The Role of Hukou, Caste, and Community.' In *China and India: Learning from Each Other – Reforms*

and Policies for Sustained Growth, ed. Aziz Jahangir, Steven Dunaway, and Eswar
    Prasad. Washington, DC: International Monetary Fund, 2005.

'Smoke clears, doubts linger at CCTV fire.' *Caijing,* 3 March 2009.

Steinfeld, Edward, Richard Lester, and Edward Cunningham. 'Lessons from
    Sulfur.' *China Economic Quarterly* (September 2008): 28–32.

Sutton, John. 'The Globalization Process: Auto-component Supply Chains in
    China and India.' In *Are We on Track to Achieve the Millennium Development
    Goals?* ed. François Bourguignon, Boris Pleskovic, and André Sapir. Washing-
    ton, DC: World Bank; New York: Oxford University Press, 2005.

Taylor, Andrew. 'Asian economies near "demographic cliff".' *Financial Times,*
    13 August 2007.

Tellis, Ashley. 'China and India in Asia.' In *The India-China Relationship: What
    the United States Needs to Know,* ed. Francine R. Frankel and Harry Harding.
    Washington, DC; New York: Woodrow Wilson Center Press and Columbia
    University Press, 2004.

Thornton, John L. 'Long Time Coming.' *Foreign Affairs* 87 (1, 2008): 2–22.

Truman, Edwin M. 'Sovereign Wealth Funds: The Need for Greater Transpar-
    ency and Accountability.' Policy Brief PB07-06. Washington, DC: Peterson
    Institute for International Economics, 2007.

UBS Investment Research. 'China's Stimulus Package Focuses on Investment
    and Consumption.' 10 November 2008.

UNICEF. *Progress for Children: A World Fit for Children Statistical Review* 6. New
    York: UNICEF, December 2007.

United Nations Conference on Trade and Development. *World Investment Re-
    port 2008: Transnational Corporations and the Infrastructure Challenge.* Geneva:
    UNCTAD, 2008.

United Nations Development Programme. *Human Development Report 2006.* New
    York: UNDP, 2006.

Wanandi, Jusuf, and Tadashi Yamamoto. *East Asia at a Crossroads.* Tokyo: Japan
    Center for International Exchange, 2008.

Wang Feng and Andrew Mason. 'The Demographic Factor in China's Transi-
    tion.' In *China's Great Economic Transformation,* ed. Loren Brandt and Thomas
    G. Rawski. Cambridge: Cambridge University Press, 2008.

Wang Tao. 'How Will China Grow? Export Slowdown, Reverse Migration, and
    Urbanization.' UBS *Asian Economic Perspectives,* 7 January 2009.

Wang Tao and Harrison Hu. 'How Will China Grow? The Re-leveraging of
    China.' UBS *Asian Economic Perspectives,* 9 December 2008

Whalley, John, and Xin Xian. 'China's FDI and Non-FDI Economies and the
    Sustainability of Future High Chinese Growth.' NBER Working Paper 12249.
    Cambridge, MA: National Bureau of Economic Research, 2006.

Wilson, Dominic, and Roopa Purushothaman. 'Dreaming with BRICs: The Path to 2050.' Global Economics Paper 99. New York: Goldman Sachs, 2003.

Wong, Gillian. 'China's Communist Party approves rural land reform.' Associated Press, 24 October 2008.

World Bank. *India — Inclusive Growth and Service Delivery: Building on India's Success*, Development Policy Review. Washington, DC: World Bank, 2006.

– *India's Water Economy: Bracing for a Turbulent Future*. Washington, DC: World Bank, 2005.

– 'Orissa in Transition: From Fiscal Turnaround to Rapid and Inclusive Growth.' Washington, DC: World Bank, 2008.

– 'Quarterly Update, June 2008.' Beijing: World Bank Office, 2008.

– 'Quarterly Update, December 2008.' Beijing: World Bank Office, 2008.

– *Unleashing India's Innovation: Towards Sustainable and Inclusive Growth*. Washington, DC: World Bank, 2007.

– *World Development Indicators*. Washington, DC: World Bank, 2008.

– Commission on Growth and Development. *The Growth Report: Strategies for Sustained Growth and Inclusive Development*. Washington, DC: World Bank, 2008.

World Trade Organization. *International Trade Statistics, 2007*. Geneva: WTO, 2007.

Wright, Teresa. 'Disincentives for Democratic Change in China.' *Asia Pacific Issues* 82 (February 2007).

Yang Binbin et al. 'Why Did So Many Sichuan Schools Collapse?' *Caijing*, June 2008.

Yee, Amy, Andrew Hill, and Paul Betts. 'India struggles to plug gaps in burgeoning IT industry.' *Financial Times*, 10 July 2008.

Yu Song and Helen Qiao. 'A preview of the upcoming National People's Congress meeting: Don't expect too many new policies.' Goldman Sachs *China Views*, 27 February 2009.

Yusuf, Shahid, and L. Alan Winters, eds. *Dancing with Giants: China, India and the Global Economy*. Washington, DC, and Singapore: World Bank and the Institute of Policy Studies, 2007.

Zhan Jiang. 'News Media, Cautious Change.' *Caijing Annual Edition 2008*. Beijing, 2008, pp. 128-29.

Zhang Haizhou. 'As old industry bites the dust, new sectors begin to bloom.' *China Daily*, 4 November 2008.

Zhang Yongsheng. 'To Achieve the Goals of China's 11th Five-Year Plan through Reforms.' Presentation to the Tokyo Club Foundation for Global Studies, 6–7 December 2006.

Zhou Xiaochuan. 'China's Corporate Bond Market Development: Lessons 'Learned.' BIS Papers 26. Basel: Bank for International Settlements, 2005.

Zhou Yu. 'The Making of an Innovative Region from a Centrally Planned Economy: Institutional Evolution in Zhongguancun Science Park in Beijing.' *Environment and Planning* 37 (6, 2005): 1113–34.

Zmarak, Shalizi. 'Energy and Emissions.' In *Dancing with Giants: China, India and the Global Economy*, ed. Shahid Yusuf and L. Alan Winters. Washington, DC, and Singapore: World Bank and the Institute of Policy Studies, 2007.

Acknowledgments

Many books describe China or India but few compare the two and what their rise will mean for the future of the global economy. My focus on the future is informed by years of experience that provide both a bottom-up and a top-down perspective on the two giants, and is organized by the growth-accounting and institutional frameworks I use.

The transformation of the two giants is especially dramatic to anyone who has lived and worked in or extensively visited them over the past few decades. In the mid-1960s, when I lived and worked there, India was a very poor country. All residents used ration cards to obtain basic food staples. New Delhi, my base, was a spacious, pleasant city with broad, leafy streets. My work in the family planning network of an NGO took me to hospitals located in northern India's towns and villages. I was frequently confronted by the deprivation of village life and the difficulties faced by young doctors and nurse midwives who were providing rural health care in isolated and destitute conditions. The Green Revolution was introducing high-yield wheat varieties and expanded food production in the northern states of Punjab and Haryana, but not everywhere. A drought gripped the eastern state of Bihar, leaving villagers with literally nothing but the roofs over their heads.

In 1978, during my first visit to China, change was very much in the air. It was October and the big poster campaign was in full swing in Beijing. I was introduced to the Four Modernizations in a chalkboard exhibit in a silk-spinning mill in Hangzhou, today a thriving center for fashion, electronics, and industry. Agriculture was just beginning the transition from collective organization to individual management, and rural medical care was still delivered by barefoot doctors whom I met during visits to communes in Jiangxi province. The schools were teaching English again, and teachers and students shyly approached foreigners to try their language skills.

In the late 1980s, when I served as associate deputy finance minister, responsible for Canada's international financial diplomacy, the G7 attempted to coordinate the economic policies of its members. That experience of policy bargaining illustrated to me the pitfalls and the value of international cooperation, especially in times of crisis, and underline today the significance of the more inclusive, but larger and more unwieldy, G20 in encouraging the emerging giants to take on collective responsibilities.

Since joining the University of Toronto in the early 1990s, I have studied and written extensively on Asian integration and the rise of China and India. The Rotman School of Management under Dean Roger Martin's leadership contributed to the book in myriad ways, providing stimulating colleagues and research support as well as the base for a series of research projects and publications on the Asian economies. The institutional framework in this book is one that I use in classes on international business in the world economy that Paul Masson and I teach to final-year MBA students. A number of students contributed their unique perspectives on the Chinese and Indian economies, based on their own experiences and those of their families and networks. They also provided invaluable connections and assistance in both countries. David Atnip in Shanghai was an invaluable on-the-ground observer; Henry Zhao in Hangzhou organized a number of valuable and insightful interviews with entrepreneurs and officials; and Sophie Liang was never too busy to contribute her interpretation of events and to help with translation.

International networks and colleagues contributed indirectly in a number of ways. One channel is the regular conferences organized by the Pacific Trade and Development network, where I am a member of the Steering Committee; a second is my long association with the Peterson Institute for International Economics in Washington, DC, where I have been an author and advisory board member. Material for most of the chapters was presented at academic and other seminars in China, India, and North America. A summer-long visit to the China Center for Economic Research in Beijing provided opportunities to interact with Chinese economists, including Justin Lin, now chief economist at the World Bank; Li Ling, his deputy at the time; Zhao Yaohui; Shen Minggao; staff at the World Bank and IMF offices; and a number of candid and helpful interviewees in banks, regulatory agencies, government ministries, and research centers who would prefer to remain anonymous. Suman Bery and Rajesh Chadha were generous hosts at the National Council for Applied Economic Research in New Delhi, providing a base for a number of interviews with enterprises based in and near that city. Ajai Bambawale and Clarence Chandran were very helpful in arranging contacts in the research and financial community in Mumbai and with leaders of the IT services industry in Bangalore. The Canadian embassies in Beijing and New Delhi and ambassadors Joseph Caron and David Malone were also most imaginative and helpful in arranging contacts and interviews.

Several background academic and policy papers benefited from attendees at conferences and from close collaborations: with co-author Anil Kashyap and with William Brainard and George Perry, editors of the *Brookings Papers on Economic Activity*; co-authors Ed Safarian and Paul Masson and editors Michael Plummer and Belton Fleisher at the *Journal of Asian Economics* and *China Economic Review*, respectively; and with Takatoshi Ito, Shujiro Urata, and Colin MacKenzie at the *Asian Economic Policy Review*.

Other colleagues who have been particularly helpful include Arvind Panagariya, who has produced an outstanding and comprehensive analysis of the Indian economy's partial transformation, and Loren Brandt at the University of Toronto, whose views and book on China's transformation have also been invaluable. I have benefited from intensive discussions with former international colleagues Toyoo Gyohten and Yoichi Funabashi in Tokyo and with Xu Sitao at the Economist Intelligence Unit in Shanghai and Beijing; from conversations over the years with Han Sung Joo and Young Soogil in Seoul and Zhang Yunling in Beijing; and from an annual policy seminar at the East West Center, University of Hawaii, under Charles Morrison's able direction. I am also deeply grateful to colleagues who were kind enough to read and comment on the manuscript or the papers on which it is based, including Loren Brandt, Arvind Panagariya, Randy Spence, Ed Safarian, Eleanor Westney, Paul Masson, Gary Jefferson, Lee Jung-hwa, Sophie Liang, Ellen Frost, and some anonymous referees, all of whom provided invaluable comments but who bear no responsibility for the final product, which is mine alone.

Able research assistance was provided by Laurina Zhang, Usman Naeem, and Jad Yaghi at the University of Toronto and Guo Xiaobo in Beijing. Jennifer DiDomenico and her colleagues at the University of Toronto Press deserve warm praise for the speed with which they turned a manuscript into a book. It was also a pleasure to work once again with Barry Norris, the best copy editor I have known.

Last, but most important, I thank Ed Carson, whose interest, encouragement, and expertise were invaluable from start to finish. Without him, the book would have remained a series of academic papers.

Index

accountability: in China, 117, 124; and economic growth, 153; elections and, 153

Achilles heel: of China, 154; of India, 52–3

acid rain, 107

advanced countries, ix; Chinese environmental weaknesses and, 140–1; economic growth of, 204n2; expertise in, 141–2; global division of labor and, 142–3; gravity shift and, 145; location of industries, 144; and manufacturing industry, 140–4. *See also* Organisation for Economic Co-operation and Development (OECD)

affirmative action, 27–8

Africa, China and, 135, 200n23

aging of population: in China, 34; in India, 39

agrarian society: in China, 6, 14; in India, 6, 23, 24, 28, 128

Agricultural Bank of China, 65

agriculture: in China, 3–4, 5, 14, 15, 98, 106, 186n17; employment in, 36, 38, 39, 41; incomes in, 43; in India, 4–5, 7, 33, 39, 40–3, 100,

159, 166–7; labor supply for, 23; productivity, 15, 43, 159

Akbar, 23

Alibaba, 90, 133

Alicollege, 90

All China Federation of Trade Unions, 37

Ambedkar, Bhimrao, 27

antimonopoly law (China), 112–13, 157

architecture: ASEAN +, 169, 173–4; global economic, 174–82

ASEAN (Association of Southeast Asian Nations), 167, 168, 171, 206n30; + 1, 171; + 3, 169, 170, 171, 172

Asia: 1997–98 financial crisis, 61, 168–70, 172; 2008–09 global recession and, 172–3; financial cooperation within, 169–70; regional institutions in, 168–73; sovereignty vs. cooperation within, 171; trading within, 170–1; U.S. and, 168

Asia Pacific Economic Cooperation (APEC), 168, 173

Asian Bond Fund, 170

Asian Bond Market Initiative, 170

59, 67; by China, 68–9, 135–6; in
enterprises, 87, 89–90; by India,
69, 136; and job creation, 21; in
pharmaceutical industry, 82; and
technology transfer, 81
Four Modernizations, xv–xvi
Frankel, Francine, 22–3
free trade: China-India, 164; in
Europe, 165, 166; in North
America, 166

G6, 8
G20, ix, xiv, 173, 174–6, 177, 184
Gandhi, Indira, 5, 25, 29, 41, 55, 62,
123
Gandhi, Mohandas (Mahatma), 24,
26, 27, 41, 100
Gandhi, Rajiv, 25–6, 29, 98, 163
Gandhi, Sanjeev, 123
Gandhi, Sonia, 54, 55, 65, 162
GE: Healthcare China, 132–3; in
India, 91, 133, 165
Geely (Chinese firm), 89
gender: discrimination, 44; and education, 36; and sex ratio in China,
199n16
geometry, variable, 171–2
Germany, unemployment in, 144
global supply chains, 128–9, 138, 139,
145–6, 149
globalization, ix, xiii–xiv, 182; Asia
and, 174–5, 184; of auto industry,
82, 131–2; China and, 59–60, 88,
94, 130, 160, 165, 173, 175–6, 182;
and division of labor, 142–3; and
environment, 104, 140, 180; of
finance, 55; G20 and, 174; India
and, 82, 91, 92, 130, 160, 164, 165,
175, 176; of industry, 81, 88; of IT
industry, 91, 92, 132; and labor

markets, 144, 181; of pharmaceutical industry, 132; U.S. and, 181.
See also international competition;
trade
Goldman Sachs, 8
gong jian, 116
government intervention: and competition, 88; and economic growth,
74, 122–3; in financial systems, 54,
56, 57, 64; in India, 25, 161; and innovation, 87; and savings, 54
governments: and banks, 56, 58–9,
65, 155, 157; in China, 18, 19–20;
and economic growth, 110; ownership of financial institutions, 65
growth. *See* economic growth
Guangdong province, 19, 79, 88, 111,
112, 125, 156
guanxi relationships, 20
Guha, Ramachandra, 25, 26
Gujarat state, 124

He, Michael, 33–4
health care: in China, 22, 104, 113,
125, 149–50; in India, 123
heavy industry: in China, 111; in
India, 25, 26, 42
Herd, Richard, 186n6, 197n29
high-tech industry: in China, 86–7; in
India, 81, 85. *See also* IT industry
Honda, 91
Hong Kong, 20–1, 59, 117
Hu Jintao, 78, 152
Huawei Technologies, 85, 134, 165
Huiyuan, 113, 157
hukou, 5, 37, 47, 100
human capital: in China, 33–8, 47;
education and, 33, 145; in India,
33, 38–53, 92; international competition and, 145. *See also* labor